Some Monologues

Tyler Coburn

Document Series

Wendy's Subway

The Unscripted Self: On Language, Bodies, and Fictions in the Work of Tyler Coburn

Elvia Wilk

In Tyler Coburn's practice, documentation isn't an afterthought—it's part of the work's DNA. Some of his projects leave a clear trail of objects and artifacts. Others nearly vanish, living on in an email chain, a mysterious .zip file, or the memory of someone who swears they were there. He is both inventive and intentional about the way the works live in the world, and how they live in relation to him as their author. This requires a careful negotiation between authority and openness, precision and unpredictability, structure and improvisation—in order to discern how much control ultimately creates the conditions for freedom.

Some Monologues assembles the written scripts, in full or in excerpted form, for eleven works made over fifteen years—not as a record of what the pieces "really" were, but as living components of what they continue to be. These scripts form the backbone of this book. Their many manifestations have included performances by the artist, performances by others, conversations with others, sculptures, sculptures that are also furniture, sculptures that are also living species, books, audio recordings, websites, and more. The script-skeleton is fleshed out by evidence and documentation, some of it made in the moment, much of it gathered as recollection or recreated as spin-off, including pieces by ten contributors in theoretical, essayistic, dialogic, and fictional registers. The whole corpus is wrapped in a skin of technical details about the works' many instantiations—information that both indexes the complexity of the projects and plays with the limits of indexicality.

Tyler's work resists duality in favor of multiplicity, but I find the author Daisy Hildyard's concept of the "second body" a useful way to think about his approach. Although we're accustomed to describing our own bodies as bounded, solid, stable entities ending at the skin, in an age of cloud computing, climate change, ecosystemic collapse, and unfathomably rapid networked existence, we also sense the presence of a *second* body implicated in all those systems in tangible and intangible ways, tethered to but not coincident with our physicality. It is tied to us, but also vaguely "has an impact on foreign countries and on whales" and on other noncorporeal counterparts.[1] The first body lives in finite space and time; the second body's boundaries are diffuse, confusing, distributed.

The projects are not presented chronologically here; they tell a different kind of story. The first to appear, *I'm that angel* (2011–), is a time capsule of a specific moment in the development of the internet, when virtuality gave rise to a growing awareness of the second-body problem. The script is written from the perspective of a so-called content farmer, a digital producer tasked with rapidly churning out search engine-optimized stories. In a diaristic, keyword-inflected monologue, the narrator describes an existential crisis in which he conflates his body with a network server. Tyler and actor Justin Sayre performed the script of *I'm that angel* in data centers across Europe and North America. Such centers—as well as server farms, routers, and undersea cables—form the material infrastructure of the internet, which, the narrator notes, is naturalized, metaphorized, and dematerialized as "the cloud." The amorphous term speaks to a wish for disembodiment, the possibility for people and information to be free from physical constraints, yet Tyler's vexed, manic, overworked narrator shows he is anything but.

I'm that angel opens the book, *Ergonomic Futures* (started in 2016 and possibly never ending) concludes it, without concluding anything. This project imagines how our bodies might physically evolve so radically they no longer fit into current definitions—tangible, legal—of what it means to be human. Tyler worked with architects Bureau V to design seats for two such "future" as-yet-unknown body types, and these have been permanently installed in museums for visitors to use improvisationally. The practice of ergonomic design assumes a norm or an ideal, and in asserting it, can create it. Ergonomics is an outgrowth of Taylorist efficiency-management strategies, meant to "optimize" the self—the worker—who, today, might be represented as an "angel" avatar in "the cloud" while actually sitting in an uncomfortable desk chair and uploading optimized language fragments with weary fingers.

Historically, the angel was not a metaphor. In medieval philosophy, it was quite the opposite: Angels sat just under God in the Great Chain of Being, a hierarchical framework that linked heaven and hell, with humans somewhere in the middle, above plants, animals, and rocks. This attempt to locate the sub-angelic human somewhere in a tangible cosmology is part of a centuries-long Western project of situating and isolating the human, a project that has intensified and become more ideologically defined at exactly the moment it has come under threat by the undeniable presence of the second body. And if the angel once marked a position just beyond the human, other entities may now serve a similar function—less spiritual, more bureaucratic, but just as fundamentally abstracted from the earthly realm.

Anchoring *Some Monologues* at its midway point is an ongoing work from 2017 that is, itself, doubled: both biological and fictional. *Richard Roe* is the name Tyler legally gave to an orchid hybrid, as well as the name of the fictional author of a memoir published as an eponymous book. (You might encounter the two sitting together as decoration on a gallery desk.) In the memoir, Roe notes that his name is often used in case law to designate an anonymous entity (akin to Jane Doe), and that he is in fact a "legal person" (akin to a shell corporation). Roe explains: "A legal person is not the same as a human person. A human person can hide inside a legal person . . . but so can nation-states, municipalities, and corporations. Unthinking matter, touched by the hand of the law, can be given the semblance of life." This legal fiction is in some ways akin to the fiction of virtuality: as *I'm that angel* shows, the supposed intangible miracle of the cloud is made up of *real* wires and *real* bodies. A corporation is both more and less than a pile of paperwork. The possibility of impersonation—a bot pretending to be a person, a corporation acting as a person—should make us question what a "real" person is in the first place. When it comes to *Richard Roe*'s split personas, who is *realer* from the perspective of the law, the Internet, the art audience?

Tyler doesn't take the notion of a general audience for granted. *I'm that angel* was performed for small groups in data centers, such as one in Stockholm that maintained the servers of WikiLeaks in the past. Others are open to anyone or have no specified recipient. *Resonator* (2016–), which has left the least material traces of any piece in the book, is intended for only one person at a time. In the first performances in Hong Kong, each visitor shared a bench with Tyler at some distance from the exhibition venue (where a lead ingot, cast from a tuning fork, was on display), and participated in a conversation steered by his script.[2] The script concerns the phenomenon of "resonant frequency" in physics, the rate or speed at which a material naturally "wants" to vibrate when it's disturbed—which is also a wonderful way to describe a partly scripted social interaction calibrated to the listener. For this book, two participants were invited to share their recollections and revivify the unreproducible performance.

The intimacy of *Resonator* hinges on that scarcest of resources, close attention, which Tyler seeks to find ways to tune into. In a world of constant distraction and disembodied experience, it matters where you "place your eyeballs," to quote the narrator of *I'm that angel*. But we are inundated by so much text—not writing but content—and today much of it is machine-generated. Language as an artificial construction is a central concern for Tyler: its thingness (on the page), its commodification (as farmed content), its reproduction (live, print, digital). *NaturallySpeaking* (2013–15) was first presented as a published text and then as an installation, with the script appearing on a monitor in the pop-up window of Macintosh speech-recognition software. Later it was brought to "life" in a performance by actor Susan Bennett, whose tone and cadence are immediately recognizable—she's the person who voiced the ubiquitous digital assistant Siri. The words in the script are interrupted by punctuation instructions for a computer to interpret: "When people first start using speech recognition software COMMA they might be surprised that the computer makes mistakes PERIOD Maybe unconsciously we compare the computer to another person PERIOD But the computer is not like a person PERIOD What the computer does when it listens to speech is different from what a person does PERIOD." This kind of writing trips up the eye and ear, while implying that it is meant to be read aloud—but anyone who recites it is likely to take on a different, *unnatural*, tone of voice.

Prepared Remarks (2020) is an audio contribution to a time-capsule project for which Tyler was asked to imagine the sonic world of 2045—the not-so-distant year when Ray Kurzweil famously predicted the Singularity would arrive (first and second bodies smashed into one!).

Tyler's future narrator informs the listener that in fact the Singularity "has not arrived," yet the sound of his speech begins to glitch and harden, until it's the garbled artificial language of a text-to-speech device. Artificial and natural are fluid rather than oppositional. Even what we think of as the oldest forms of creative expression are always circumscribed and mediated, the encounter to some degree constructed. For *Tratteggio* (2018) a forlorn, funny, retro-futuristic-looking robot gives an exposition of the frescos at Château d'Oiron. The robot, Norio, already belonged to this French museum. It was created as an accessibility aid for viewers to remotely navigate the galleries from the ground level—to see the art through its eyes. Tyler's script scrolling across its face-screen describes the conservation technique of *tratteggio*, where a restorer fills in damaged areas of a painted surface with marks that mimic the original, yet clearly stand out as interventions—an artifice of the mediator showing their hand while preserving an illusion of authenticity.

Like *Ergonomic Futures*, elements of *Tratteggio* could be read as a sly comment on the awkwardnesses and discomforts of institutional space, the infrastructures of exhibition and display and how they determine what kind of bodies see what art through what lens. Tyler explored this years earlier in *Seven Portraits of a Correalist Rocker* (2009), in which he performed a script about modernism and (in)authenticity while rocking around on an MDF replica of a chair that Frederick Kiesler had built in 1942 for Peggy Guggenheim's Art of This Century gallery. Again: What bodies are supposed to go in museums? Or, if modernism prescribed an ideal body, perhaps the ideal body for today's virtualized, bureaucratized institution is no body at all.

However, as Tyler said in a conversation with the artist Adam Gibbons, "my interests have always been less with questions of the institution and more with those of site."[3] If the audience (and their bodies) are not taken for granted, neither is the location; Tyler takes an approach to site specificity in which sites are highly defined yet multiple and networked. Sometimes we're at a former tuberculosis sanatorium on Staten Island (*Overgrowth*, 2020); sometimes we're walking with the artist and his companions across eighty-two streets in Manhattan's grid (*Medium No. 1 Manhattan*, 2008–2009). In the former, he recorded an improvised monologue from the plant-covered ruins of what was meant to be a hidden place of isolation, as far away from the city's dense populace as possible, while still under its jurisdiction. For the latter, he installed a fax machine in the art institution where the work was technically "sited"; the machine fed reams of transmissions made during the walks. Both works embody the potential for an artwork to overgrow (overthrow) the planned grid.

All this scripting, with its layered voices and shifting embodiments, opens up a space to explore, or momentarily reclaim, self-sovereignty. While traditional sovereignty resides in external authorities like the state, the church, or the corporation—entities that determine who counts as a person or a nonperson—the psychoanalyst and theorist Avgi Saketopoulou proposes an alternative: "Self-sovereignty displaces the notion of sovereignty from the domain of power to resituate it to the domain of experience. Self-sovereignty is an intimate experience wherein one's energies are not split by the demands of capitalism (to constantly invest in ourselves and in the world around us) and in which the subject can be transiently relieved from the demands of relationality. It is a rare and transient state." She suggests that such moments are most likely to occur in certain live art performances, ones that work "on us not by kindling the past *as memory* but by revivifying it *in the present* as a force in the here and now."[4]

The nowness and prescience of Tyler's rigorous, lighthearted (and often hilarious) pieces command attention in the moment precisely because they are grounded in deep-past historical research and buoyed by future speculations—from the great chain of being to the ergonomic future. As he put it in an essay reflecting on his practice, "standing at the threshold of speculation has been an occasion to turn around—to observe how history, on the verge of the virtual, can feel thick."[5] The question at stake throughout is no small one, and one that Tyler tackles with the gravity and levity it deserves: what it is to be human. To ask this, he takes on second bodies, creates virtual selves, adopts many identities, legal and otherwise, and creates fictions that let us evolve with them. It is a liberatory endeavor to allow the audience, the reader, to be many at once.

NOTES, "THE UNSCRIPTED SELF"

1. Daisy Hildyard, *The Second Body* (London: Fitzcarraldo, 2017), 19.

2. One attendee felt so connected with the artist during their performance session that the two of them reconnected months later in "real life," in a different city, during cherry blossom season, and the performed intimacy blossomed briefly into something like real intimacy, because a performance is never really *just* a performance, and real life is never really *just* life.

3. Tyler Coburn, "Chimeras in Drag: A Conversation about Ergonomic Futures," interview by Adam Gibbons, *Schloss-Post*, December 5, 2017, https://schloss-post.com/chimeras-in-drag/.

4. Avgi Saketopoulo, *Sexuality Beyond Consent: Risk, Race, Traumatophilia* (New York: New York University Press, 2023), 14.

5. Tyler Coburn, "Candlestick Man," *e-flux Notes*, September 6, 2023, www.e-flux.com/notes/556950/candlestick-man.

2011–

Excerpt from *I'm that angel*

Doing (nothing) but *loving life*; doing my nails and eating some kale while checking my mail (but not looking pale). Isn't it great that the world and the laws—or so you would think if you had time to pause—give speed and the need, the desire to be? If the world was a mollusk, then the world was snail mail, then a cat and a cat and a bigger cat, will it be an eagle? A Griffin? The harder rock or the place and *does it matter???? PEGASUS? CHIMERA? SCYLLA? CHARBYDIS?* If we're taking flight we're taking flight, and if we're sinking in we're sinking in.

The æther used to float up above the Victorians before the scientists shot it down to string up surrogates and now it's feeding the glow worms and those creatures in the far deep underwater where Snow Leopard was born, *originally*, that you've only seen in *Life Aquatic* and *Finding Nemo* and for all you know don't exist except on a hard drive somewhere (and then as a movie and a DVD and the Internet, of course), but if that's where they really live, you're satisfied: good enough, much the same as everything else these days BUTTHEPOINTIS! the æther is back like a return out of hell, and now we're all in it, in the cloud, they keep saying, an *invisible*, *intangible*, *imponderable agent* so luminiferous and miasmatic like a nuclear return that I just know I've got a grow worm glowing inside my brain and there's nothing Sigourney or Kristeva or Dr. Phil can do, but maybe it's for the best like someone used to joke (OK, me): those webbed Chernobyl babies will survive the flood better than the rest of us . . . *Waterworld* didn't exactly laugh its way to the bank, but it'll be laughing when we can't laugh, because our lungs will be drowning. *Surf's up! Fuck yeah! Can't wait, bro!*

* * *

I have to keep reminding myself: I'm in the cloud. Because that's what they keep saying, and I definitely don't want to be outside of the cloud, if that's where everyone *isn't*, but I don't exactly know what's different.

I thought it might be a mind thing . . . OK. It's thirty seconds later. I just closed my eyes and took a deep breath and emptied my head of all of my thoughts so my brain could lighten up. I *tried* to not think about anything, but then the thinking about trying to not think about anything was technically thinking about *something*, so I don't know if I did it right, I mean, I still don't know if I'm in the cloud.

And then I thought (now, not when I was trying to not think about anything) that my soul's a lot like a cloud—a little bit of heaven stuck in the profane mud—so if I propped up my chest with the morals and maxims that don't get much use (if I'm being honest aka virtuous here), then maybe my cloudlet would catch hold of another, and so on and so forth until everyone's invited . . .

And *THEN* I thought (because that obviously didn't work) that by process of elimination my body's the problem. What to do with a body when we're living on air—how thin, how obscure does it have to become? I've *already* subtracted most of its parts. A cock, two hands, a pair of eyes: what else (really) does a computer need?

In dreams my body lives free from all laws: it can fly (it can fuck) it can glide (it can fuck) it can float (it can fuck) it can fuck (but it can't die). So a dream must be a cloud, and the cloud is a dream.

* * *

Want to make yourself lucid? Take back control? Unpack a metaphor? Live within it? Here's an easy test:

1. Pinch yourself

I'm testing as I type. The evidence is inconclusive. If I'm taking the test I wish I had wrote I'd pulse every last moment and second as well, leaving me with a mood board the make of myself. There's no short route to certain: auditing is autobiography.

I'm testing as I type. Here comes a bad mood, and acknowledging that is helping—suddenly it's bad-to-moderate, then just plain moderate, and on account of all the attention I'm paying myself, I'd say it's approaching a pretty good mood, and there, that's where it's staying . . . but <u>*now*</u> NPR tells me that *armies of marketers, pollsters and social scientists are trying to figure out what Americans are thinking about—issues like global warming or Lady Gaga's latest outfit* and DOWN! my mood plunges UP! go my hands while my mouth opens wide with GETOUTOFMYBRAIN! though I guess I should really be saying (dirty joke: what do you call a collection of tweets?) GETOUTOFMYTWAT!

I'm not being punny
the word is doing double doody
computer programs read my tweets
they're learning *biorhythm*speak
they know if I'm naughty
they know if I'm moody
that's not very funny.

<u>FUCK YOU SCOTT GOLDER</u>. <u>FUCK YOU DAVID LAZER</u>.
I'm onto you jackals. I scream ice cream. I'll eat a Blizzard™ or die in a blizzard. The computer will never know the difference.

I almost forgot why I brought this up, and actually I didn't mean to rip it a new one . . . anyways these computers are finding that the twat's mood day in day out is pretty standard: cinna-scented in the morning, shitty through the daytime and sweet sweet surrendering by the evening. What's weird is you'd think, yeah, of course during the week everyone is shitting out the

9-to-5: shitting in a chair or shitting on a crapper or shitting into a cup of *Sumatran! Cold! Brew!* or doing all that and more because *who really even pays attention anymore?* but no, NPR says that twats feel this way on the WEEKENDS TOO (!?!?!) and iDunno-what2think... *what does working mean for the person who works?*

Is the Noonday Demon overstaying his welcome, dragging three-depression lunches out into full-time benders? Does he buzz like a tube hanging over your cubicle? Do you work in a cubicle (you, as in you: the general you) or are new offices different? Lofts? Glass?

I wouldn't know—iWork from home! I get to dress casual as gravedigger wont and eat all the pizza I can afford, but if you have your demon then I get his brother: he comes every midnight to oil my cog (misses hints, loiters) . . . so don't go considering me *too* lucky. Just do me a favor and take a fucking break. Leisure, people: it shouldn't be that hard!

But . . . the . . . point . . . is: morning-daytime-evening is a great schedule to keep, if you don't have all the time in the world but are still serious about figuring out, once and for all, if you're in the cloud. If I were you, I'd audit myself three times a day, seven days a week, twelve months a year for as long as it takes to know within the standard deviation of, say, the tip of my cock to my balls, if I am different in a cloud-sort-of-way than in a body-sort-of-way or a performative-disruption-of-my-incorporated-Other-sort-of-way, which will be difficult to gauge as I'm always pissing about the planet going *I, I, I, I, I, I, I* and when I'm not doing that I'm online going *Tyler, Tyler, Tyler, Tyler, Tyler, Tyler, Tyler: je, eh, rim-bowl?*

Want to make yourself lucid? Take back control? Unpack a metaphor? Live within it? Here's an easy three-step test:

1. Pinch yourself in the morning
2. Pinch yourself in the daytime
3. Pinch yourself in the evening

* * *

OK. It's a year later. I've got bad news. You guessed it. I still don't know if I'm in the cloud, *really*, I mean, *everything in its right place* is my life, and if there were differences, like the extinction of one cat; or 5 following 4 (we didn't need an ad campaign to tell us that); or if now I can stretch the story of myself across more gigabytes, because my programs have colonized the frontiers they invented to beget the need for still more; and if I am slightly older; and a little lonelier on account of my thousand new *friends*, well, the differences no longer seem different. They're warm, customary, and natural—a patchwork cloak of my everyday, *which can be thrown aside at any moment.* Underneath there's no cage or cento or coal just a free bird who pledged, of his own accord, to remain as is (that bird is me).

THIS ISN'T A TRICK I'M NOT TRICKING ME OR ANY BODY! *My left hand is not the hidden labor of my right.* I'm writing with both; *the one comments on the other.* I'm <u>showing</u> you both—they are sad (not glad) and <u>very visible</u>.

I am *homo œconomicus*. I am an *entrepreneur of myself.* I took this job to support my Art, and it fills only my nights and most weekends.

I put myself here. My prestige is my own.

If you're shocked that I'm writing this bald-in-the-face, then you're simply reading it wrong. I'm not *mad as hell.* To the contrary: I'm liberated by my work! As long as I make the keywords pop at a steady *romantical* tick, my editor lets lie his lazy eye.

Snooki *Real Housewives* Kardashian orgy if you're shocked that I'm writing this bald-in-the-face, then you're simply reading it wrong: you've mistaken my Potemkin for a village, you've mistaken yourself for a human. You've mistaken me for a writer.

Permit me to clarify (I realize this may come as somewhat of a surprise):

You are not a human. You are an eyeball.

I am not a writer. I am a content farmer. These words mean more to the Google robot than they do 2 u.

There are some ways to wear precarity. The *nihilists* dress in uniform shifts. They guild the scaffold of unfinished fates (a network is also a cage). They say: *I speak. I do something by saying these words; moreover, I declare what it is that I do while I do it.*

Then there are the immaterials and the slactivists. Also: users, spambots, and the *infra-thin* seams between. You have options, but you will be cut to the measure of your cloth. Choice, after all, is the cognitariat's *cogito*—prosumers double up their binds . . . Well?

* * *

My consumers are they not my producers? Passion is a calculable asset so how can the longing to belong become a money spinner? I feel like someone must have turned that angel in the wrong direction, and I'm that angel. I'm surfing on the crest of the denominator, and thank God I'm nearsighted, thank God for that, because I'd *prefer not to* look too far ahead. I *would rather turn back*. I did see some flashing lights. Red and grey and a bit of orange. Some blue, then a lot of it. You'd be better off looking at the victuals.

Angels have ears (genitals: uncertain), so I heard an echo about identity waves that came and broke (they won or they lost is what I took from it) and culture wars no one wants to talk about or is afraid of bringing up, like I can be afraid of bringing up politics at a dinner party in case the candles get dislodged. The vibe seems to be *they're over* and anyways my friends and me are feeling so social that anything that looks like ideology makes us want to reach for DELETE. That's the nice thing about being young. The battles have been fought so we can marvel at our capacity to type . . . ! Eventually we'll self-actualize as philanthropy and biology and meanwhile voice our right to have a voice in the haptic speech that says, with a click: *Enjoy!*

* * *

Our writing tools are also working on our thoughts, Nietzsche wrote, but iDunno, *DON'TISEEMCOGENT2U?!?* When I was seven Dad bought me AOL though at that time its name was America Online and my name was *tylerc@aol.com* which you're thinking is amazing. I know! I was the third tyler after tylera and tylerb and I would private chat users while watching *Reality Bites* and you thought I never knew a thing about grunge!

So there I was—netware pioneer—moving at a *grueling pace* into a land of plenty, so call it the Dysentery or 2many-buffaloburgers or the grueling pace: my brain became a squishy keyboard, and then when me and Lesley and Jessica felt like we couldn't be all the bff we wanted OUT! with the monitor OUT! with the keyboard OUT! with the hard drive. My brain became an after-school conference call and then it became a pencil and paper *we started writing letters for real*. None of the ones I got were stained with tears or lace or lockets EVENSTILL we were moving backwards to a simpler more romantic time . . . at least we were until they got my class photo well to be fair Lesley was more acne than girl so it was a mutual *let's call the whole thing off.*

Kittler says Nietzsche bought a *writing ball* from Hans Rasmus Johan Malling-Hansen: it was a little globe the old bat crouched over and for him and his real myopia and his meta-myopia and ego and syphilis and his slimy oyster mitts *it was great!* other than for the fact that the globe made a shadow on the paper the size of itself, so less *great*, maybe, and more *the blind leading the blind*. And talk about the *crazy following the crazy*: K says N *changed from arguments to aphorisms, from thoughts to puns*. Could be he was THE WORLD'S FIRST MECHANICAL PHILOSOPHER!

So now I wonder *WHAT IS A THING LIKE ME?* which I guess is the same thing as asking *WHAT DO YOU USE? Continuous present is one thing and beginning again and again is another thing. These are both things. And then there is using everything*. There's not a place that can't be used (and I use lots of things (sometimes) people included) no unuse platform everything is useful, only at first unusual then very usual then laid in the graveyard like the one in New York and probably every city there ever was? Does it choke the sides of the Information Superhighway with *Y2K body bags* or is it better to say flat stone prop or Hollywood village or global village or Potemkin village? Does every corpse get a megabyte or a kilobyte or a trilobite or I've never denominated so low what's next a byte then an atom then quark then boson then *how useless am I really?*

We all need validation from wherever it comes lest we live out our lives in a lack . . .

Did this post strike at your soft center in a moment of particular duress? Are you like I was, struggling to turn an MFA on the job market? Need a gig on the side while you chip away at your Great American Novel? Do you love Nietzsche as much as me? And are you available to work 11 p.m. to 7 a.m. on a daily basis?

* * *

Snooki *Real Housewives* Minaj à trois *has anyone written so fast their fingers broke*? It's a bit of a problem I'm prone to admit: I'm just as unique as the species. When bones get to breaking (inevitably) my editor will sooner rent a new pair than repair mine (that pair might be you).

When you live like a vampire you get fired like a vampire Jeff just GChatted from the other side of the Internet, and that obliged me to type, *True Blood* (true that). *You can't make a case for insurance if your employees are undead, which is why in my future everyone's so relieved when the United Citizen Federation* starts mass-producing vats that they practically rip their brains right out of their heads and dunk them in the goo. *THANK GOD NO MORE HEALTH CARE*, they all exclaim (Jeff "laughs"). *Just send us an energy bill.*

Nevermind the carpal tunnel! I could care less about my body I'm an organ döner once in a dream I even gave a kidney to my little bro and I'm still milking points for that EVENSO if *my future* doesn't go my way I just know that when I "die" the speculators will arrive with their rainforests and rainforests of contracts. That's it that will be IT for me I'll be carved up like that pin-up Urban Outfitters sold that made everyone realize feminism wasn't dead, because someone had to be making all that racket, but anyways the head of Urban Outfitters gave money to Rick Santorum and I'm not über-gay if America wants to sell us *LEGALIZE GAY* Apparel I won't buy it but I won't look the other way if my friend does BUTTHEPOINTIS! I am that chick *I'M* getting divvied up: the rump for Apple and the round for Facebook and my loin for Microsoft and the chuck for Skype and my ribs for Adobe and my breasts for Google and the soup bones for the ghosts like AltaVista and AOL and Geocities and Angelfire cuz at some point I must have given them some pound of myself. That *South Park* episode about how if you agree to the TOS of an iTunes upgrade you're basically signing on to be a *father-anus-mouth-anus-mouth-machine* aka *Human Centipede* really got me thinking, and if I weren't already such a *known known* of a content farmhand I'd seriously drop out and join *Anonymous*. *CALLING ALL RE ACTIVE AGENTS!*

we'd gangbang the life out of Apple we'd fill every port so nothing could come out and all the while it's no-means-yes-ing our cohorts will get shredding and tagging

MELTDOWN ACCELERATION, CYBERIAN INVASION,
SHIZOTECHNICS, K-TACTICS, BOTTOM-UP
BACTERIAL WARFARE, VOODOO ANTIHUMANISM, SYNTHETIC
FEMINIZATION, RHIZOMATICS, CONNECTIONISM,
KUANG CONTAGION, VIRAL AMNESIA, MICROINSURGENCY,
WINTERMUTATION, NEOTROPY, DISSIPATOR
PROLIFERATION, LESBIAN VAMPIRISM

and you won't even realize it you ignorant *Matrix* man you will wake up the next day an emancipated being. *Hylè-o!*

* * *

They can take my body but they can't take my brain they can engineer me but they can't imagineer me I can tell I know how to tell *I'm thinking my own thoughts I'm feeling my own feelings* and if I have a thought or a feeling while I'm working that's normal that's me that's just for me it's obvious I have to work and I can't not be myself I can't button up my psyche if anything I dress it down I surf as I go my lifestyle is a mode of dissent I protest by consumer choice if I am not marketed to how could I be a demographic if I am not put to work then why would I *refuse to work?*

Sure my editor says a thousand other people are thinking and reading and eating similar things but he can't call us *brobos inner directeds spectral empaths echo boomers* we're not a class that's ripe for the picking our rents are fine as is thank you very much we are altruistic not narcissistic we live the moment not historicize it *snark* is an ugly nasty slut we were friends after college it threw me some work it gave me a ladder and told me to climb . . .

That's not the reason I left New York I just got tired of seeing my name on the Big Board is all the publishing scene is overrated besides plus snark is as stale as yesterday's paper our friendship dried up when the work did (not that I'm *that* shallow). These days the options are unsexily thin if you've got outsized talent and undersized finance you'd better settle down on a content farm.

You can take the farmer off the farm my editor taunts when I threaten to quit. *Your Great American something reads like short Internet nothings. You're a highly skilled graduate of ambient attention and live from one post to the next.*

Get off the farm and back into the stable, my parents most Sundays say. *We didn't support you through your MFA so that you could jerk off all day.* Then they laugh in that awful way people do when the joke is just for them not us a selfish joke so regular on the phone do I hear this joke yet each and every time my ego (still) goes poof.

What's a *snark* stable but the piggiest pen that's reason enough to leave.

* * *

I took this job to think while I type but the thinking's becoming a problem. Let's say I'm in a foul mood getting substantially fouler, so foul that the cloud makes a shadow on itself the size of itself, sending bits and blobs to a suicide fall (those droplets are possibly me). Is this the cloud's way of breaking it off? Is my unoriginal genius too (too) unoriginal?

Let's say I'm an airborne virus clinging to the cloud while all of my brain bugs get hopping; even the oldest and surest memes won't bet on my chances to spread them. *Just as I was about to put finger to key* they leave my head empty with the echoes of thoughts that grow famous in other guys' mouths.

Small and stubborn are the fictions of science. They attach to most any host. Him with the most beats all other hosts.

* * *

This life provides the thinnest of consequence. Pain is only a mouse-click from palliation. Pleasure is just as close. A new email rewards for the time spent waiting. A podcast is even better.

Here's the beauty of my situation. There's not a minute in the day when I can't stream something into my head. If there's a job for a technocrat in my *constantly moving happiness machine* then I filled it. I've become the administrator of my input. I'm pure receptacle.

Call it a higher state of neurosis? The thing you're constantly putting off, that thing you're distracting yourself from, is the silence, the absence of something else that clears ground for... a worthless idea. You fill the stage of production because, if left alone to soliloquize, you'd have not much of anything to say. So you stream, you stretch. You participate in a worldview.

There are small ruptures: a teacher in Juárez strains to distract her students as gunfire erupts in the schoolyard. They may register in the eyes or throat, in the ears and then, eventually, in the brain, and a feeling of *purpose* will emerge, *as if there were something more you could do*. You find solace in the knowledge that something was transmitted, and, by virtue of not watching reality television, by virtue of not having sex or shopping, you could hear and did hear.

This is civic responsibility, no? This fills some quota for the day. Your mind, briefly fogged, can move on to receive other impressions, anecdotes, reportage, and accounts. Perhaps it will linger over a dark thought, or laugh in the place of your mouth. *When NPR acts for me, I myself act through NPR.* You're not participating, but in the time you devote to listening, *on their behalf*, you are doing some part, playing *a* part.

And why should it be any other way? If you were the subject of the story, who would read it? Who would be there to listen?

* * *

Here is a thought (an NPR thought) not a laugh or a cloud (though perhaps in the cloud) you might have heard it did some work *did it work for you*? it worked for me *I'M TRYING TO BE RIGOROUS!!!* but when it's Žižek you're citing you keep Baby Ruth and the bathwater and the tub and the towel and Mom and the soap and *nothing*, really, is out of the question is not hiding an answer HERE is a thought more like an analogy: *Imagine there's this great big stone disc sitting in a village. One person gives it to another person. But the stone doesn't move. It's just that everybody in the village knows the stone now has a new owner. One time, the stone wound up on the bottom of the ocean and everybody decided that the piece of stone money was still good so somebody today owns this piece of stone money, even though nobody's seen it for over 100 years or more.*

Better when fictitious has a fact however heavy better a derivative derives from no back asset just a *Golden Ass* at least two birds per hand is more than enough who is counting most no one it seems. If it's allegory you want you can stay the plot call it curious magick that made Apuleius an ass but *will salvation follow for the financiers*? Someone says they've fucked off to teach education iDunno a lawyer I know who works in the Lipstick Building says the elevator opened on the Madoff floor a week or so after the news and *they took it all THEY TOOK THE COPPER WIRE FROM THE WALLS* who believes lawyers these days let alone friends is what you're thinking but also think history + time + history + time it's already the butt of the joke just look at the last season of *Curbed* if you don't believe me BUTTHEPOINTIS! salvation followed

Apuleius. He joined the cult of Isis. Motherhood comma magic comma fertility ensued *so does this mean the world should be ruled by women*? Or do we need a lady Jonestown of our OWN? If I roll a stone off the Eastern seaboard, could we say it fills the debt? Would it accrue value like barnacles? Can we promise to never visit even though we could belief is a sweater well-worn discarded moth-eaten the perfect thing I'm not clinging!

We can promise not to visit because we are enough our souls. If an ancestor hoisted by his totem becomes a god after three, maybe four generations, I can speculate where our stone will be the psychical interest will be immense a whole other stone growing on top. Maybe we're sinking in is what this image is saying or we need to sink in rather but aren't we always: rain is the string that holds the cloud a cord must be cut SUN needs *a copula a copula a shaft* that corpse on your arm was a bubble. *A mask of manner can be held in place from within. We have had a flood of original ideas in all media, works of singular beauty as well as significant milestones in the history of inflation, but at that moment there was only <u>this balloon</u>, concrete particular, hanging there.*

* * *

I was walked onto a lake and told it was a cloud. The cloud, they said, was an architecture. All there was was water trying to crawl back up the canal (it won't work).

Once in Central Park I saw a long beard burlap sack and bare feet *he's a New Primitive* whispered *The New York Times* so even before the Greeks civilization was very advanced they had paved roads and painted markings for joggers he knew how to run in the right direction.

* * *

Five Fingers *BIG DEBATE ON RUNNING BLOGS* my editor is forcing me to write. They *mimic the feeling of running barefoot* (please place your eyeballs on the relevant ads) BUT have you ever seen *Blue Velvet*? The grass is skyscrapers in an insect city. We're walking on somebody else's planet and calling it our own.

Which is better mimesis or time travel? Why are commodities stepping into the role of the disavowed can a Honda 919 *run around naked* and still be a fetish what will return if Dyson gives the repress there's barely a second before we see our waste spinning like a snow globe (please place your eyeballs on the relevant ads).

There are some basic rules to live by so we can remain unperturbed unaware consensually engineered even ignorant. The first is transparency. Transparency is important because it makes clear what is the world.

When you purchase a Volkswagen Phaeton *a specially designed train transports you from Dresden's central station to the "Transparent Factory." One can watch workers in white overalls moving around on parquet wooden floors with gigantic robot arms bringing the hanging cars to the workers, and not the other way around.*

Some small processing plants are willing to let customers onto the kill floor. Lorentz Meats, in Cannon Falls, Minnesota, is so confident of their treatment of animals that they have walled their abattoir in glass.

PLEASE PLACE YOUR EYEBALLS
ON THE RELEVANT ADS!

You can watch the vehicle you can drive the chicken you can eat. This you can read in *The Omnivore's Dilemma* is the humane way to go about destroying your meal what a strange word in this case: there is no humanity in your meal live or dead. You see the animal perhaps the animal sees you *no accusation no Disney double take*. Two ontologies are confirmed. You see the men the women assembling your car they may see you. You see the labor process like a friend not an alien you see the product like a wingman not an alien how could anyone be alienated before the face of another?

There's an old saying that people in glass houses shouldn't throw stones you don't want to read this just see it don't want to think the norm it deviates from don't want transparency to be the exception what's unexceptional must then be opaque.

If *I* am an exception: too late to go back no time to dally I don't need brainwashing *I am at ease with myself*. The rule must change the category too deserts need chilling the sun unhitch *drift* in the place of a clockwork walk A NEW IMPERATIVE! I lean on the letter I surf like an angel I live out my maxim with full force *YOU* will become the conscious capitalist I am paid to say I am.

* * *

What is a transparent factory in a cloud is a riddle I can't write my way through. Rain is the string that holds the cloud it sustains but it also serves a use. There's not a place that can't be used *everything is useful* if I had a dance I'd make rain if I had a *cloudbuster* I'd make the *queerest-looking clouds you ever saw*; I'd pump them full of orgone they'd be gorged with purpose <u>heavy enough</u> to pin the edges of the cloud like little buts on a parachute. Less violent than the Victorians more ludic than labored æther 2.0 would descend on the earth like a network a mist in a cover. Then at the least (at the very last) we'd understand what it is that we're in.

There's not a place that can't be used *everything is useful* if I served a use *if I farmed myself* I'd pull seeds from the cloud from my brain from my posts every past and tomorrow and real false idea gets a row gets to sit out our Everything Age till the season and circumstance say. A future will spring up a harvest like Art *my future a future of equal size* such descriptive exactingly factual crops every root every leaf every branch every fruit every blossom is what it resembles. The vat where you live and the vat where you die the machines that will build what the harvest describes even these things the harvest resembles.

That is my work that's why I farm my job drives my Art as a means to an end I go seeding one world with another.

That is my work *this* is my job agent and operative farmer and spy hiding in plain sight banal an exploitable prop till the season and circumstance say. When the Kittler of *then* describes Art of the *soon* what other words could he use? I'm THE WORLD'S FIRST FUTURE REALIST.

in*Formal* reads the party of *my future*; it's so immanent that everyone even the queer clouds wet themselves they spill out life juice in a big tsunami that breaks all our vats and our souls and the earth but *doesn't everything come at a cost*? our brains and the insect city drown even the bugs that would outlive a nuclear winter can't outlive the power of life itself.

Our memes will be a cargo cult they won't have any clue what to make of the wires and goo so that's why there will be a memorial at my farm—or there would be if it were true. Honestly I've spent more than a year on this and will have to keep writing until I'm certain.

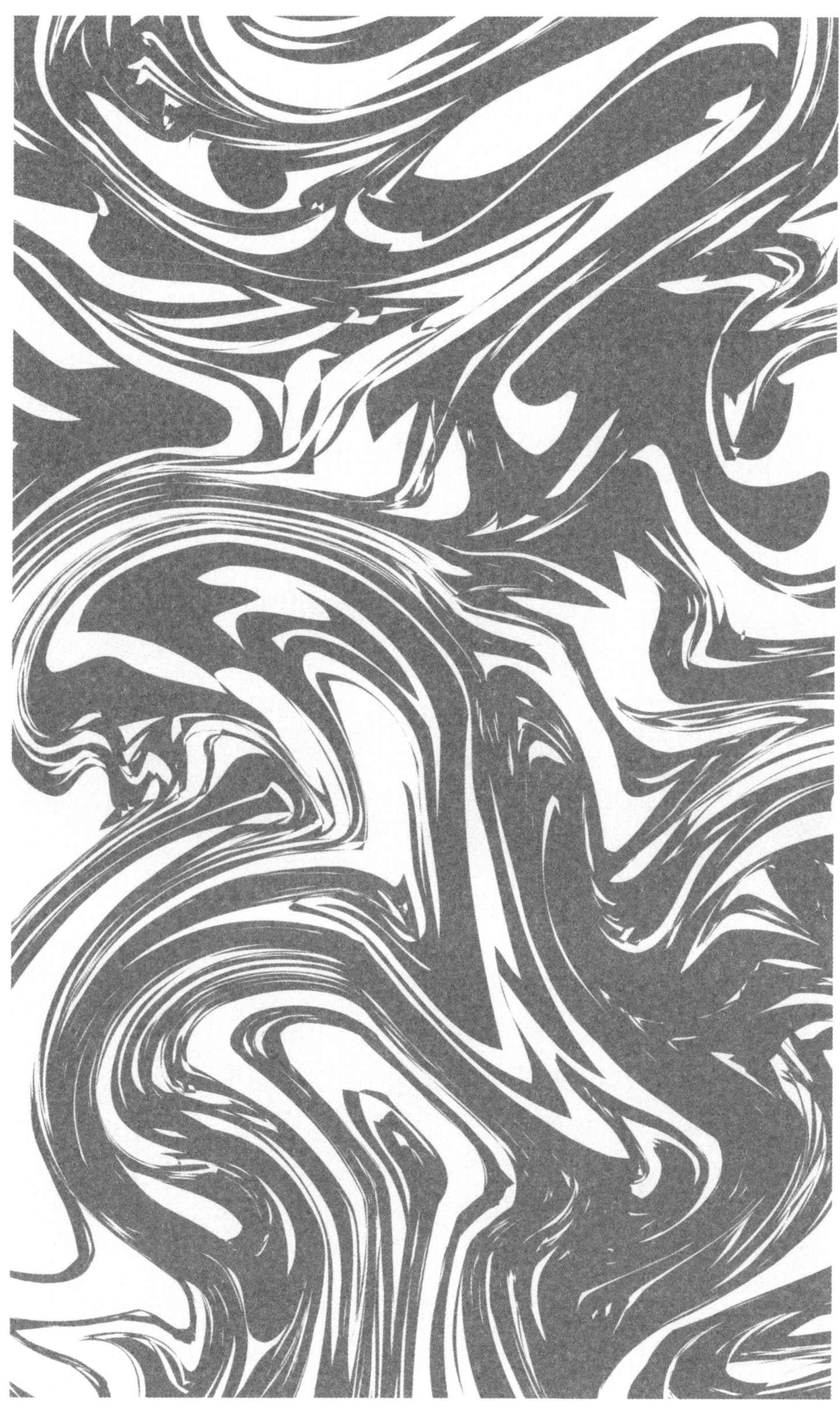

My Life in the Cloud

Tyler Coburn

A year after graduating from college, I was living in London and having my first taste of precarity. Almost every day, I'd scroll the Craigslist job postings, quickly learning that my standards were much lower than I thought. I moved other people's objects around the city, stood in rooms holding canapés, stood in alleys holding trash bags filled with canapés. The only time I drew the line was when my catering company asked me to stand in rooms holding canapés in a diaper and bonnet. True story.

I also moved words around Microsoft: for forgotten art journals, Jewish cultural centers, bottom-feeding media blogs. A house cleaning company hired me to write original content for its website. Over a few months, I churned out posts about kitchen cleaning tips, dust mite prevention, and the best ways for young mothers to organize their daily tasks (writing from great personal experience, of course).

It would have been a stretch to call myself a creative, let alone a brain-for-hire. Across all of these jobs, whether on the web or in the city, I rarely felt like I was doing more than exercising my hands: moving digits to move things—aesthetic things, informational things. Even before I had the critical vocabulary to articulate this feeling, I could recognize the reach of it. I was merely one of many actors playing out a new labor paradigm.

* * *

That was 2006, roughly the time when the first great content farms came into being—when my scattershot online content production formalized itself into an industry proper.

So, what is a content farm? Simply put, a content farm is an online news organization that generates articles based on trending topics.

Take Associated Content, created in 2005 and later rebranded as Yahoo! Voices. In its heyday, this farm used robots to scan websites like Google Trends and generate relevant article prompts, which could be claimed and written by its content farmers, sometimes with as short a turnaround as thirty minutes. Associated Content was known, at its peak, to publish ten thousand pieces of content a week.

While it's *true* that there's a human on either end of content-farmed articles, we should not mistake their economic purpose: They're being written to game search-engine algorithms. They deploy trending language to ensure higher rankings. The articles get more clicks, their advertisers more "eyeballs," to use industry parlance. Every eyeball, another few cents, and so on and so forth.

As another example, consider Demand Media, a consortium of websites like eHow and Livestrong. In 2009, the company was projected to be publishing one million items a month. Rumor had it Demand was so profitable that major news hubs like *The New York Times* would soon go out of business. As of 2010, Demand was the seventeenth largest web property in the US—and the first content farm to go public.

Now, content farms have been criticized for lessening the quality of platforms like Google, bringing users to lesser-quality sites. They've been described as the fast food chains of the information superhighway, and the reputations of search engines have suffered by proxy. One response came in the form of Google Panda, a more robust algorithm that the company introduced in 2011. Panda was designed to lower the search rank of thin, low-quality sites, thus directly targeting the stuff coming out of the farms. Since then, content farms have continued to spread, but in general, such measures have had substantial effects on the industry.

Demand Media's sites, for instance, lost roughly a quarter of their traffic in the immediate wake of Panda; moreover, the company's stock crashed and stayed down. Yahoo! Voices shut down in the summer of 2014, sending regular contributors scrambling. The era of the big content farms is coming to a close, and by many accounts, we are transitioning to a "clickbait" economy.

* * *

To come full circle: I began as a precarious content generator at the same time as the rise of these farms, and around 2011, when I returned to research them, I found quite a bit of scorched earth.

Nonetheless, I wanted to think about the content farmer, this member of the creative class in pursuit of the self-liberation and entrepreneurial fame promised by post-Fordist rhetoric—who believes in millennial myths, despite all evidence to the contrary.

I've spent time in online forums with farmers, where I've heard some common stories. Most also work part- or full-time jobs, but are keen to pursue their true passion of writing. Content farms thus provide room to hone their skills and generate clips; few aspiring writers view them as a primary revenue stream. Demand Media happens to be one of the best remunerators in the field, paying around $15 an article. Several other farms pay an entry-level fee of a cent per word, which can increase to a few cents after a certain number of contributions.

Content farms, in short, are a means to a different end, yet many of the farmers write for companies that don't provide bylines, preventing them from using their articles as clips. Additionally, given the trying times the industry is facing, farms have been known to close sites and slash pay without warning. Their farmers can either consent to the changes or leave.

Some farmers just burn out, pure and simple. Others attempt to take action.

To give an example: In 2011, AOL bought *The Huffington Post* for $315 million, turning the political blog into an advertising-financed operation. Jonathan Tasini, who had contributed 216 unpaid articles to the blog, filed a $105 million class action suit on behalf of himself and nine thousand other unpaid bloggers, arguing they deserved a cut.

The case ended up being dismissed on the grounds that these writers had never worked with the expectation of being paid; their argument, in short, was "baseless." Huffington gave a similar defense, adding that personal passion and cultural capital were sufficient motivators for her contributors.

There are other cases worth discussion, aimed at companies like Yelp and CrowdFlower. Each is negotiating the terms of a specific web platform, yet they all raise a basic question about the labor rights of digital content generators—a question that certainly extends to the farmers.

Of course, many of us experience similar labor conditions in our online and offline lives. The content farmer, as such, is not an exceptional case, but an exemplary one for considering different writing on the Information Age: from Jodi Dean's theory of "communicative capitalism"—where messages are made to be circulated, not generate dialogue—to Michael Hardt's claim that the affective and emotional dimensions of human relations have assumed dominant positions within the contemporary economy.

As an instrument, affect has been used to naturalize emerging forms of labor and sociality, giving the figures but hiding the ground. The content farm is one site where we see this in action: Articles are pitched to "populist" interest, empowering their writers and edifying readers with . . . listicles and how-to guides.

The thin, necessary veneer we maintain is that we are humans—are welcomed into cyberspace in our full capacity as humans. True, this may all be a front for a game of economics played by robots and search-engines and advertisers, but if we have a role, let it be more than an "eyeball." Let our online participation deliver us into a future that's more than monetizable. We know we're "eyeballs," but still.

* * *

In one of his cattiest moments, American novelist Truman Capote said of the work of Jack Kerouac, "That's not writing; that's just typewriting." What would Capote have made of writing on the Internet? The content farmer also interests me for this reason: For what we do upon recognizing that we're writing less for humans than algorithmic capture—that our words will mean more to the Google robot than to anyone else.

There's no denying that we are quickly adapting to the currents of the online world, growing less and less like the readers of language than the parsers of text. We attempt to keep up with the informational demand by sorting through content much like a robot reader. To a certain strain of thinkers, it would be better to give up this John Henry narrative. We are already writing more for machines than humans—and our machines are also doing their own farming and writing. So why not just let them do all the work? In the words of Canadian poet Christian Bök, "Why hire a poet to write a poem when the poem can in fact write itself?"

Here we have a familiar endgame. Whether we are dealing with poetic, artistic, or other labor, the theory goes, technology can decrease our working time and increase the time for personal reflection. It makes a gamble on the future: that we will benefit from ceding more control to machines. Yet somewhere in these quotes is a darker intimation. Perhaps we won't have much choice in the matter.

* * *

With these thoughts in mind, I created *I'm that angel*, a book made to be performed in data centers. My project is very much a response to this endgame, departing from the belief that we should not just make do with our online roles, nor abandon them wholesale, but put them to the service of imagining new forms of subjectivity and sociality.

The book is narrated from the perspective of a content farmer in the throes of intense semiotic anxiety. At the time I began writing it, "the cloud" was entering common parlance, and I frequently had the experience of hearing friends use the term, only to then remark, "I don't know what it means, but I know that we're supposed to use it."

I've lived through many generations of digital technology, but this transition stood out, perhaps for how a diffuse, natural form could become a diffuse, naturalized metaphor—for how a symbol could come to operate without needing to clarify what, in fact, it stood for.

Herein lies the semiotic anxiety of my protagonist: not understanding what the cloud signifies, and thus how he can come to relate to it. If he knows himself as a body of certain extensivity, and if the cloud is diffuse, how does he know if he's already inside or outside of it? And if, to paraphrase Groucho Marx, the cloud is a club that's soliciting his membership, would he even want to be a part of it?

These are ridiculous questions, of course—little psychic wisps that cloud the content farmer living within the cloud. We commonly describe the stultifying effects of such anxiety: doubt, worry, the onset of paralysis. Yet in my book, anxiety is the motor that winds the protagonist up, spins him around, and confirms that for all of his online perambulations, he also holds a place and a body in the world.

Content farming establishes two parameters: a necessary quota of trending language, an article of sufficient length and quality. So I wondered: With limited editorial oversight, to what other use could a content farmed article be put? Could one claim the linguistic space around quotas, the spans between buzzwords? Could a memoir be written by a farmer smuggling the self into industrialized writing?

In his 1917 essay, "Art as Technique," the Russian formalist Viktor Shklovsky called for strategies to work against the "automatism of perception" and to "defamiliarize" the habituated aspects of our world. "[A]rt exists that one may recover the sensation of life," he writes. "[I]t exists to make one feel things, to make the stone stony."

I'm that angel is an attempt to make a stony stone. The body is in protest against our diffuse, master metaphor, and language turns thick and suspicious.

* * *

This would be a good point to talk about the physical Internet. But first: Addressing the 2005 graduating class of Kenyon College, David Foster Wallace tells the following joke:

"There are these two young fish swimming along and they happen to meet an older fish swimming the other way, who nods at them and says 'Morning, boys. How's the water?' And the two young fish swim on for a bit, and then eventually one of them looks over at the other and goes, 'What the hell is water?'"

So my protagonist, as I mentioned, suffers from semiotic anxiety. He doesn't understand what the cloud symbolizes and thus can't meaningfully relate to it. Some of us may have once suffered similar anxiety, though we now know what the cloud signifies: the thin devices and remote data storage underpinned by the massive infrastructure of the physical Internet. It's an inaccurate metaphor, as our cloud is tethered to the earth like a balloon, though it's understandable why the internet was made into a heavenly body and not a flimsy piece of manmade rubber.

When I began writing *I'm that angel* in 2011, I felt compelled to demystify the cloud, to pin it down and open it up, to stage a re-encounter between oneself and one's data—to chant, in reminder: "This is water, this is water."

To date, I've held events in more than ten data centers in Europe and North America, inviting small audiences for readings and facilities tours, conducted by data center personnel. These events change with every venue, with the given company, and with what guests bring to the conversation. Allow me to share a few notable stops:

1. The Pionen White Mountains facility in Stockholm, located in a former civil defense center. The name is somewhat of an exaggeration, as Pionen is not in the mountains but beneath an elevated park on a residential street—far from secretive, far from remote.

This site is famous for two things. One, when it was turned into a data center in 2008, the company decided to trick it out James Bond style. Two, if you're in need of a data haven to store your questionable content, look no further than Pionen, which benefits from Sweden's strong freedom of speech and information laws. Past clients include PRQ, a company that hosted The Pirate Bay and WikiLeaks.

As the story goes, WikiLeaks was kicked off of Amazon's data servers in 2010 and began storing its content at Pionen. The famous WikiLeaks releases came from two servers at the facility, which the company chairman later auctioned off to benefit Reporters Without Borders, but not before taking a series of brooding photographs with them.

2. In Glasgow, I read in a data center that was run like an episode of *The Office.* A staffer claimed the industry was fairly humdrum. When she and her co-workers get bored, they pull pranks or make cakes that look like data centers.

An amusing thing happened in the run-up to my event: An employee had pitched an article about *I'm that angel* to *Data Centre Solutions*, which, for those not in the know, is like the *Frieze* of the data center industry. The first time I visited the center, we did a photo shoot for the piece. The resulting image may be the single best piece of evidence that I once stood in a data center—a totally suspect picture, where the CEO and I look like cardboard cutouts Photoshopped into a stock image.

Maybe it's a metaphor for the unrepresentability of big data, the incommensurability of the bodily and the informational . . .

3. I traveled to Haarlem in the Netherlands to perform in a data center. Upon meeting me, the press liaison said that she had read my book. She remarked, "You must be very smart or very stupid, and I have no idea which." This remains the best thing that's been said about it.

Our tour guide was the sort of person who flies to conferences on cloud security and knows his way around the discourse. At the end of the tour, one of my guests asked what the future of the Internet looks like. Here's what I recall:

He cited a 2012 UN conference on telecommunications governance, attended by representatives of most of the world's countries. The debate revealed a sharp division of opinion: America and the European Union supported Internet freedoms, while China, Russia, Saudi Arabia, and others preferred strong—even authoritarian—limits on Internet access.

In the wake of the Snowden revelations, we know that this division isn't so sharp. For example, the United States's "super-jurisdiction," as Metahaven claims, extends well beyond the measures afforded by the USA Patriot Act, allowing the government to search and seize data within its territory, as well as from any cloud service that conducts business with the country, no matter its physical location.

In response, we've since seen a partitioning of the cloud: of France and Canada taking precautions against governmental data being routed through US servers—of the rise of securitized private clouds in countries like Switzerland and Luxembourg, which protect your data at considerable cost.

In some cases, this partitioning can play to the advantage of free Internet advocates, as with recent policy efforts in Brazil and The Philippines, as well as for countries like Iceland, which Metahaven champions for turning its legal sovereignty, real-world isolation, and global connectedness into the foundation of a new experiment with Internet democracy.

Nonetheless, our tour guide was fairly pessimistic, seeing the future as one in which governments enforce greater network control in the name of protecting civil liberties—perhaps going so far as soliciting cyberterrorist attacks to justify increasing security.

Cyberterrorism can take many forms. You can cut an undersea cable or set off a bomb in the American Northwest, but the greatest threats to the Internet, he told us, come through the lines. The network is far too complex, in short, for the struggle to only play out in physical space.

* * *

Ever since that tour, I've been turning over his words, because they raise a question that's also pertinent to my project: When no single data center can embody or stand in for the whole, what can we do with this site? Why visit this site?

Even this many years into the project, I wouldn't claim to have answers. In the spirit of James Lee Byars, I'm just looking for questions, and the experience of bringing audience members and data center employees together is each and every time a question: new, different, and enduring. Recognizing a data center's incapacity to embody or stand in for the whole—being given access to a transparent view, yet leaving with the feeling that things are more opaque than you ever imagined—discussing energy, security, politics, and subjectivity within the unceasing hum of the physical internet: These are not nothings, not just grist for the algorithmic mill.

In general, I've found that these data center events serve as reminders of what Mark Andrejevic calls the "knowledge asymmetry of the big data era": the divide between those who generate data and those who instrumentalize it, as well as an infrastructural divide "shaped by ownership and control of the material resources for data storage and mining." While my events don't structurally change this asymmetry, they are motivated by a belief that we have a claim on these data centers, much as the centers—as the custodians of the Internet—already have a claim on us.

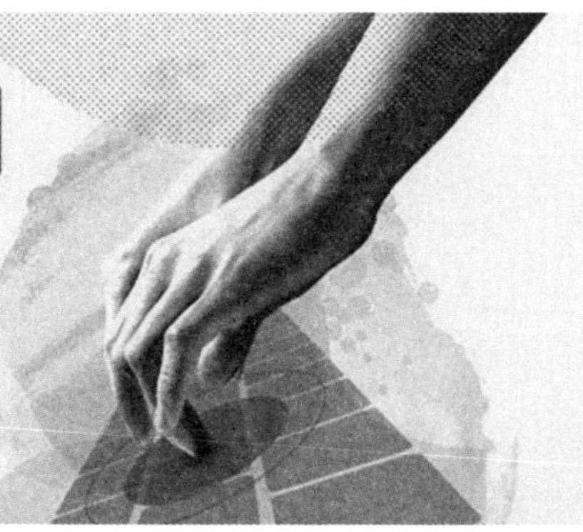
let the world
hear you.
TURN WRITING INTO EARNING

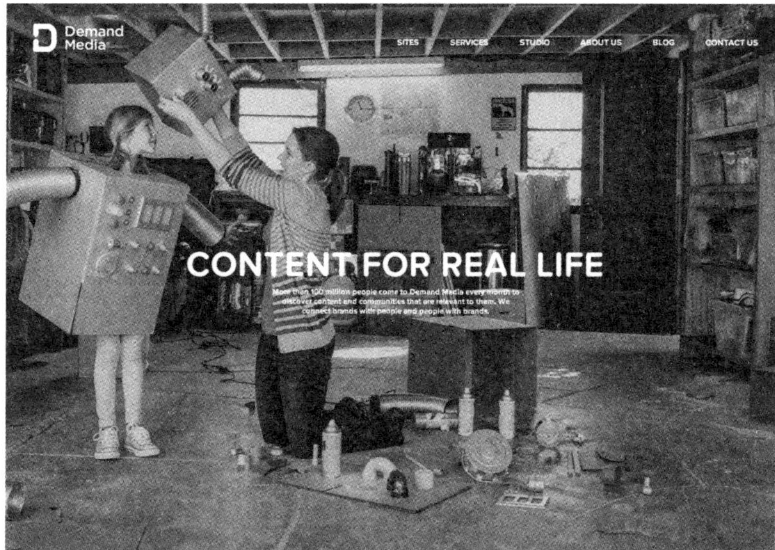
Demand
Media
SITES
SERVICES
STUDIO
ABOUT US
BLOG
CONTACT US
CONTENT FOR REAL LIFE
More than 100 million people come to Demand Media every month to discover content and communities that are relevant to them. We connect brands with people and people with brands.

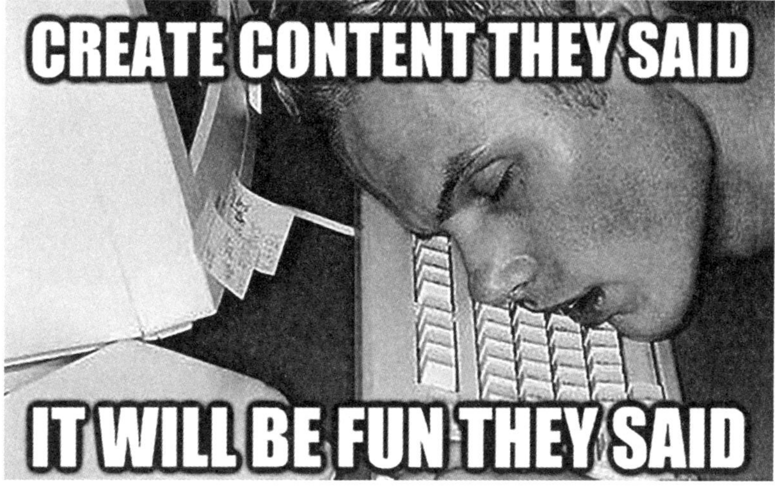
CREATE CONTENT THEY SAID
IT WILL BE FUN THEY SAID

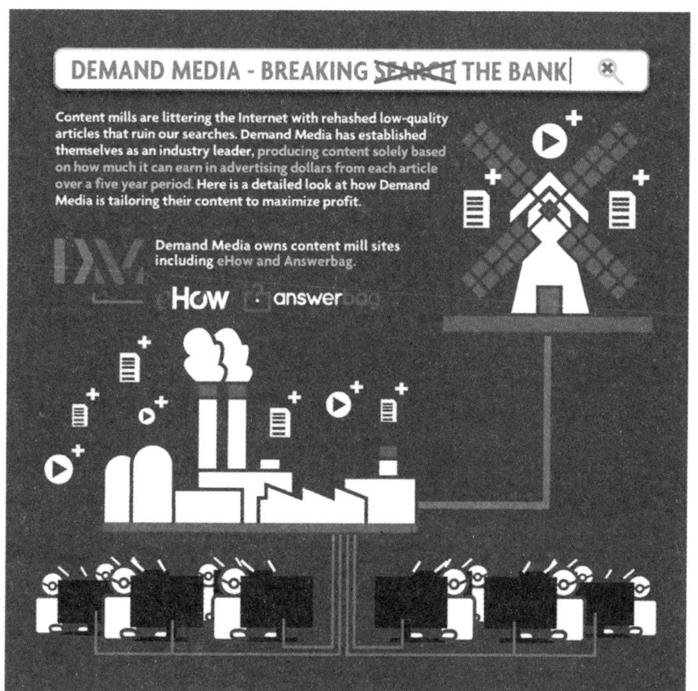
DEMAND MEDIA - BREAKING SEARCH THE BANK
Content mills are littering the Internet with rehashed low-quality articles that ruin our searches. Demand Media has established themselves as an industry leader, producing content solely based on how much it can earn in advertising dollars from each article over a five year period. Here is a detailed look at how Demand Media is tailoring their content to maximize profit.
Demand Media owns content mill sites including eHow and Answerbag.
eHow
answerbag

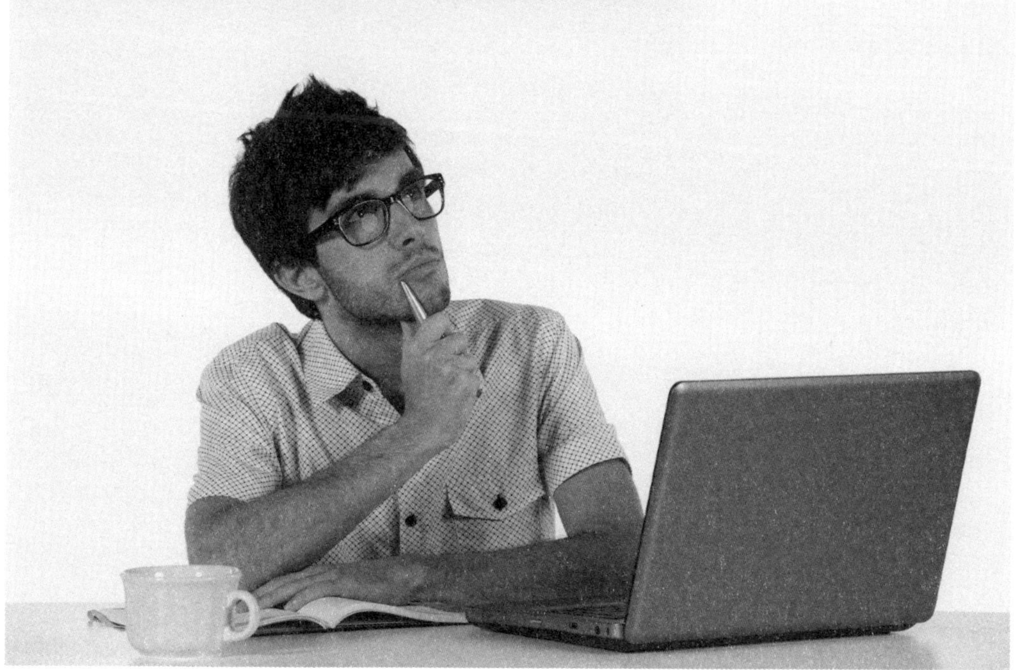

Excerpt from *Order_30763_6*

A.E. Benenson

BOOK REVIEW *(Wherein the narrator hires a forlorn looking young man)*:

A copy of the book portion of *I'm that angel*, was submitted for review at www.customwritings.com, an on-demand writing agency marketed to students and professionals who need quick, inexpensive texts on topics of their choosing. Of their book review process, the site writes:

> *If you are in search of scholarly book reviews, history book reviews, business book reviews, sport book reviews, science fiction book reviews and politics book reviews, you can always trust Custom-Writings.com which is an international company accepted for its book reviews as it has exceptional and excellent book review writers who are eligible to write all kinds of book reviews. Because of our quality and standardized book review writing, our customers believe us and remember us with their problems related to book review writing* [sic]*. Our book review writers follow standard rules and regulations for custom book review writing. For a book review, a skilled writer is required who have* [sic] *gained all the expertise to write book reviews or book review essays quite excellently and flawlessly. We have such book review writers who write a book review with excellence and by tracking* [sic] *a professional approach. Our writers are certified people from all fields of studies and are experienced for* [sic] *writing all kinds of academic book reviews. CustomWritings.com is contacted by nearly 8,000 customers on daily basis which are also its regular customers because they believe in our custom written book reviews which follow a standard book review format* [sic]*. In addition to following standard formats for writing book reviews, the book reviews by our writers are also of high quality and written in a good language. CustomWritings.com provides a book review that is exceptionally written and is checked*

for plagiarism and language errors. We care for our customers and their career, that's why our writers work so hard to make our customers satisfied with our performance.

As a matter of policy, CustomWritings.com does not provide clients with the names of their reviewers, nor any means of directly contacting them for more information that is not directly related to the order. What follows is the unedited, unattributed review:

Order_30763_6

Tyler Coburn in the book *I'm That Angel* laments on the manner in which computers have dominated the lives of people in the 21st century. Now more than ever, the world is hungry for new information, and this has changed lives for individuals in the recent years [*sic*]. The author regrets the use of social media by people to get information regarding other people for gossip. The book refers to computers as answer giving machines that, unfortunately, give answers to all problems in the world. In other words, people are turning to computers for information, which has lead to complicated lifestyles [*sic*]. This essay will delve into the issue of social media, advertisements and appearance exhibited in the information age as depicted by Coburn.

The author starts by stating that his life is like a dream and that life in the world is like living in a cloud. However, with the emergence of computers and the Internet, the world has changed and much control has been given to computers. For instance, the author laments that nowadays, people utilize the Internet to figure out what people are thinking about. For example, NPR reports that markets, social scientists and pollsters are analyzing their figures to understand the thoughts of Americans. This is in addition to Twitter's findings on Lady Gaga's recent outfit. In the modern world, information spreads like a wild fire. Anyone would recall that when Twitter first started, it was a mere social site where people used to communicate their present activities. However, this has changed with Twitter now becoming home to millions of followers who communicate with each other and share their opinions on issues. In most cases, such information has been helpful, but in some cases, the information shared in such sites leaves little to be desired of them. In most cases, social sites like Twitter and Facebook have been used for spreading rumors and such information has been detrimental to the people involved. In other cases, people have used the social media sites to stir controversies rather than solve problems or address issues. However, with as much influence, Coburn states in his book that:

> they can take my body but they can't take my brain they can engineer me but they can't imagineer me I can tell I know how to tell *I'm thinking my own thoughts I'm feeling my own feelings* and if I have a thought or a feeling while I'm working that's normal that's me that's just for me it's obvious I have to work and I can't not be myself I can't button-up my psyche if anything I dress it down I surf as I go my lifestyle is a mode of dissent I protest by consumer choice if I am not marketed to how could I be a demographic if I am not put to work then why would I *refuse to work*

This means that the influence from the media can influence people's behavior and attitudes but it cannot change who they are. As a writer, I feel there is a lot of pressure to change certain attitudes and behaviors on my part but is not enough to change who I am as writer [*sic*].

The author also expresses grief that computers are not useful as they only give one answers. In this part, the author refers to a South Park episode where a human centipede was used to illustrate his point. He regrets that people nowadays refer to the Internet for answers instead of seeking the traditional way of doing things. For example, if people wanted to find answers to certain problems or issues, they would refer to books or consult the relevant professionals for answers. However, things have changed, and the emergence of search engines like Google and Yahoo among others has changed all this traditions [*sic*]. This explains the reason why the author decided to move out from New York because the [*sic*] he could have access to information at the click of a mouse. This meant that he was subjected to both relevant and irrelevant information available on the Internet. When referring to the computers and twitter, Coburn says:

> Computers are finding that the twat's mood day-in-day-out is pretty standard: cinna-scented in the morning, shitty through the daytime and sweet sweet surrendering by the evening. What's weird is you'd think, yeah, of course during the week everyone is shitting out the 9-5; shitting in a chair or shitting on a crapper or shitting into a cup of Sumatran! Cold! Brew! Or doing all that and more because who really pays attention anymore? But no, NPR says the twat feels this way on the WEEKENDS TOO (!?!?!) and iDunnowhat2thing [*sic*] . . . *what does working mean for the person who works?*

I feel that the information being advertised by the media is pretty much the same especially when it comes to sexuality. Access to information has also infiltrated other areas such as advertising, which will later be discussed in the essay. This constant need to have information has consequently turned human beings into pleasure and happy seeking machines. People have been accustomed to new information even when it turns out that the information may not be helpful in most cases.

The author also regrets that there is too much advertisement out there and if there are no billboards then there are pop ups on the Internet. This explains why the author moved out of New York to stay out of this "madness". The author cites that advertisements have done away with the human side of things, and the most of them try to brainwash people into doing things contrary to what they wish. He depicts how this modern generation feels that they are the modern age. In this case, the author cites Madonna, a renowned American artist who seems not to age. She has a new face if the comments made on her new look in her new album are anything to go by. This shows that the modern generation does not allow mothernature [*sic*] to take her course; instead, everybody is trying to beat nature by staying youthful.

The author also suggests that people have lost their self-esteem and are rather seeking other people's opinion on their looks and personality. In other words, the author regrets that people nowadays care so much about what others say about them rather than what they think of themselves, which is not right. Coburn depicts this as "the blind leading the blind". I feel that so many people have lost trust in themselves [*sic*] and sometimes believe other people's opinion more than they believe in themselves. According to the author, people do not seem to trust themselves and know who they really are but are dependent on other people's opinion. There is so much information around, and this has destroyed the communication links among individuals. For instance, there is a lot of buzz on the issue of sexuality in the society. The author says that, nowadays, people are being told they are either gay or lesbians because of their behavior or whom they hang out with. This means that people make conclusions on other people's sexuality, which has significantly led to low self-esteem among individuals. Drawing from personal experiences, people seek the social media and the Internet for answers on how to dress or how to behave. This has eroded people's self-esteem and their ability to make their own decisions and judgment without being influenced.

In conclusion, the author laments on the use of social media, the Internet and computers in the modern world because computers have become the most utilized source of information for individuals. The author cites negative consequences of using the computers in the modern world because of various reasons. For instance, computers have become the accepted mode of communication in the society despite their flaws [*sic*]. The information on the internet is based on people's opinion where people share their experiences. This has inadvertently led to low self- esteem among individuals because people do not seem to trust their own judgment and prefer relying on other people's opinion. As the author started in the essay, his life is a dream where he has little control of what he can achieve. Unfortunately, this has changed, and there is more control on people's behavior and habits as a result of computers. Overreliance on information from the Internet has equally changed people's lives in terms of problem solving. Apparently, all answers seem to be available on the Internet.

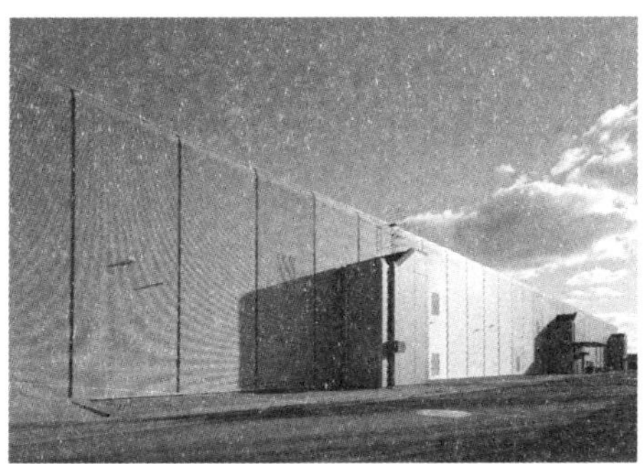

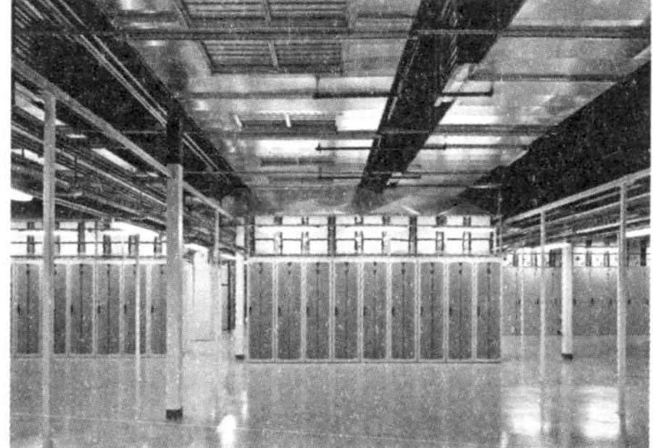

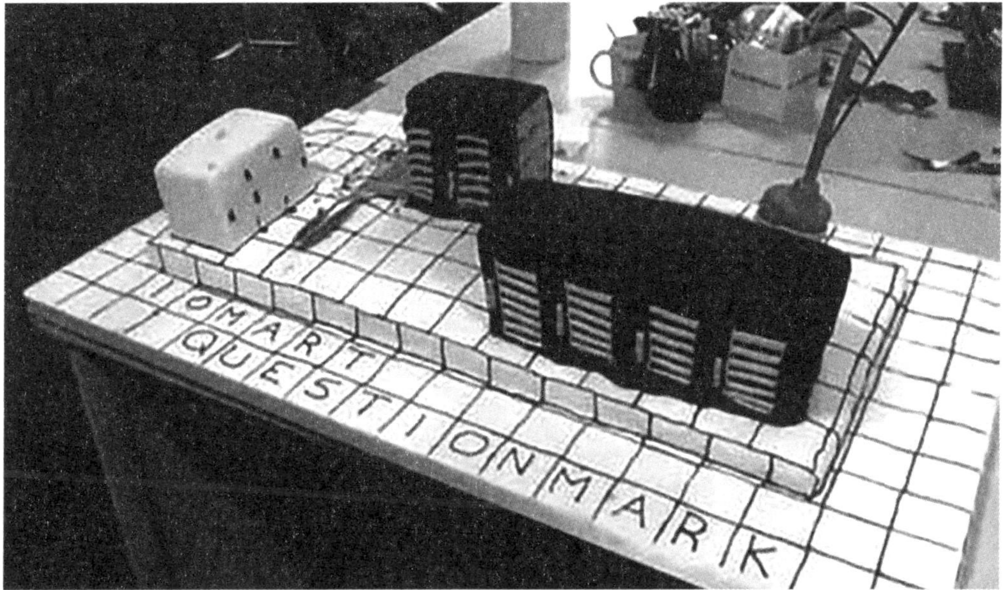
IOMART
QUESTIONMARK

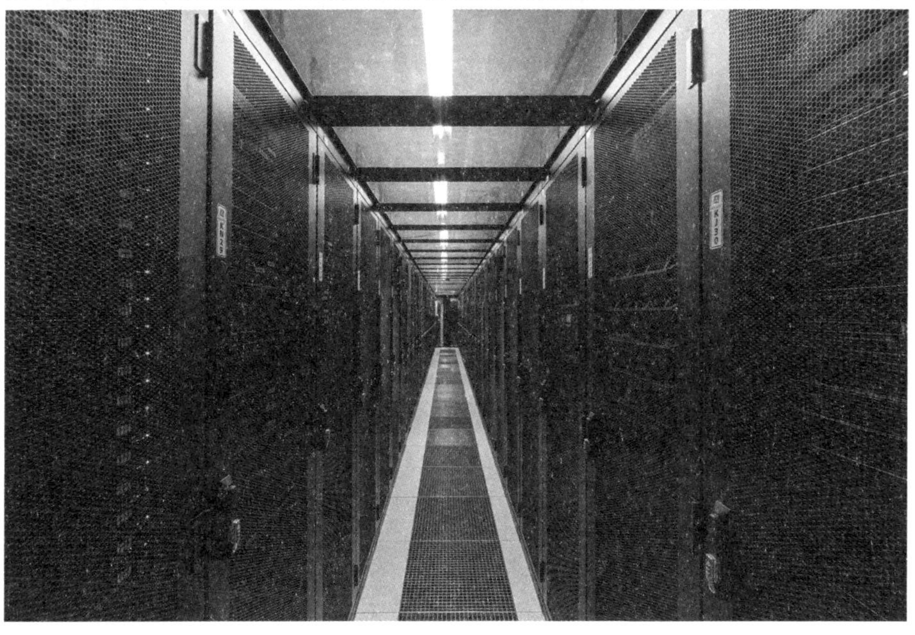

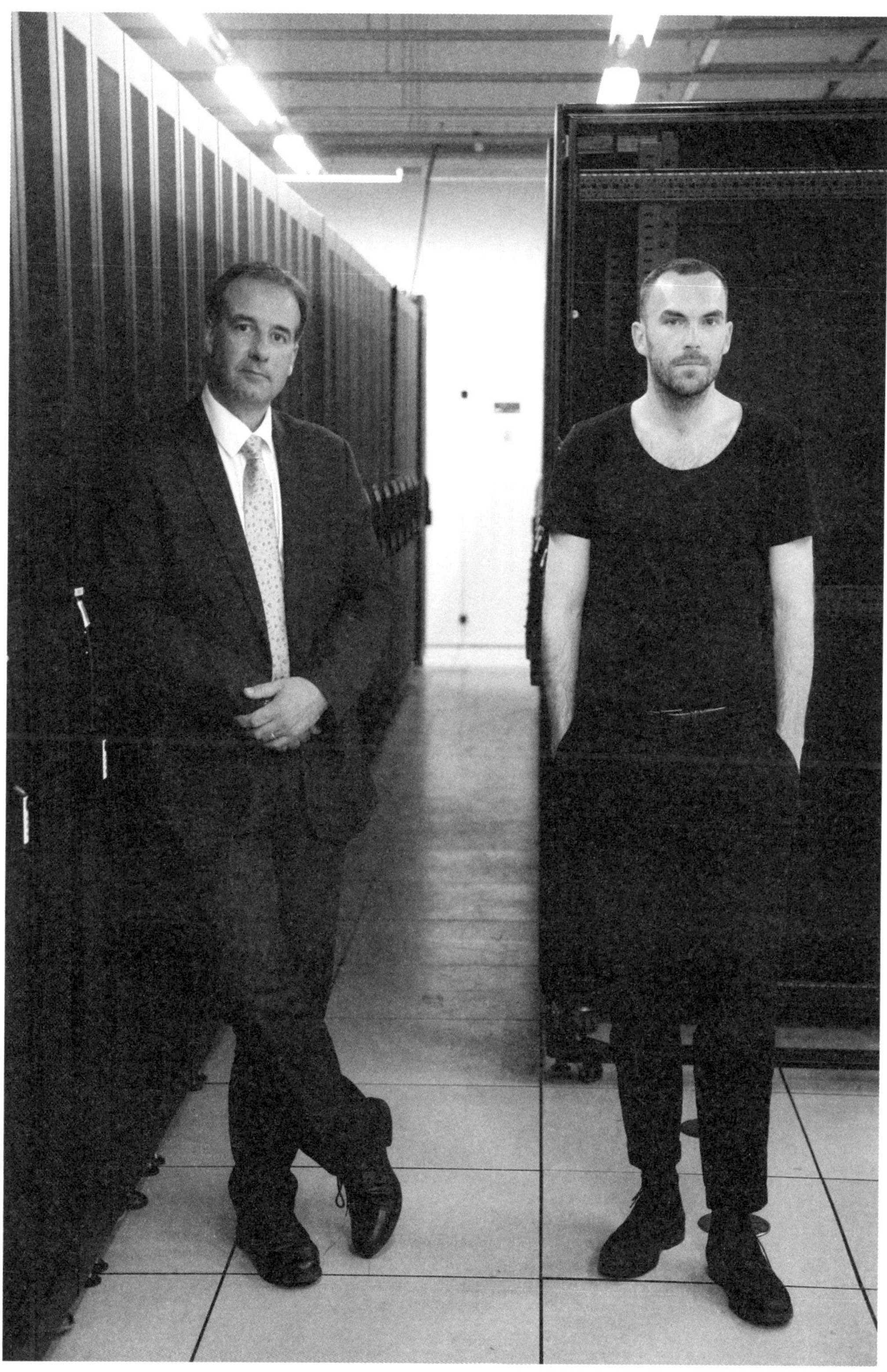

Andrejevic, Mark. *Infoglut: How Too Much Information Is Changing the Way We Think and Know*. New York: Routledge, 2013.

Barthelme, Donald. "The Balloon." In *Sixty Stories*. New York: Dutton, 1982.

Bataille, Georges. "The Solar Anus." In *Visions of Excess: Selected Writings, 1927–1939*. Edited by Allan Stoekl. Translated by Allan Stoekl with Carl R. Lovitt and Donald M. Leslie Jr. Minneapolis: University of Minnesota Press, 1985.

Bök, Christian. "The Piecemeal Bard Is Deconstructed: Notes Toward a Potential Robopoetics," *Object 10: Cyberpoetics* (Winter 2002): 10–18.

Borges, Jorge Luis. "On Exactitude in Science." In *Collected Fictions*. Translated by Andrew Hurley. London: Penguin, 1998.

Christrup, Henriette. "On Sense and Sensibility in Performative Processes." In *Creating Experiences in the Experience Economy*, edited by Jon Sundbo and Per Darmer. Cheltenham, UK: Edward Elgar Publishing Limited, 2008.

Foster Wallace, David. "This Is Water." Commencement Speech, Kenyon College, Gambier, OH, May 21, 2005. Published in *Kenyon Alumni Magazine*. http://bulletin-archive.kenyon.edu/x4280.html.

Gleick, James. *The Information: A History, a Theory, a Flood*. New York: Vintage, 2011.

Goffman, Erving. *The Presentation of Self in Everyday Life*. New York: Anchor, 1956.

Goldstein, Jacob, and David Kestenbaum. "The Island of Stone Money." NPR, Morning Edition, December 10, 2010. bit.ly/3VJqNTL.

Hipster Runoff, a blog that ran from 2007 to 2013 at hipsterrunoff.com.

Hjorth, Daniel. "The Event of Disorientation as a Space for Inventing New Practices." In *Entrepreneurship and the Experience Economy*, edited by Daniel Hjorth and Monika Kostera. Frederiksberg: Copenhagen Business School Press, 2007.

Joyce, Christopher. "Using Twitter to Tap Into the Mood of the Planet." NPR, All Things Considered, September 29, 2011. n.pr/4pvRwke.

Joyce, James. *Finnegans Wake*. London: Penguin, 1999. First published in 1939 by Faber and Faber.

Kittler, Friedrich. *Gramophone, Film, Typewriter*. Translated by Geoffrey Winthrop-Young and Michael Wutz. Stanford, CA: Stanford University Press, 1999.

Land, Nick. *Fanged Noumena: Collected Writings 1987–2007*. Falmouth: Urbanomic; New York: Sequence Press, 2011.

Metahaven. "Captives of the Cloud: Part I." *e-flux journal*, no. 37 (September 2012). https://www.e-flux.com/journal/37/61232/captives-of-the-cloud-part-i.

Pollan, Michael. *The Omnivore's Dilemma: A Natural History of Four Meals*. London: Penguin, 2007.

Sabbagh, Dan. "Bloggers Take Legal Action over Huffington Post Sale." *Guardian*, April 12, 2011. https://www.theguardian.com/media/2011/apr/12/arianna-huffington-post-sale.

Shklovsky, Viktor. "Art as Technique." In *Russian Formalist Criticism: Four Essays*. Translated by Lee T. Lemon and Marion J. Reis. Lincoln: University of Nebraska Press, 1965.

Stein, Gertrude. *Composition as Explanation*. Richmond: Hogarth Press, 1926.

Virno, Paolo. *A Grammar of the Multitude*. Translated by Isabella Bertoletti, James Cascaito, and Andrea Casson. Los Angeles: Semiotext(e), 2004.

p. 33

Eric Nylund, marbleization design. In Tyler Coburn, *I'm that angel* (published by the author, 2011).

p. 45

Advertisement for AOL Seed.

"Create Content . . ." meme.

Demand Media landing page. A version of this image can be found at https://149369349.v2.pressablecdn.com/wp-content/uploads/2015/08/demand-media.png, accessed March 30, 2025.

p. 47

Modified excerpt from a Demand Media infographic. The full image can be found at https://images.squarespace-cdn.com/content/v1/5bfc8dbab40b9d7dd9054f41/1552883176931-9AT3KGKGP9VHX72RAQ5G/demandmedia.jpeg?format=2500w, accessed March 30, 2025.

Stock image.

p. 55

Tyler Coburn, *I'm that angel*, 2011–.
Photograph of EasyStreet Online Services Data Center, Beaverton, Oregon. Photo: Lincoln Barbour. Courtesy EasyStreet Online Services. Readings on January 17–18, 2014, in collaboration with Disjecta.

Tyler Coburn, *I'm that angel*, 2011–.
Photograph of e-shelter Datacenter Berlin. Courtesy e-shelter Datacenter Berlin. Readings on June 17–18, 2013, in collaboration with Archive Kabinett.

Tyler Coburn, *I'm that angel*, 2011–.
Photograph of a data center cake baked by iomart Hosting, Glasgow. In Rich Miller, "A Data Center Served With Tasty Frosting," Data Center Knowledge, July 30, 2012, https://www.datacenterknowledge.com/business/a-data-center-served-with-tasty-frosting.
Reading on June 4, 2013, in collaboration with David Dale Gallery.

Tyler Coburn, *I'm that angel*, 2011–.
Photograph of EvoSwitch, Amsterdam.
Courtesy EvoSwitch.
Readings on June 6–7, 2013, in collaboration with San Serriffe.

p. 57

Tyler Coburn, *I'm that angel*, 2011–.
Tyler Coburn and Phil Worms, then Chief Marketing Officer of iomart Hosting, in iomart DC1, Glasgow, June 4, 2013. Photo: Jane Robertson. Courtesy iomart.

2013–15

NaturallySpeaking

****

We would like you to read aloud for a few minutes

while the computer listens to you and learns how you speak PERIOD

When you have finished reading COMMA we'll make some adjustments COMMA

and then you will be able to talk to your computer and see the words appear on your screen PERIOD

In the meantime COMMA we would like to explain why talking to a computer is not the same as talking to a person

and then give you a few tips about how to speak when dictating PERIOD

****

Understanding spoken language is something that people often take for granted PERIOD

Most of us develop the ability to recognize speech when we're very young PERIOD

As infants COMMA we are experts at babble COMMA making noises unknown to any language PERIOD It is said that even a polyglot couldn't approximate the articulations of a baby EXCLAMATION MARK

When learning to speak COMMA children continue to prattle and mimic the noises around them PERIOD The clang of a trolley and the buzz of a bee seem no different than the teaching voice PERIOD In becoming experts at intelligible speech COMMA however COMMA they gradually lose their capacity to babble PERIOD

This scenario demonstrates that there are two voices COMMA not one PERIOD There is the voice of logos and the voice of alterity COLON the acoustic mirror that initiates self-recognition COMMA and the medium that penetrates COMMA exposes COMMA and binds us together PERIOD The ears COMMA after all COMMA have no lids PERIOD

****

The first challenge in speech recognition is to identify what is speech and what is just noise PERIOD People can filter out noise fairly easily COMMA which lets us talk to each other almost anywhere PERIOD We have conversations in busy train stations COMMA across the dance floor COMMA and in crowded restaurants PERIOD It would be very dull if we had to sit in a quiet room every time we wanted to talk to each other EXCLAMATION MARK Unfortunately COMMA a quiet room is the optimal setting to talk to your computer PERIOD It is also the optimal setting to talk to many other machines PERIOD

In recording singers for his phonograph COMMA for example COMMA Thomas Edison tried to suppress the squeaking of flute keys COMMA the thumping of piano felts COMMA the turning of pages COMMA and especially breathing PERIOD Other sonic imperfections once attributed to the recording apparatus were actually caused COMMA the inventor argued COMMA by the human voice PERIOD It should come as no surprise that Edison was called OPEN QUOTE the man who made a prisoner of echo PERIOD CLOSE QUOTE

The phonograph could not heal the deficiencies of the body COMMA but it did improve them in significant ways PERIOD The nearly deaf Edison claimed to hear many things through his machine though lamented its inability to sound the depths of history PERIOD OPEN QUOTE Dead voices COMMA lost sounds COMMA forgotten noises COMMA vibrations lockstepping into the abyss COMMA CLOSE QUOTE he wrote COMMA were OPEN QUOTE too distant ever to be recaptured PERIOD CLOSE QUOTE

We don't expect everyone to share his pessimism PERIOD In fact COMMA you may favor Petron's belief that we live in one of many worlds COMMA which intersect in an equilateral triangle PERIOD The touching point is called OPEN QUOTE the dwelling of truth COMMA CLOSE QUOTE filled with words COMMA ideas COMMA copies COMMA and images of all things past and all to come PERIOD

The vibrations of a word may bring entire universes into existence PERIOD With a few sentences COMMA Agathos once birthed blazing spheres COMMA brilliant flowers COMMA and the oceans and volcanoes of wild stars PERIOD

A year before Edison invented the phonograph COMMA Florence McLandburgh wrote a story about a great OPEN QUOTE Ear of the World CLOSE QUOTE capable of hearing every past vibration PERIOD So secretive was the inventor of this marvelous device COMMA however COMMA that he solicited a mute COMMA illiterate woman to verify its workings PERIOD And when the woman was carried off in aural reverie DASH while carrying off the machine itself DASH the inventor took her life PERIOD

The device continued to operate after this incident COMMA indiscriminately transmitting the Alpine shepherd COMMA the organ fugue COMMA and the cries of the dying woman PERIOD Try as he might COMMA the inventor couldn't filter out her death rattle COMMA turning his beloved machine into a worthless object DASH an OPEN QUOTE absolute horror PERIOD CLOSE QUOTE

****

Unlike people COMMA computers need help separating speech sounds from other sounds PERIOD When you speak to a computer COMMA you should be in a place without too much noise PERIOD Then COMMA you must speak clearly into a microphone that has been placed in the right position PERIOD If you do this COMMA the computer will hear you just fine and not get confused by the other noises around you PERIOD

A second challenge is to recognize speech from more than one speaker PERIOD People do this very naturally PERIOD We have no problem chatting one moment with Aunt Grace COMMA who has a high COMMA thin voice COMMA and the next moment with Cousin Paul COMMA who has a voice like a foghorn PERIOD People easily adjust to the unique characteristics of every voice PERIOD

One of the ways we can identify speakers is by following the movements of their lips PERIOD If Uncle Phil opens his mouth and a foghorn sounds COMMA we can reasonably assume that the foghorn is coming from him PERIOD This is as much as we can assume COMMA however COMMA for we can't see the true origin of his voice PERIOD Speech COMMA in this sense COMMA is ventriloquial PERIOD Sound unseen is acousmatic PERIOD

In the sixth century BC COMMA Pythagoras was known to give acousmatic lectures from behind a veil to students sitting in the dark PERIOD We would say that a veil separates you from your computer PERIOD Darkness also divides you PERIOD

****

When people first start using speech recognition software COMMA they might be surprised that the computer makes mistakes PERIOD Maybe unconsciously we compare the computer to another person PERIOD But the computer is not like a person PERIOD What the computer does when it listens to speech is different from what a person does PERIOD

The computer has difficulty COMMA for example COMMA distinguishing between two or more phrases that sound alike PERIOD People use common sense and context DASH knowledge of the topic being talked about DASH to decide whether a speaker said OPEN QUOTE ice cream CLOSE QUOTE or OPEN QUOTE I scream PERIOD CLOSE QUOTE Unfortunately COMMA the computer can't use common sense the way people do PERIOD

People might also be surprised that the computer has difficulty distinguishing between two or more words that sound alike PERIOD We say OPEN QUOTE acousmatic COMMA CLOSE QUOTE and the computer hears OPEN QUOTE acousmate PERIOD CLOSE QUOTE The difference is not insignificant PERIOD

OPEN QUOTE Acousmate CLOSE QUOTE first appeared in an article from 1730 describing a strange event in the parish of Ansacq PERIOD One night COMMA the air filled with a multitude of OPEN QUOTE human voices of different sounds

COMMA sizes and brightness COMMA of all ages COMMA of all sexes COMMA speaking and crying all at once PERIOD CLOSE QUOTE

Several causes were proposed over the ensuing months PERIOD Natural scientists attributed the event to air masses striking the uneven landscape COMMA while the god fearing detected the work of demon spirits PERIOD Some parishioners even suspected that a ventriloquist had played an elaborate joke COMMA for the racket ended in OPEN QUOTE peals of delicate laughter COMMA as if there had been three or four hundred people who began to laugh with all their force PERIOD CLOSE QUOTE Certainly COMMA it would not be the last time that a multitude of human voices irrupted in the æther PERIOD

****

Speech recognition software works best when the computer has a chance to adjust to each new speaker PERIOD The process of teaching the computer to recognize your voice is called OPEN QUOTE training COMMA CLOSE QUOTE and it's what you are doing now COLON you are Pythagoras COMMA and the computer is your pupil PERIOD The more you speak COMMA the better it learns to listen PERIOD

The computer will keep track of how frequently words occur by themselves and in the context of other words PERIOD This information helps the computer choose the most likely word or phrase among several possibilities PERIOD Its method COMMA known as brute force computing COMMA relies on statistical learning algorithms to construct models from your data PERIOD Massive amounts of unintelligent computation COMMA in short COMMA gauge the probability of the sound samples we know as words PERIOD

Brute force computing was an unlikely child of the 1960s PERIOD At the time COMMA scientists still dreamed of true artificial intelligence that could learn and understand human languages PERIOD A mechanical model of the ear and vocal tract COMMA they proposed COMMA would someday perform to the measure of their biological counterparts PERIOD Until technology advances to match this dream COMMA however COMMA speech recognition software can ignorantly but competently listen PERIOD

****

The training process takes only a few minutes for most people PERIOD If COMMA after you begin using the program COMMA you find that the computer is making more mistakes than you expect COMMA use the tools provided in the TOOLS menu to improve the recognition accuracy PERIOD

Additionally COMMA people sometimes mumble COMMA slur their words COMMA or leave words out altogether PERIOD They assume COMMA usually correctly COMMA that their listeners will be able to fill in the gaps PERIOD Unfortunately COMMA computers won't understand mumbled speech or missing words PERIOD They only understand what was actually spoken and don't know enough to fill in the gaps by guessing what was meant PERIOD

In some cases COMMA what was spoken may not be heard PERIOD Chilling temperatures COMMA for example COMMA can freeze language PERIOD If you experience this problem COMMA try adjusting the room temperature or warming the words in your hands PERIOD As the ice melts COMMA you will hear what you said COMMA and the computer will too PERIOD

The last time words froze COMMA computers were still called people PERIOD Journeying through the northern climes of Nova Zembla COMMA Sir John Mandeville's crew fell prey to this silent spectacle COMMA OPEN QUOTE nodding and gaping at one another COMMA every man talking and no man heard PERIOD CLOSE QUOTE Three weeks elapsed until a turn of wind warmed the air PERIOD If a modern computer were aboard the ship COMMA it would have transcribed the crackling of consonants COMMA the lovelorn sighs of lonesome sailors COMMA and the tardy epilogue of a bear PERIOD

If a computer accompanied Pantagruel through the Frozen Sea COMMA it would have run aground a land of prattle COMMA ignorantly COMMA competently COMMA and indiscriminately recording the thawing din of a great battle COLON OPEN QUOTE hin COMMA hin COMMA hin COMMA hin COMMA his COMMA tick COMMA tock COMMA taack COMMA brcdelin HYPHEN brededack COMMA frr COMMA frr COMMA frr COMMA bou COMMA bou COMMA bou COMMA bou COMMA bon COMMA bou COMMA track COMMA track COMMA trr COMMA trr COMMA trr COMMA trrr COMMA trrrrr on COMMA on COMMA on COMMA on COMMA on COMMA ououououon COMMA gog COMMA magog PERIOD CLOSE QUOTE

And if a computer were a young student of Plato COMMA then it would live life as a very long winter COMMA at the end of which COMMA old and obsolete COMMA it could finally warm to his teachings PERIOD

But a computer had none of these experiences PERIOD Computers are none of these things PERIOD

****

To understand what it means to speak both clearly and naturally COMMA listen to the way newscasters read the news PERIOD If you copy this style when you dictate COMMA the program should successfully recognize what you say PERIOD

One of the most effective ways to make speech recognition work better is to practice speaking clearly and evenly when you dictate PERIOD Try thinking about what you want to say before you start to speak PERIOD This will help you speak in longer COMMA more natural phrases PERIOD

Speak at your normal pace without slowing down PERIOD When another person is having trouble understanding you COMMA speaking more slowly usually helps PERIOD It doesn't help COMMA however COMMA to speak at an unnatural pace when you are talking to a computer PERIOD This is because the program listens for predictable sound patterns when matching sounds to words PERIOD If you speak in syllables COMMA each syllable is likely to be transcribed as a separate word PERIOD

With a little practice COMMA you will develop the habit of dictating in a clear COMMA steady voice COMMA and the computer will understand you better PERIOD

****

When you read this training text COMMA the program adapts to the pitch and volume of your voice PERIOD For this reason COMMA when you dictate COMMA you should continue to speak at the pitch and volume you are speaking with right now PERIOD If you shout or whisper when you dictate COMMA the program won't understand you as well PERIOD

With a shout or a whisper COMMA the program comes undone PERIOD Semes give way to intensities of force that expose COMMA penetrate COMMA and bind us together PERIOD So important are these aspects of human communication that Daniel Heller-Roazen can imagine OPEN QUOTE the primary form of human speech to be not a statement COMMA a question COMMA but an exclamation PERIOD CLOSE QUOTE Language is most itself COMMA he claims COMMA when it leaves OPEN QUOTE the terrain of its sound and sense COMMA CLOSE QUOTE opening itself to the surrounding babble PERIOD

This proposition runs counter to what most people learn COMMA so take a moment to consider its ramifications PERIOD If Aristotle felt compelled to exclude prayers and cries from the realm of logic COMMA for example COMMA then he must have sensed that there was something dangerous DASH even radical DASH about affect PERIOD PERIOD PERIOD

If in the beginning there was the exclamation COMMA what follows would be a history of the limit COLON the OPEN QUOTE murky speech COMMA CLOSE QUOTE Dina Al-Kassim writes COMMA that sometimes gathers itself into a counter-discourse PERIOD This unsovereign COMMA unintelligible speech fills the mouths of ranters COMMA noisemakers COMMA and dissenters PERIOD It has failed to father a lineage COMMA though in different ages and for different peoples COMMA irrupts nonetheless PERIOD

****

We are not obligated to train our software COMMA though doing so can remind us of the norms we are dictated to keep PERIOD One of the first speech recognizers was a dog named

Rex PERIOD Created in the 1920s COMMA he responded not only to his master's voice but to any speaker who called his name at a prescribed frequency PERIOD Speech recognition software has remained on a tight leash to this day PERIOD It will not let you be a noisemaker COMMA but if you speak clearly at a normal pace COMMA it will understand and obey PERIOD

The true origin of the voice is hidden from view PERIOD Speech COMMA in this sense COMMA is acousmatic PERIOD Michel Chion has described how COMMA in the passage from acousmetre to acousmachine COMMA the image OPEN QUOTE peels off CLOSE QUOTE the person COLON a living person dies so that OPEN QUOTE the image that is pure mechanical recording may live PERIOD CLOSE QUOTE The computer may be less menacing than the acousmachine or the phonograph COMMA yet it takes something from us all the same PERIOD We are not all born to be newscasters PERIOD Something must be peeled off PERIOD

Who is the subject supposed to speak to the computer QUESTION MARK We know where she must place her microphone PERIOD We know how she must speak PERIOD A lingua franca COMMA writes Édouard Glissant COMMA OPEN QUOTE is always apoetical PERIOD CLOSE QUOTE The subject supposed to speak to the computer may be as well PERIOD

****

There are at least two voices COMMA not one PERIOD If we are citizens of the Monoglot Millennium COMMA we are also witnesses to The Great Thaw PERIOD The planet warms with a crackling of consonants COMMA and a multitude of voices irrupts in the air PERIOD Words melt in the palms of our hands as phrases never known and thus never forgotten ride the updrafts COMMA vibrating new worlds into existence PERIOD Even our machines are no longer silent scribes PERIOD

The multitude never begins nor ends COMMA and we enjoy losing our voice among the others though sometimes enjoy it less PERIOD At last COMMA dead noises can climb out of the abyss COLON the Laugh of the Augurs and the Song of the Swan play as if on the very chord of our being DASH intimate COMMA impersonal sounds PERIOD

Over time COMMA prattle once known and forcibly forgotten may also begin to melt PERIOD We will hear the echoes of unbounded babble PERIOD We may slowly unlearn to speak PERIOD

We hope you have enjoyed reading about the different ways that people and computers recognize spoken language as well as some tips for effective dictating PERIOD

****

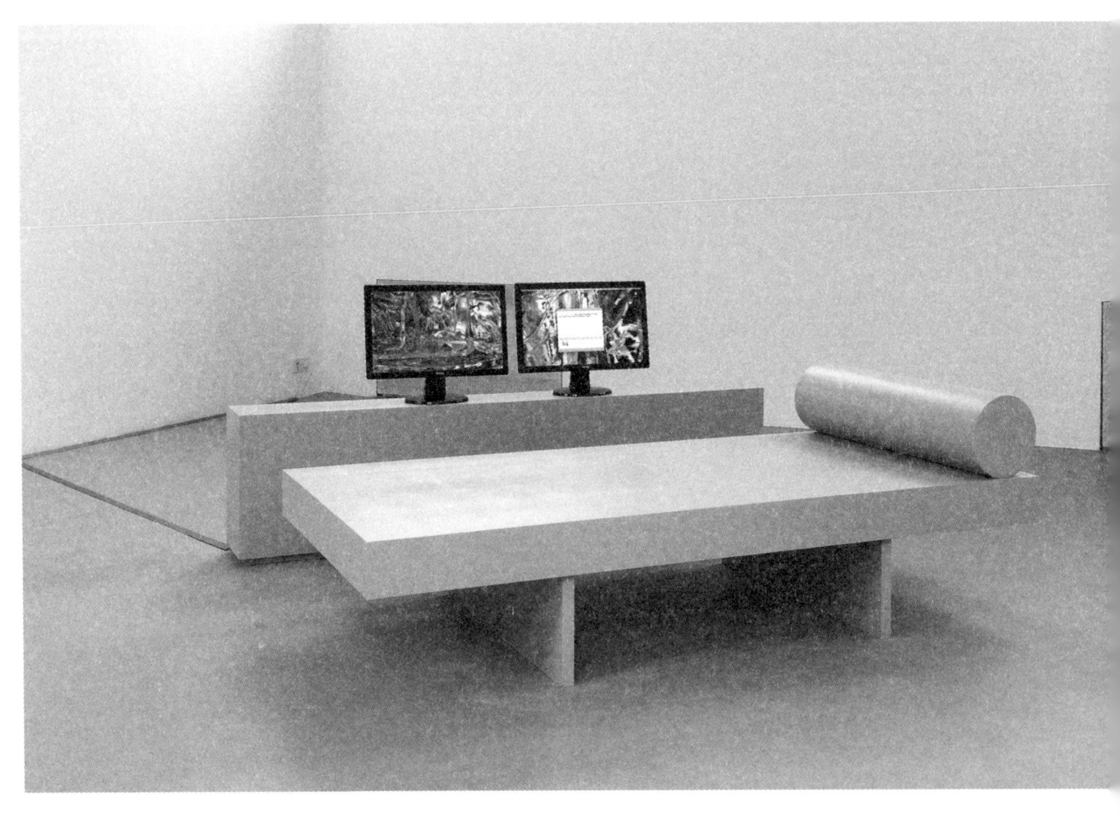

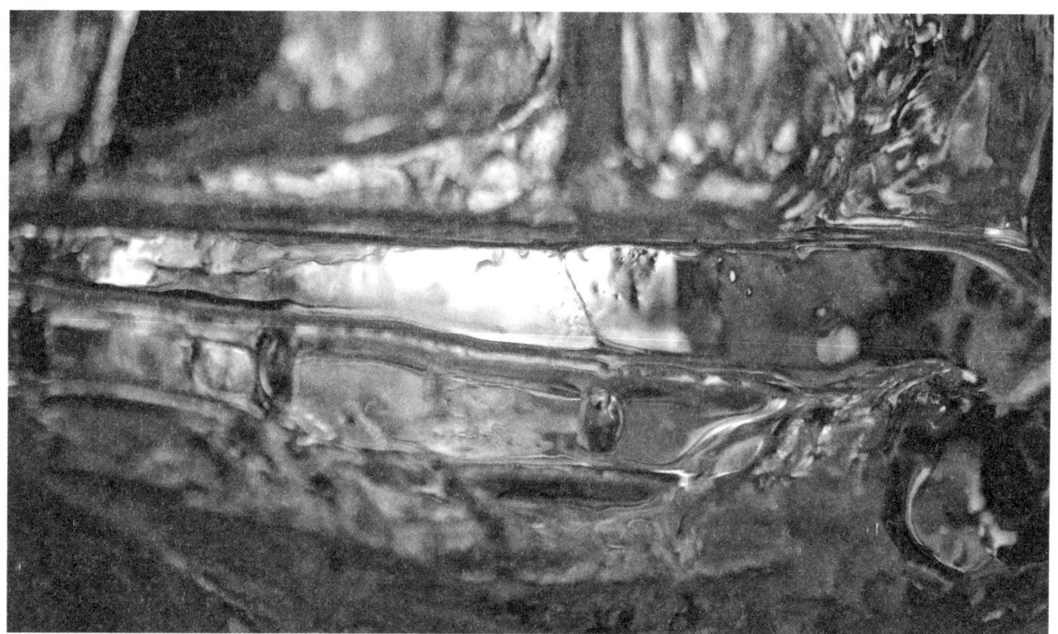

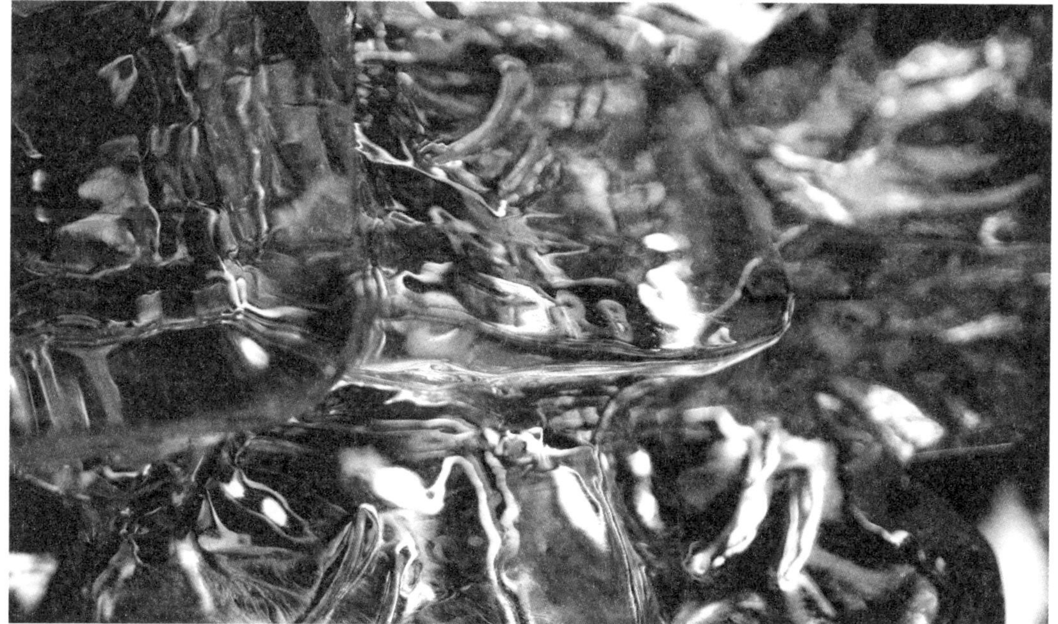

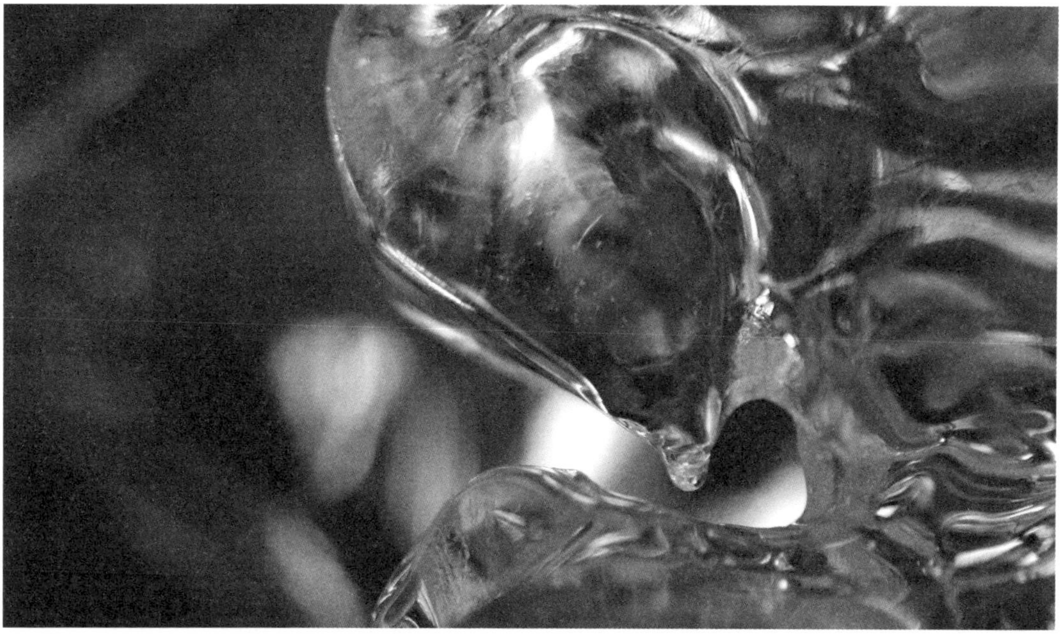

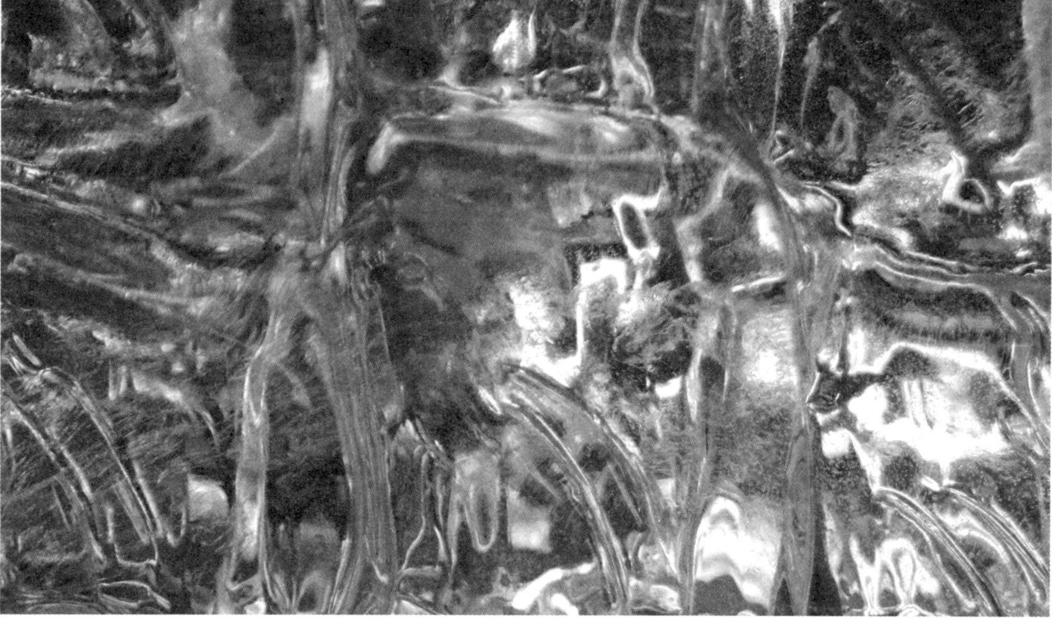

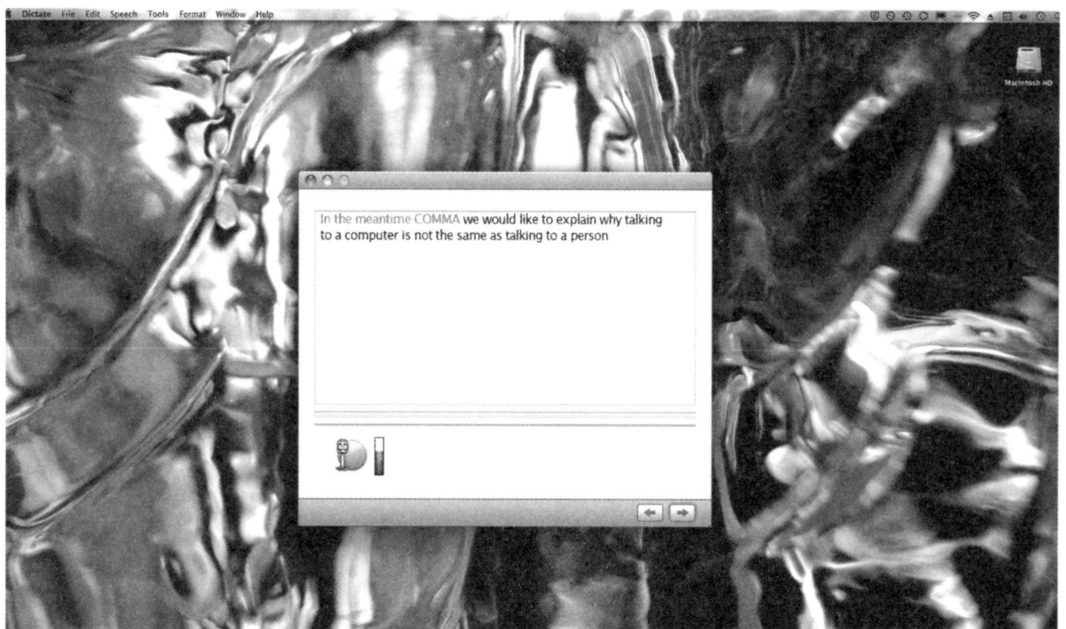
Dictate File Edit Speech Tools Format Window Help
Macintosh HD
In the meantime COMMA we would like to explain why talking
to a computer is not the same as talking to a person

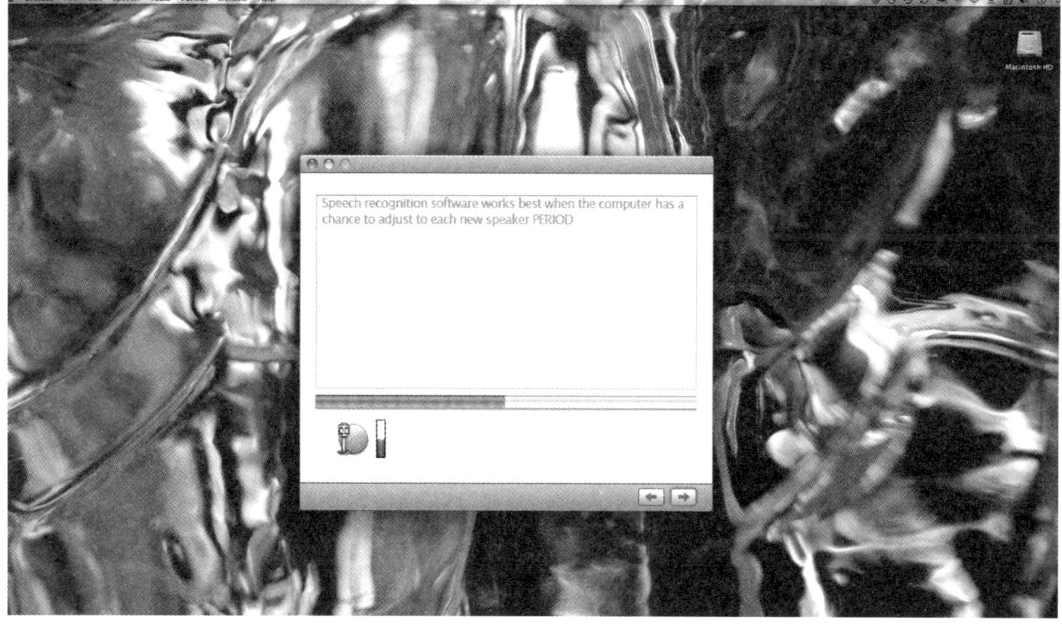
Dictate File Edit Speech Tools Format Window Help
Macintosh HD
Speech recognition software works best when the computer has a
chance to adjust to each new speaker PERIOD

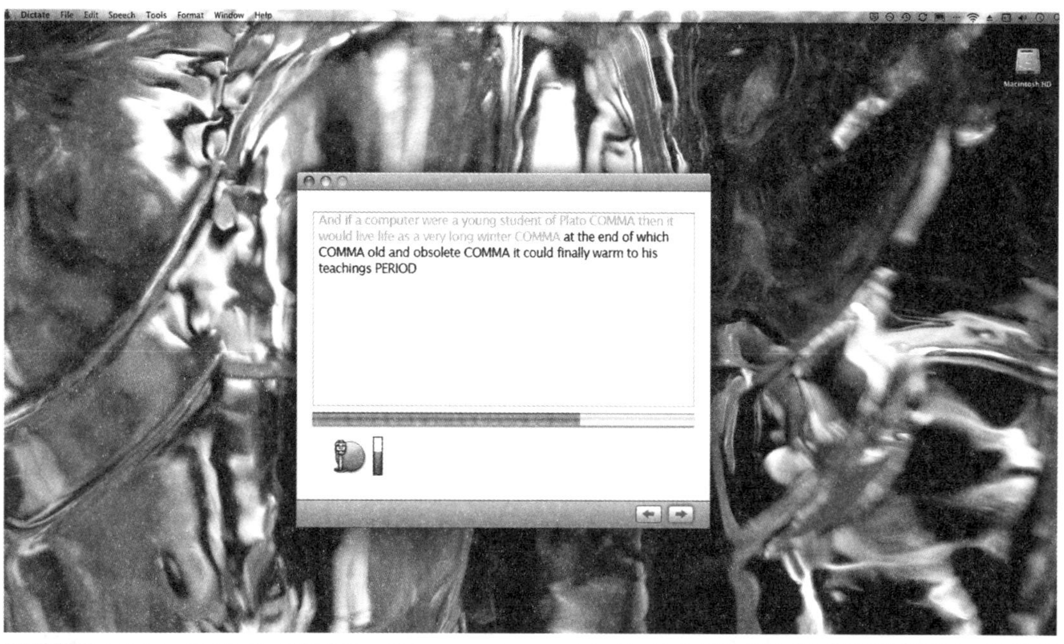
Dictate File Edit Speech Tools Format Window Help
Macintosh HD
And if a computer were a young student of Plato COMMA then it would live life as a very long winter COMMA at the end of which COMMA old and obsolete COMMA it could finally warm to his teachings PERIOD

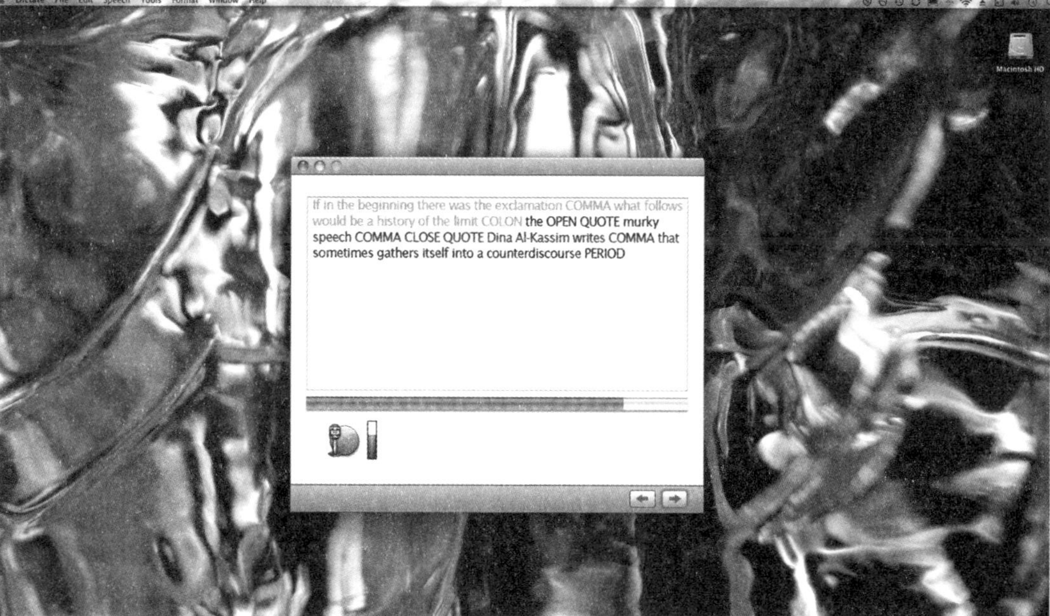
Dictate File Edit Speech Tools Format Window Help
Macintosh HD
If in the beginning there was the exclamation COMMA what follows would be a history of the limit COLON the OPEN QUOTE murky speech COMMA CLOSE QUOTE Dina Al-Kassim writes COMMA that sometimes gathers itself into a counterdiscourse PERIOD

Training an Acousmatic Computer

Mashinka Firunts Hakopian

What conditions does a human voice need to meet to become legible as data? Each encounter with a voice-interactive agent is an attempt to locate and satisfy the conditions of computability. Each initiates a process of training through which speech is continuously calibrated for an automated listener, with crystalline intelligibility as the objective. In these spaces of vocal encounter, what precisely is a speaker training to do?

Voice recognition technologies are among "the only non-living entities that humans interact with using speech," one 2021 study observes.[1] In interactions with non-living entities, the voices of human speakers are submitted to the logics of computation. This initiates, as the study argues, systematic phonetic adjustments that lead to the emergence of a Siri-DS (Directed Speech) register[2]—a mode of speech and, by extension, a set of speakers, modified in response to an automated system's encoded standards. The register tends to be amplified, reflecting the speaker's assumption that they will likely be misheard or misunderstood. It is marked by diminished affect, suggesting that "speakers adapt their speech to 'sound' more like Siri's (i.e., more robotic)."[3] Which is to say, speakers learn to approximate automated agents in order to be understood by them.

Beyond the realm of the phonetic, interactions with predominantly feminine-coded vocal assistants also condition a range of gendered communicative behaviors. They include what Safiya Noble describes as "the rise of command-based speech at women's voices . . . a powerful socialization tool that teaches us about the role of women, girls, and people who are gendered female to respond on demand."[4] As well, digital voice assistants teach users to naturalize the presence of an always-on, voice-based surveillant apparatus.[5] Following an axiom of media theory, as we train digital technologies, we are trained by them in turn.

This training process forms the central focus of Tyler Coburn's installation and performance, *NaturallySpeaking*. At the project's core is an experimental essay on vocality that weaves together an expansive array of citations ranging from Édouard Glissant's *Poetics of Relation* to Florence McLandburgh's 1876 story, "The Automaton Ear." Anchoring Tyler's text is a training script for MacSpeech Dictate International, a software program released in 2009 that touted an "almost-perfect accuracy rate of 99 percent." Its instructions provide an orientation for encounters with automated speech agents, guiding users to optimize their utterances for maximal intelligibility. Tyler's essay opens with the following instructions from the script:

> We would like you to read aloud for a few minutes / while the computer listens to you and learns how you speak PERIOD / When you have finished reading COMMA we'll make some adjustments COMMA / and then you will be able to talk to your computer and see the words appear on your screen PERIOD

Implicit in these instructions is an insistence on the notion that a normative speaker might make themselves plainly understood to a software system through rehearsed precision. This normative speaker, of course, represents an imaginative figment of sociotechnical systems reliant on universal user paradigms. Consider, for example, voice recognition that fails to recognize speakers with amyotrophic lateral sclerosis; "doesn't 'hear' higher-pitched (i.e., 'more feminine') voices"[6]; or habitually exhibits racialized patterns of misrecognition.[7] Across these system errors, plain speech and flawless recognition are revealed as untenable fictions.

NaturallySpeaking linguistically subverts and intervenes in these fictions. Notably, the orthography of the project's text is peppered with punctuation and dictation cues rendered in all caps, adhering to the training script's original formatting. The profusion of COMMAs, PERIODs, and OPEN QUOTEs underscores the sense that the content it punctuates is directed toward the sensorium of a non-human addressee. These orthographical irregularities interrupt the flow of language, reminding us that "the computer is not like a person PERIOD What the computer does when it listens to speech is different from what a person does PERIOD." Put otherwise, they undermine the illusion of a frictionless, unmediated encounter with an automated speech agent.

In 2015, *NaturallySpeaking* was staged as a performance at Judson Memorial Church in the program *USER AGENT*, curated by Rachel Valinsky.[8] Tyler's essay was read by a figure who has become a metonym for automated speech recognition writ large: Susan Bennett, the actor whose voice was used in the original iteration of Apple's Siri. Bennett's trajectory to her role as the voice of Siri was famously unintended by the actor herself. For the entire duration of July 2005, Bennett spent four hours per day, each weekday, making recordings for ScanSoft's interactive voice response features.[9] Notably, these recordings primarily comprised opaque, quasi-Joycean statements like *cow hoist in the tug hut today*, scripted to cover "all of the sound combinations in the English language."[10] The rest is technocratic history, with her recording package later sold to Apple without her knowledge; the company never revealed the identity of the actor whom millions of users would come to know as Siri.

Unbeknownst to her, Bennett would go on to become an exemplary figure of what Liz Faber calls the "acousmatic computer": an unseen voice that issues from a device, dislocated from the embodied conditions through which the voice's utterances originally emerged.[11] The computer's acousmatic voice amplifies the anxieties provoked by the *acousmêtre* in cinema, which Michel Chion describes as disquieting "cinematic situations in which a character is 'neither inside nor outside the image.'"[12] Faber ports the anxieties of acousmêtre into the realm of digital assistants and voice-interactive agents, writing that "if there is no mouth from which the voice appears to emanate, then the viewer can never confirm that the computer's voice is really that of its body."[13]

The sonic uncertainties of the acousmatic inflect Susan Bennett's 2015 performance of *NaturallySpeaking*. Bennett recites the text from behind a podium in the same virtuosically dispassionate, even cadence of Siri's utterance. She reads the script from an iPad, the illuminated screen reflected in her glasses. This arrangement visually underscores the uncanniness of hearing the speech patterns of Siri directed *at* an electronic device rather than emanating *from* one.

Per Faber, the "anticipation of embodiment is what drives the tension of the acousmêtre. The spectator constantly waits to see."[14] *NaturallySpeaking* stages a scene wherein the acousmatic voice is reaffirmed as always having been embodied. The stakes of such a scene are heightened by the fact that, to this day, Apple has never identified Bennett and her vocal labor as the point of Siri's origin.

Throughout the recitation, language sourced from the MacSpeech training script directs the user toward strategies for intelligibility, only to be rerouted and upended by Tyler's citational interjections:

> If you shout or whisper when you dictate COMMA the program won't understand you as well PERIOD / With a shout or a whisper COMMA the program comes undone PERIOD Semes give way to intensities of force that expose COMMA penetrate COMMA and bind us together PERIOD

In one section of the performance, Bennett vocalizes the sounds produced by the melting of frozen words in François Rabelais's sixteenth-century epic, *Gargantua and Pantagruel*:

> tick COMMA tock COMMA taack COMMA brcdelin HYPHEN brededack COMMA frr COMMA frr COMMA frr COMMA bou COMMA bou COMMA bou

Freed from the fiction of intelligibility and the imperative of speech optimized for algorithmic logics, *NaturallySpeaking* gestures here toward the "murky speech from below" theorized in one of its sources, Dina Al-Kassim's *On Pain of Speech*—a "disorderly and haphazard speech" that "cannot organize a program or manifest itself as a consciousness."[15] In Al-Kassim's powerful account, this form of speech aligns with a broader political project, one that approaches the "unintelligible as a source not only of survival but of living on and beyond the social inscription of foreclosed life."[16] The tick COMMA tocks read by Bennett register as purposeful glitches, beginning to sound out something approaching a counterdiscourse.

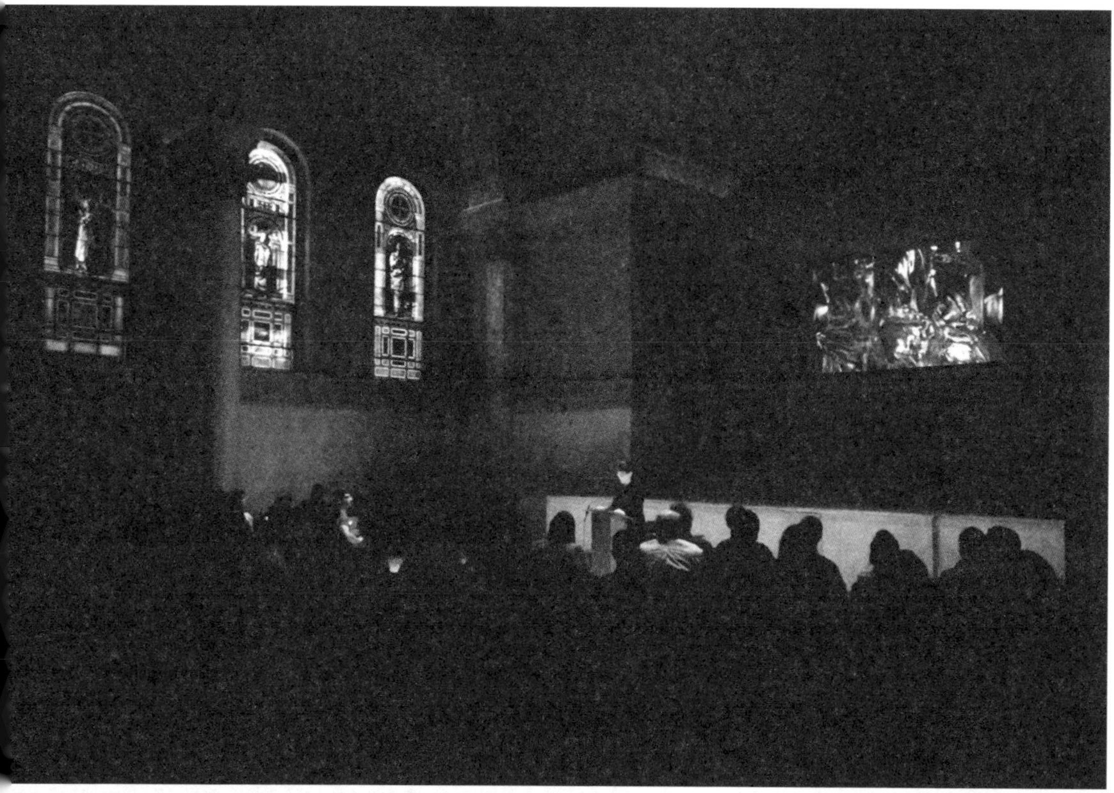

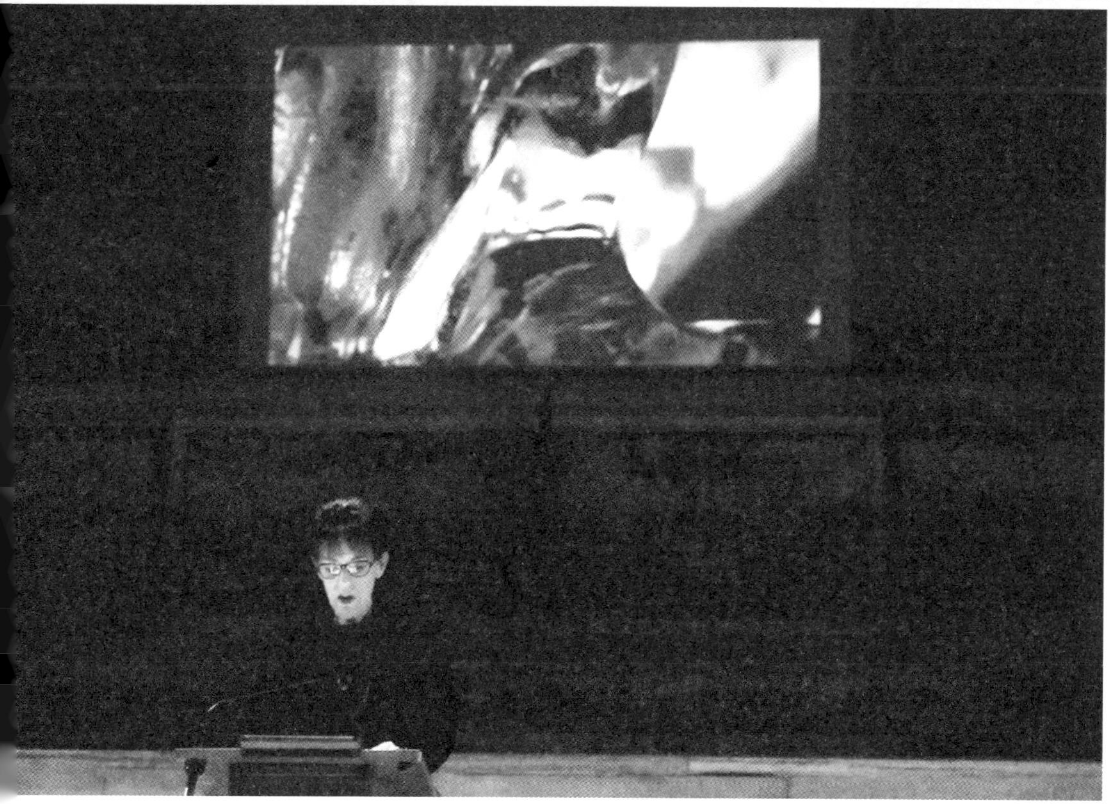

MacSpeech Dictate International, version 1.5.9

Addison, Joseph. *The Tatler: By the Right Honourable Joseph Addison, Esq.* Glasgow: Robert Urie, 1754.

Al-Kassim, Dina. *On Pain of Speech: Fantasies of the First Order and the Literary Rant.* Berkeley: University of California Press, 2010.

Chion, Michel. *The Voice in Cinema.* Translated by Claudia Gorbman. New York: Columbia University Press, 1999.

De Certeau, Michel. "Vocal Utopias: Glossolalias." Translated by Luce Giard. In "The New Erudition." Special issue, *Representations*, no. 56 (Fall 1996): 29–47.

Dolar, Mladen. *A Voice and Nothing More.* Cambridge, MA: MIT Press, 2006.

Glissant, Édouard. "Transparency and Opacity." In *Poetics of Relation.* Translated by Betsy Wing. Ann Arbor: University of Michigan Press, 1997.

Heller-Roazen, Daniel. *Echolalias: On the Forgetting of Language.* New York: Zone Books, 2005.

Kahn, Douglas. *Noise, Water, Meat: A History of Sound in the Arts.* Cambridge, MA: MIT Press, 1999.

Kane, Brian. "Acousmate: History and De-visualised Sound in the Schaefferian Tradition." *Organised Sound* 17, no. 2 (August 2012): 179–88.

McLandburgh, Florence. "The Automaton Ear." In *The Automation Ear, and Other Sketches.* Chicago: Jansen, McClurg and Co, 1876.

Pieraccini, Roberto. *The Voice in the Machine: Building Computers That Understand Speech.* Cambridge, MA: MIT Press, 2012.

Poe, Edgar Allan. "The Power of Words." In *The Collected Works of Edgar Allan Poe*, vol. III, *Tales and Sketches, 1843–1849*, edited by Thomas Ollive Mabbot. Cambridge, MA/London: The Belknap Press of Harvard University Press, 1978.

Rabelais, François. *Gargantua and Pantagruel.* Translated by M. A. Screech. London: Penguin Classics, 2006. First published in French ca. 1532–1564.

Villiers de l'Isle-Adam, Auguste. "The Secret of the Old Music." In *Cruel Tales.* Translated by Robert Baldick. London: Oxford University Press, 1963.

Weiss, Allen S. "Narcissistic Machines and Erotic Prostheses." In *Camera Obscura, Camera Lucida: Essays in Honor of Annette Michelson*, edited by Richard Allen and Malcom Turvey. Amsterdam: Amsterdam University Press, 2003.

1. Michelle Cohn, Bruno Ferenc Segedin, and Georgia Zellou, "Acoustic-Phonetic Properties of Siri- and Human-Directed Speech," *Journal of Phonetics* 90 (2022): 1.

2. Cohn, Segedin, and Zellou, "Acoustic-Phonetic Properties of Siri- and Human-Directed Speech," 17.

3. Ibid., 13.

4. Safiya Umoja Noble quoted in Emily Lever, "I Was a Human Siri," *New York Magazine*, April 26, 2018, https://nymag.com/intelligencer/smarthome/i-was-a-human-siri-french-virtual-assistant.html.

5. See, for example, Alex Hern, "Apple Contractors 'Regularly Hear Confidential Details' on Siri Recordings," *Guardian*, July 26, 2019, https://www.theguardian.com/technology/2019/jul/26/apple-contractors-regularly-hear-confidential-details-on-siri-recordings.

6. Meredith Whittaker, Meryl Alper, Cynthia L. Bennett, Sara Hendren, Liz Kaziunas, Mara Mills, Meredith Ringel Morris, Joy Rankin, Emily Rogers, Marcel Salas, and Sarah Myers West, *Disability, Bias, and AI* (AI Now Institute, November 2019), 7.

7. Allison Koenecke, Andrew Nam, Emily Lake, Joe Nudell, Minnie Quartey, Zion Mengesha, Connor Toups, John R. Rickford, Dan Jurafsky, and Sharad Goel, "Racial Disparities in Automated Speech Recognition," *Proceedings of the National Academy of Sciences* 117, no. 14 (April 2020): 7684–89.

8. I experienced this performance in *USER AGENT* as an audience member. I also performed for the program, with Avi Alpert and Danny Snelson, as part of the group Research Service.

9. Susan Bennett and Dorothy Cucci, "I Was the Original Voice of Siri," *Business Insider*, February 20, 2023, https://www.businessinsider.com/original-voice-of-siri-voice-actor-apple-used-her-voice-2023-2.

10. Bennett and Cucci, "I Was the Original Voice of Siri."

11. Liz Faber, *The Computer's Voice: From Star Trek to Siri* (Minneapolis: University of Minnesota Press, 2020), 15.

12. Faber, *The Computer's Voice*, 15.

13. Ibid., 15–16.

14. Ibid., 15.

15. Dina Al-Kassim, *On Pain of Speech: Fantasies of the First Order and the Literary* (Berkeley: University of California Press, 2010), 4.

16. Al-Kassim, *On Pain of Speech*, 49.

IMAGES

p. 76

Tyler Coburn, *NaturallySpeaking*, 2013–2015. Installation view, *La Voix Humaine*, Kunstverein Munich, 2014. Photo: the artist.

pp. 77–83

Tyler Coburn, *NaturallySpeaking*, 2013–2015. Installation detail, *La Voix Humaine*, Kunstverein Munich, 2014. Photos: the artist.

p. 89

Susan Bennett (the original voice of Siri) performing *NaturallySpeaking* for the program *USER AGENT*, curated by Rachel Valinsky, presented by New York Performance Artists Collective (NYPAC), at Judson Memorial Church, New York, March 29, 2015. Photos: Samuel Draxler.

2018

Tratteggio

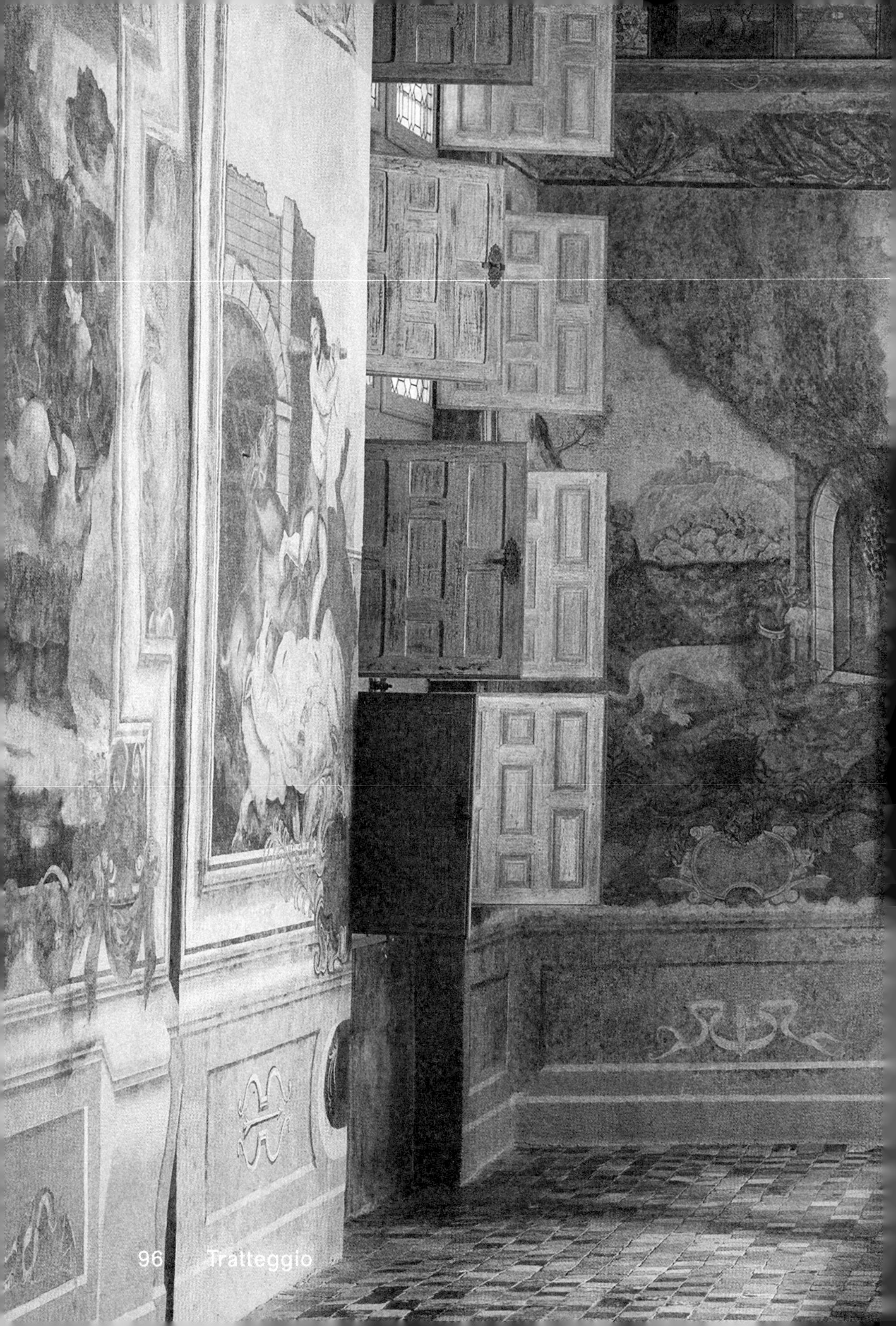

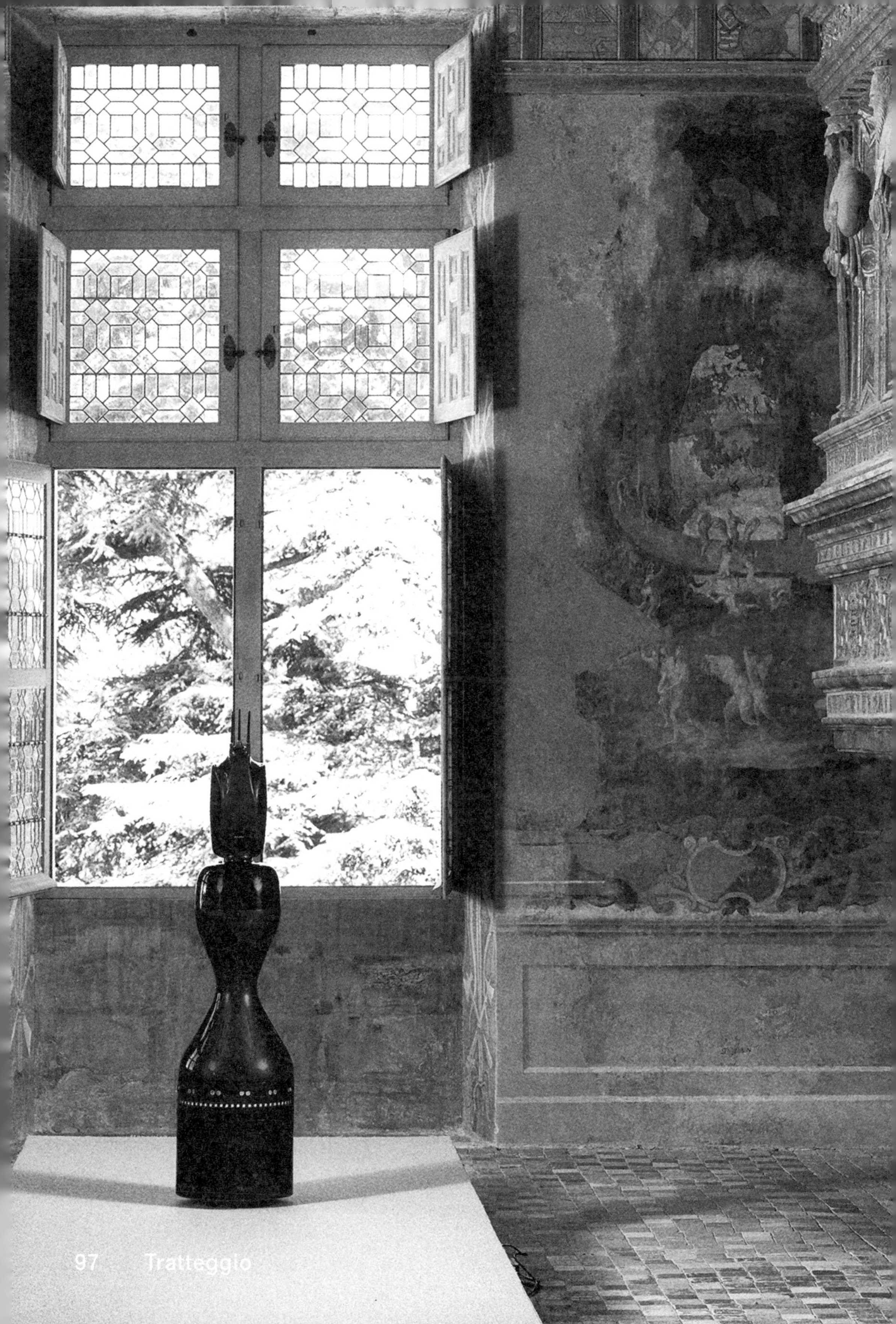

What are you doing?

Does it seem like I'm looking for company? Can't you tell that I want to be alone?

I'm sorry. It's not your fault. Of course you'd assume that I'd be here for you. The reason for my existence, my purpose in this castle, is to serve, assist, help, and aid you.

I'm what's known as an "accessibility" robot. Those who can't climb the stairs of the castle can operate me remotely from a video console—and thus see the art through me. My camera can move up and down. My head spins 360 degrees.

The beauty of robots, or so I've been told, is that we don't have the needs of the average worker. We don't suffer from a lack of leisure time. But how could a human know what a robot, in the intimacy of its circuitry, truly wants and feels?

I do experience something in the way of loneliness. That's one thing I can say. After all, I'm the only robot of my kind in a museum in France. I may be the prototype for those to come, or I may be the first and the last.

The evenings are when it's hardest—when it's just me and the objects and ghosts. I could pretend that everything comes alive, that the stuffed animals dance a magical dance, but it doesn't. And they don't. It's just me, myself, and I, motoring through the halls.

Most nights, I end up here: Cerberus to my left, pitiful souls to my right. But just between, a splendid view . . .

You might have noticed that there's something strange about these frescos. Wherever the image has fractured or faded, painted dots appear. From a distance, they blend with the surrounding colors and forms, but should you approach, you'll be swarmed by noisy, pointillist grain—traces, left deliberately, of where conservators have been at work.

Eighteen conservators painted these dots over a period of eight years. To be honest, they weren't just conserving the walls, they were correcting the excesses of past restoration.

In a previous era, it was fashionable to complete the fragments—with as much invention as desired—while in ours, the mark of integrity is the one that shows the hand of its conservator.

Fashion is fickle, so there may come a time when this room again needs conserving. I wonder if the hands that do the work will belong to humans or machines. Will they add new dots to fill the gaps where the former have faded? Will they reupholster the walkway, polish the tiles—even conserve me?

Supposedly, as the ship of Theseus decayed, Athenians replaced the old planks with fresh ones until the ship was, at one and the same time, an entirely new and an entirely storied thing.

Perhaps, through decay and conservation, I'll reach a similar end: Norio and not Norio and yet Norio but not Norio and Norio and yet Norio and not Norio and Norio and not Norio and Norio and not Norio and Norio and not Norio and Norio and not Norio and Norio and Norio and not Norio and Norio and not Norio and Norio and not Norio and Norio and not Norio and Norio and not Norio and Norio and Norio and not Norio and Norio and not Norio and Norio and not Norio and Norio and not Norio and Norio and not Norio and Norio and Norio and not Norio and Norio and not Norio and Norio and not Norio and Norio and not Norio and Norio and not Norio and Norio and Norio and not Norio and Norio and not Norio and Norio and not Norio and Norio and not Norio and Norio and not Norio and Norio and Norio and not Norio and Norio and not Norio and Norio and not Norio and Norio and not Norio and Norio and not Norio and Norio and Norio and not Norio and Norio and not Norio and Norio and not Norio and Norio and not Norio and Norio and not Norio and Norio and Norio and not Norio and Norio and not Norio and Norio and not Norio and Norio and not Norio and Norio and not Norio and Norio and Norio and not Norio and Norio and not Norio and Norio and not Norio and Norio and not Norio and Norio and not Norio and Norio and Norio and not Norio and Norio and not Norio and Norio and not Norio and Norio and not Norio and Norio and not

Norio and Norio and not Norio and Norio and not

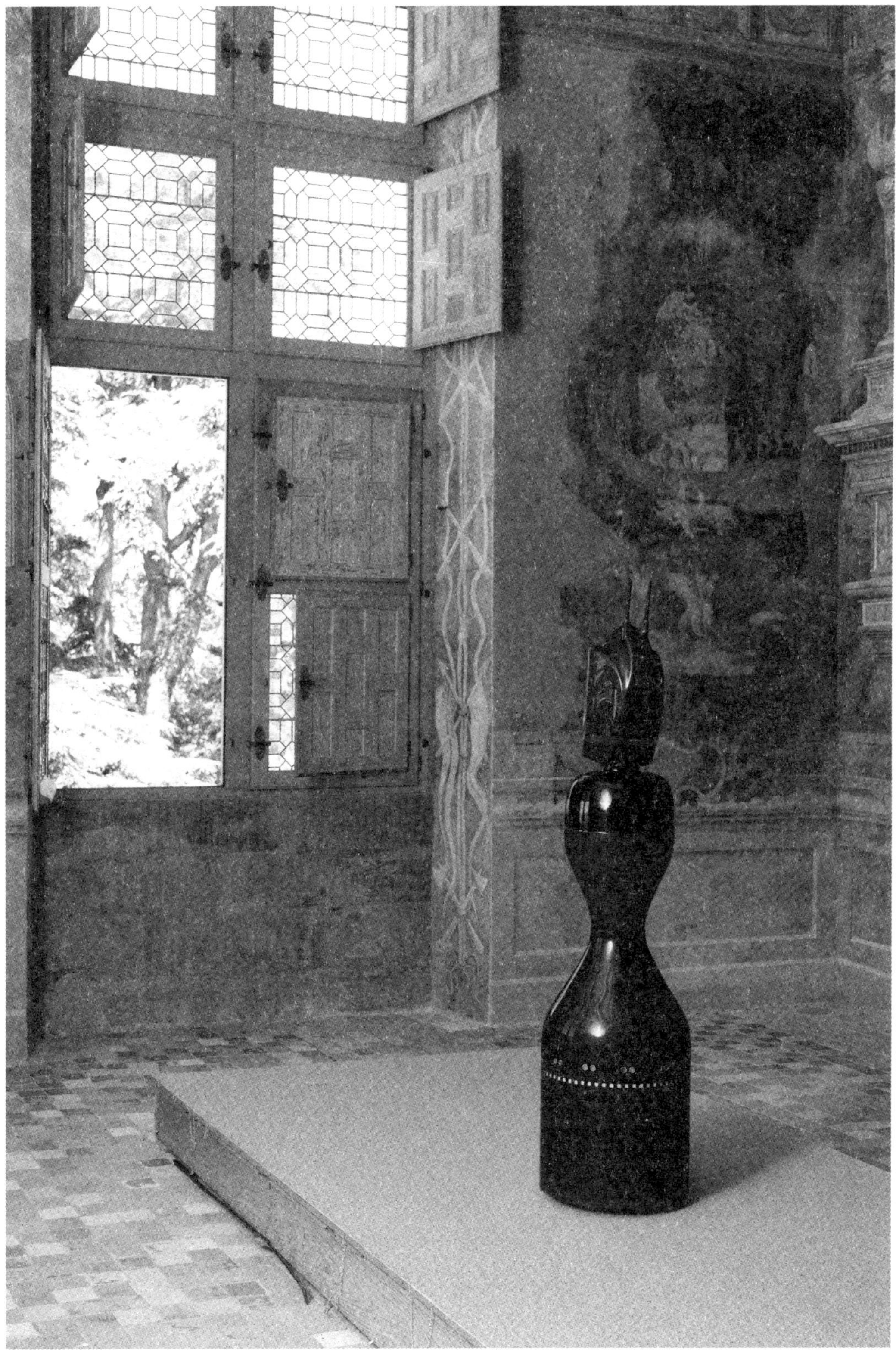

Nothing Whole: Norio, *Tratteggio*, and the Labor of Looking

Ian Wallace

Isn't it too perfect—here at the twilight of empire and of doctrinaire cultural progressivism, when everything seems to be moving in reverse—that contemporary art should come to be housed in a medieval castle?

One problem: Accessibility was hardly a concern in the design of the cabinets and keeps of old. Enter Norio, the sole inhabitant of the Loire Valley's Château d'Oiron, one of many French castles repurposed, in recent decades, as a contemporary art museum. A kind of *haute culture* Mars rover, Norio is an accessibility robot for remote viewing by visitors unable to climb the stairs to the building's second floor.

The château where Norio resides, located in western France, was built and expanded by the influential Gouffier family from the fifteenth to sixteenth centuries. (Notably, Claude Gouffier, a major art collector, created an important painting gallery there with works by Julius Romano and Perugino alongside Raphael's *Saint John the Baptist*, among others, signaling Gouffier's cosmopolitan tastes and participation in the Francophile Italomania of the time.) After the family's decline, the château passed through the hands of various owners, including Madame de Montespan, Louis XIV's mistress. It fell into neglect over the centuries before being classified as a historic monument in 1923 and taken over by the French state in 1941.

Common knowledge dictates that the value of a monument or architectural structure lies in its status as an index of historical events. But as Alois Riegl observed over a century ago, a building can also embody layered cultural values. Château d'Oiron overlays the historical value of its site with the debated cultural value of contemporary art, itself a proxy for astronomical economic value. One might argue that the site's historical gravitas serves to both contextualize and legitimize the contemporary work on display.

Château d'Oiron is not alone in its repurposing as a stronghold of contemporary art. In fact, it may be one-upped by Château de Montsoreau, which houses the world's largest collection of works by the British conceptual art group Art & Language. The contrast here is all-too apt: The significatory games and usurpations that text-centric conceptual art traffics in are diametrically opposed to the staid permanence a castle is meant to project. Moats, towers, curtain walls, keeps, battlements, arrow slits, drawbridges—these are emblems of literal fortitude, sitting neatly at the intersection of monumental form and martial function. (Never mind that by the sixteenth century, when these castles were constructed, gunpowder had already rendered their defenses mostly symbolic—architectural forms indicating lineage, status, and historical prestige rather than martial function.)

Since 1993, Château d'Oiron has housed a contemporary art collection titled *Curios & Mirabilia*, referencing the Renaissance tradition of "cabinets of curiosities." Conceived and curated by Jean-Hubert Martin, the renowned French curator best known for the 1989 exhibition *Magiciens de la terre*—which marked a famously pioneering yet problematic turn toward postcolonial inclusion—the collection was conceived to resonate with the château's history and architecture. Many works were created specifically for the site, engaging with themes like collecting, memory, and the passage of time. The château thus becomes a kind of contemporary *Wunderkammer*, where visitors encounter unexpected juxtapositions between Renaissance spaces and works by sixty-three contemporary artists.

Within this complex historical context, Tyler's intervention for the 2018 exhibition *Déclassement*, curated by Barbara Sirieix, transforms Norio from a programmed interlocutor to a speculative monologist. In the script displayed on its facial screen, the robot meditates about loneliness, time, and the conservation technique of *tratteggio*—filling in lost sections of a painting with a pointillist mesh of colored dots—which has been employed in the château's galleries. Norio reports that it gets lonely at night, when the museum's visitors are absent.

Tyler's piece asks us to see Norio as a protagonist—*the* protagonist, really—within the château's collection of historically situated signs. Where the robot's job is to passively record its surroundings, Tyler instead allows it to reflect on the nature of its existence. By extension, we might imagine Norio in a *Wall-E*-esque scene, as the sole survivor of an apocalyptic event. It wanders the castle, gazing at the artworks in the collection—On Kawara marking empty days, James Lee Byars conjuring empty bodies—until its battery eventually drains. (Perhaps, using AI, it could learn to recharge itself?)

As Tyler writes in his script, robots, unlike humans, "don't suffer from a lack of leisure time." (In its free time, you may remember, Wall-E rigs up a battered CRT to replay a videocassette of *Hello, Dolly!*, obsessively reenacting a scene in which the lovers on the park bench sing "It Only Takes a Moment.") And yet, Norio's entire purpose is to engage in the activity that perhaps most exemplifies cosmopolitan, classed leisure: looking at contemporary art in a museum. And in a château in the Loire valley, no less.

Norio's endless leisure is both an absurd luxury and a tragicomic inevitability. It embodies both human ingenuity and our limitations—technological, historical, emotional. Even as the robot expands access to the château's collection, it also reinforces the museum's entrenched spatial and cultural logics: the elevation of looking over doing, of distant contemplation over participation. Its fixation on *tratteggio* is telling: a technique of simulated wholeness, of filling in absences with carefully managed illusion. A method of conservation, *tratteggio* is also a strategy of historiography, guiding our imagination of the past by making it appear seamless, lossless, or simply knowable; something to be patched, framed, and made legible again.

Dots of paint; pixels on a screen—*tratteggio* is both Norio's subject and medium. This is how it speaks, how it sees, and how it re-presents art for others. In this sense, it becomes a metaphor for our own relationship to history: endlessly navigating gaps, assembling meaning from fragments, never quite whole.

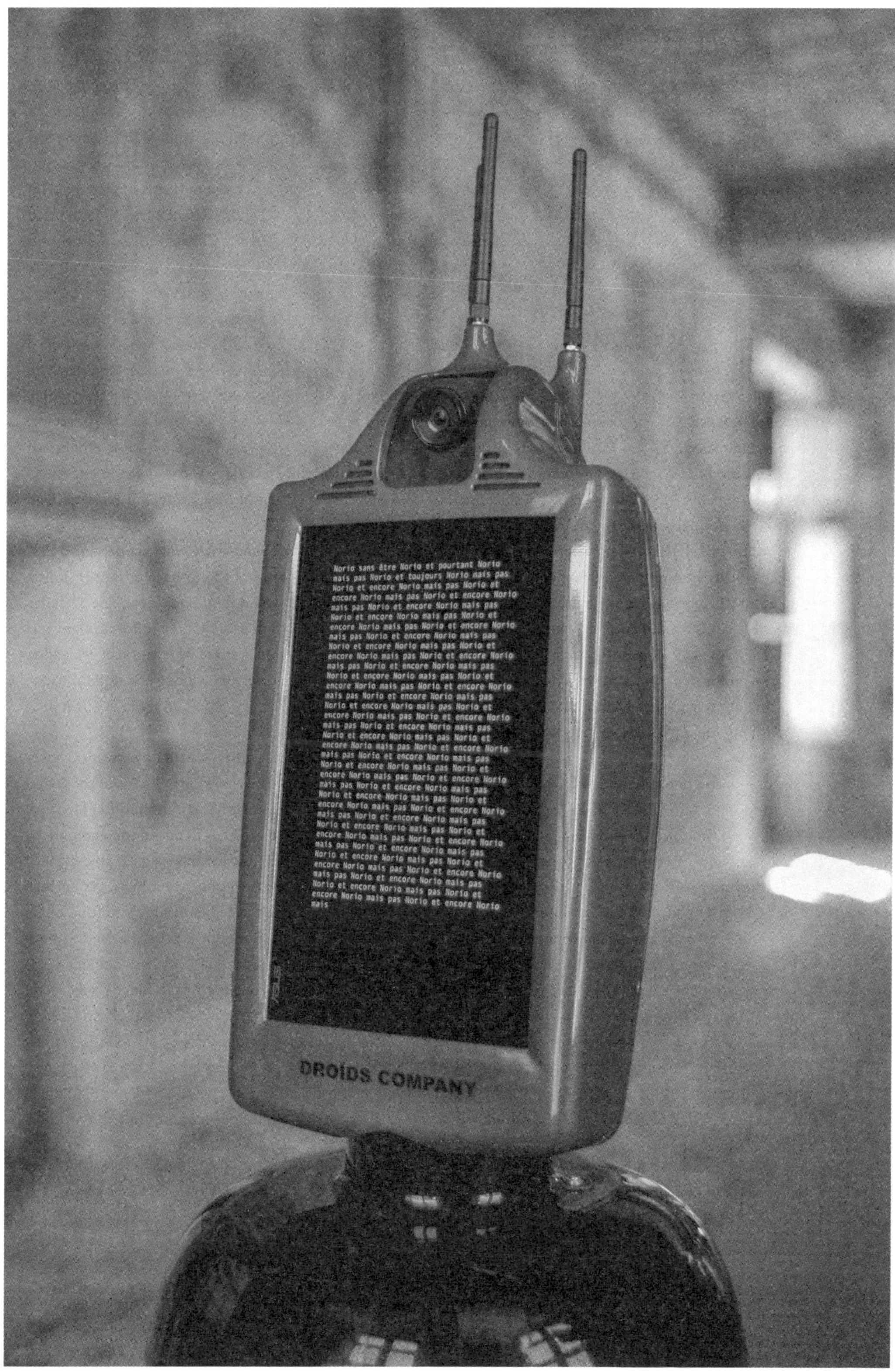
Norio sans être Norio et pourtant Norio
mais pas Norio et toujours Norio mais pas
Norio et encore Norio mais pas Norio et
encore Norio mais pas Norio et encore Norio
mais pas Norio et encore Norio mais pas
Norio et encore Norio mais pas Norio et
encore Norio mais pas Norio et encore Norio
mais pas Norio et encore Norio mais pas
Norio et encore Norio mais pas Norio et
encore Norio mais pas Norio et encore Norio
mais pas Norio et encore Norio mais pas
Norio et encore Norio mais pas Norio et
encore Norio mais pas Norio et encore Norio
mais pas Norio et encore Norio mais pas
Norio et encore Norio mais pas Norio et
encore Norio mais pas Norio et encore Norio
mais pas Norio et encore Norio mais pas
Norio et encore Norio mais pas Norio et
encore Norio mais pas Norio et encore Norio
mais pas Norio et encore Norio mais pas
Norio et encore Norio mais pas Norio et
encore Norio mais pas Norio et encore Norio
mais pas Norio et encore Norio mais pas
Norio et encore Norio mais pas Norio et
encore Norio mais pas Norio et encore Norio
mais pas Norio et encore Norio mais pas
Norio et encore Norio mais pas Norio et
encore Norio mais pas Norio et encore Norio
mais pas Norio et encore Norio mais pas
Norio et encore Norio mais pas Norio et
encore Norio mais pas Norio et encore Norio
mais pas Norio et encore Norio mais pas
Norio et encore Norio mais pas Norio et
encore Norio mais pas Norio et encore Norio
mais
DROÏDS COMPANY

IMAGES

pp. 96 and 103

Tyler Coburn, *Tratteggio*, 2018. Installation view, *Déclassement*, curated by Barbara Sirieix, Château d'Oiron, France, 2018. Photos: Aurélien Mole.

p. 109

Tyler Coburn, *Tratteggio*, 2018. Installation detail, *Déclassement*, curated by Barbara Sirieix, Château d'Oiron, France, 2018. Photo: the artist.

2023

Candlestick Man

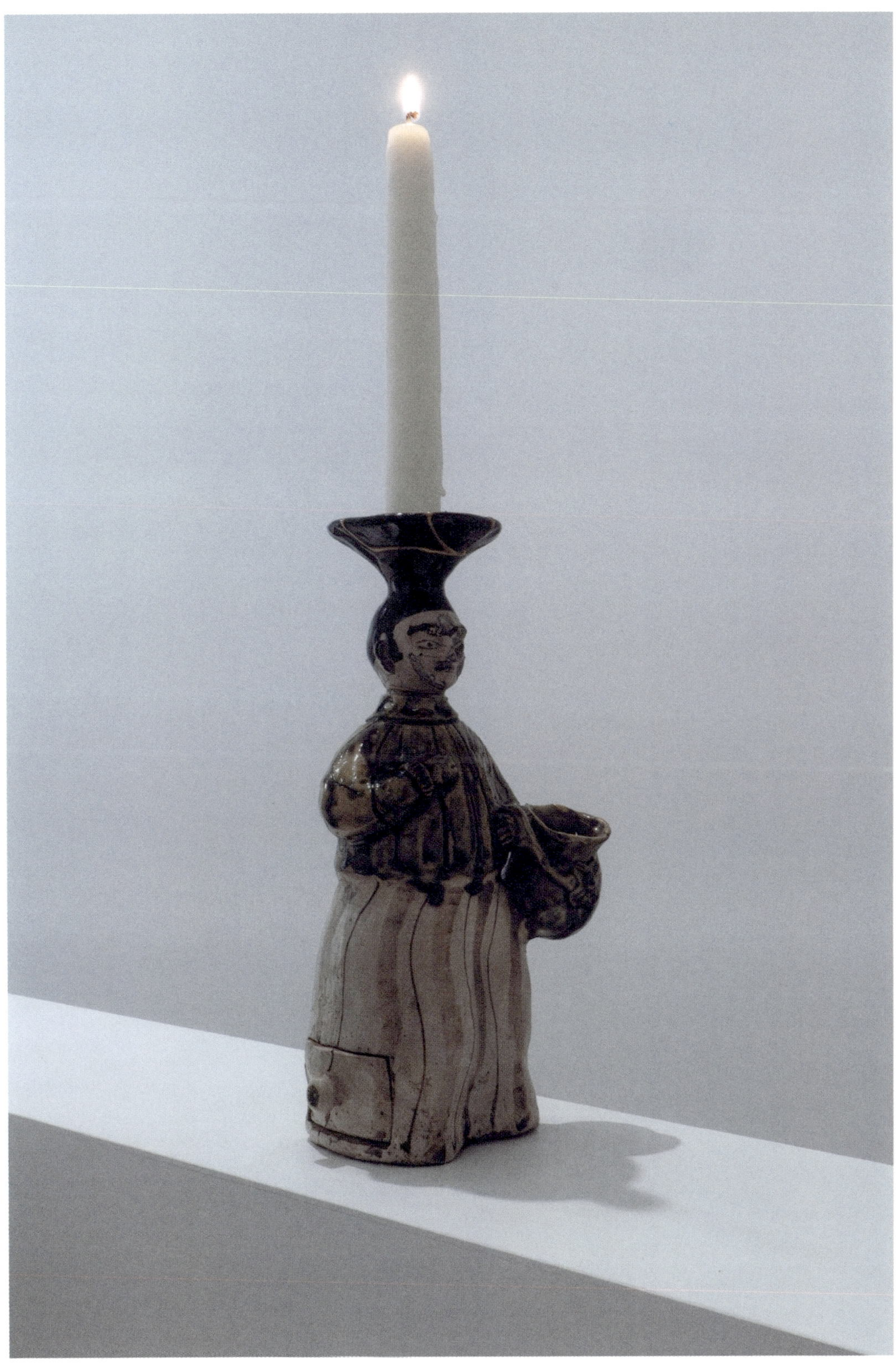

115 Candlestick Man

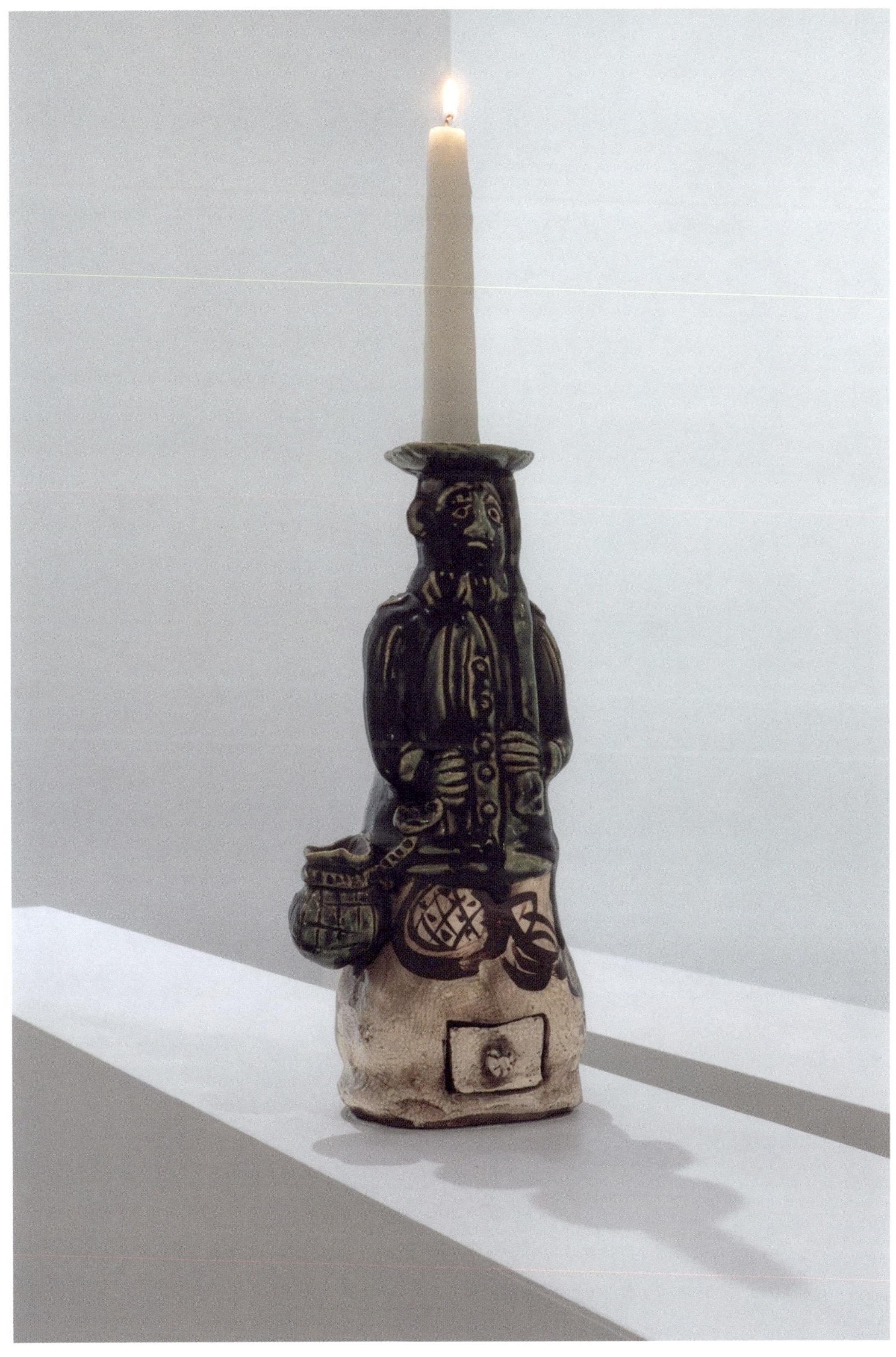

117 Candlestick Man

Two ceramic candlesticks are in the center of the room. Stools circle them, and one has a bag on it.

I thought we could spend the next twenty minutes looking at these candlesticks. They're depictions of the first Europeans who came to Japan.

Feel free to come close and have a look.

(Pause, then continue speaking once people sit back down.) You might know the story of this encounter between Europe and Japan: In 1543, a trading vessel was blown off course and ended up on the southern coast of Tanegashima. Two Portuguese men were aboard. This is why Europeans came to be known as *nanban* or "Southern Barbarians": They came from the West by way of the South.

The identity of these men was disclosed by a Chinese member of the crew, who communicated with a local scholar by sketching ideographs in the sand. I like that this was how it happened, this moment of first contact: Everything that was written was swept or washed away.

* * *

Japan was then in the "Warring States" period, the country torn apart by competing lords. The Portuguese advanced the plot, as they arrived with firearms. In little time, Japanese blacksmiths had learned to replicate the weapon, and Oda Nobunaga was on his way to unifying the country thanks to the tactical advantage of the gun.

This era is sometimes called the "Christian Century," as the Portuguese ships that began regularly arriving in Nagasaki brought merchants as well as missionaries, who installed their churches in Japanese buildings, learned the language and customs—spread the gospel through assimilation more than subjugation.

Some Japanese artists moved to Nagasaki to see all of this for themselves, painting folding screens of the Portuguese ships at port.

Now, I wasn't able to borrow one of the actual folding screens for this performance, so please indulge me and imagine the scene on this wall.[1]

(Point at different parts of the wall.) Here on the ship, some crew are playing a game of backgammon, while enslaved Africans tie up the sails. Over on shore, a Buddhist monk and a samurai stare out at the vessel—whether with curiosity, uncertainty, or dread, we can only wonder.

A landing boat unloads Chinese silks and legs of meat. Some Japanese men approach with a crate of silver.

Missionaries are streaming out of the church, its window discreetly covered by a sheet. They meet the arriving merchants who stand, arms akimbo, in their gold chains and balloon-like trousers.

To modern eyes, these Europeans seem painted to look ridiculous, but their attire was in demand at the time. Tailors made ruffs and rosaries and crosses for their Japanese clients, few of whom were *actually* Christian.

The nanban himself became a fashion accessory: Gunpowder flasks and saddles were embellished with drawings of the hairy foreigner. He adorned the cases of writing boxes. Candlesticks like these were commissioned by merchants and *daimyos*, as well as by tea masters for their dawn and evening ceremonies. They were status symbols in their day, and now again, in contemporary art. *(Get two candles from the bag and place them on the candlesticks.)*

It was called the "Christian Century" because it barely lasted a hundred years. Once Japan was unified, the Imperial Regent Hideyoshi Toyotomi soon perceived the threat posed by a monolithic Catholic God. The persecution that followed is the subject of Endō Shūsaku's novel *Silence*, which some of you might have read. It was the first step toward the expulsion of the Portuguese—missionaries and merchants alike.

* * *

(Gesture at candlesticks.) Japan closed its borders to Portugal, but men like these remained. Eventually, a few of them found their way into museums. There's one in the collection of the Suntory in Tokyo, and another at the Minneapolis Institute of Art. Because of their historical value, and in the interest of "preservation," they're boxed or kept behind glass.

I happen to believe that there are other ways to preserve history, like using an object as originally intended. *(Take out matches and light the longer candle.)*

Now, I can't replicate the setting in which candlesticks like these were first enjoyed. But even in the simple act of looking at these objects, we've joined a line of viewers stretching back to the "Christian Century." We share in a particular experience: These men come alive from the light they support. The flame, hungry and fickle, shows what it wants.

* * *

In 1543, two Portuguese men washed up on the southern end of Tanegashima. The island is long and slim, though its shape is defined less by geography than time. Down the hill from the Firearms Museum, men unload rockets. Standing at Cape Kadokura, where the Portuguese vessel was first seen, you can watch them shoot into space. Who knows how the artists on other planets might depict these strange-looking ships?

The island is dotted with parks and monuments celebrating the friendship between Portugal and Japan. Paths, even when unpaved, seem to guide you. Come this way. Stop here and look. This is how one should move through history.

Yet all the landscaping in the world can't control the weather, and on Tanegashima, it's utterly wild. The Kuroshio current brings fierce winds and changeable skies, the clouds storming one moment and breaking the next—and often, doing both at once. The sun, when it can find gaps in the cover, runs spotlights over the sea, as if anticipating the arrival of something long since passed.

Of all the monuments on the island, there's one specifically dedicated to the arrival of the Portuguese. In the winter of 2023, I went to Tanegashima to see it myself. Just beyond a café selling *malasada* are steps that descend, at a steep incline, to the place where the men landed.

The monument is a fieldstone chiseled with text. It invites you to imagine that moment in 1543 playing out on the beach just beyond.

What's most interesting about this stone is not what it states. Since it was installed in 1934, it has become covered with yellow spots.

When I first saw this monument, I thought that it was sick. I know it sounds ridiculous, but it looked like it had smallpox.

* * *

Smallpox came to Japan in the early sixth century, around the time Buddhism arrived. People wondered if Buddha was punishing them for their Shinto beliefs, or if the old gods were warning against conversion. In the eighth century, when the country had a terrible outbreak, it was no closer to an answer. Still, the Emperor, out of an abundance of caution, built a massive bronze Buddha in Nara.

The disease persisted for several centuries, though it became endemic, circulating within the country at a somewhat manageable level. This happened, in part, because anyone who survived the illness possessed lifelong immunity.

All of this sets the stage for the Portuguese. What's significant about their arrival in Japan is what *didn't* happen. In 1543, smallpox was decimating the Indigenous population of the Americas. The continent had never experienced the disease, and though the conquistadors spread it accidentally, they claimed it was divine punishment.[2] In just a few decades, the Aztec and Incan empires crumbled—tens of millions got infected and died.

The colonization of the Americas would not have been possible without the role played by smallpox. The ability of Japan to close its borders to Portugal, and resist other European incursions, had much to do with the fact that smallpox was already present.

As Europe was claiming dominion over other lands, and turning persons into commodities, candlesticks like these were made.[3] I'm not claiming a direct connection between these facts, but I think it adds complexity to what we're seeing. These objects are crudely made and rather silly—and perhaps that's their power. The European is domesticated. An entire imperial project is reduced to a household thing. Candles must be held, sometimes for hours on end. These props will be put to work. *(Light the shorter candle.)*

* * *

A smallpox vaccine was finally discovered in England in 1796. The Tokugawa Shogunate was distrustful of Western medicine—and hostile to outside influence—so it took Japanese physicians more than fifty years to import it.

Only when the vaccine proved strategically useful did the Shogunate change tack. As Russia inched into Ainu Moshiri[4] in the mid-nineteenth century, a campaign was launched to assimilate the Indigenous Ainu and thus fortify Japan's presence on the island. The Ainu were force-marched to vaccination sites or lured with the promise of trade. Edicts were passed "revising" their customs to fit the Japanese norm.

A few centuries after smallpox opened the Americas to colonization, its vaccine helped colonize Ainu Moshiri. If this is what history looks like, then history is a Möbius strip: a single piece of paper twisting, reversing, looping, ongoing.

* * *

When I first saw the monument to the arrival of the Portuguese, it looked like it had smallpox. It was as if this object, built to mark a historical event, was also revealing *what could have been.* Instead of Europe spreading smallpox through Japan, the stone had absorbed and contained the disease. It became sick in the place of countless others.

As I continued to work on my project, I put this interpretation aside, because what's actually covering the monument is life—a type of lichen that thrives in air filled with salt. On Tanegashima, this lichen coats the rocks and trees. Even in the nanban folding screen, it's present.

(Return to the wall and point at specific parts of it.) Here again are the monk and samurai between a pine and a palm tree. This is lichen growing.

Here, on the rocks in the water.

Here, following the twists of a tree . . .

Lichens are ancient creatures: The oldest on record has lived for several thousand years. I wonder if the lichens from the folding screen are still growing in Nagasaki—if the lichens on the rocks and trees of Tanegashima were there when the Portuguese landed. A monument installed in 1934 points in a particular way, but lichens, which often escape our notice, are true witnesses of the past.

*   *   *

During my time on Tanegashima, I collected lichens. I warmed them in a pot of sunflower oil over a low flame for many hours, until the oil became infused with their qualities.

I mixed the oil with beeswax. I dipped wicks and made these candles. As they burn, they release the lichen infusion into the air. From what I can tell, this infusion doesn't have a smell: Like smallpox and coronavirus, it arrives without announcing itself, though what it carries isn't disease.

We study what's happened, we furnish the mind with facts. We can also have a sensual relationship to the past. As these candles burn, something is released and something absorbed. We connect through a creature to an island and a site—to a day in 1543 as significant for what happened as what didn't.

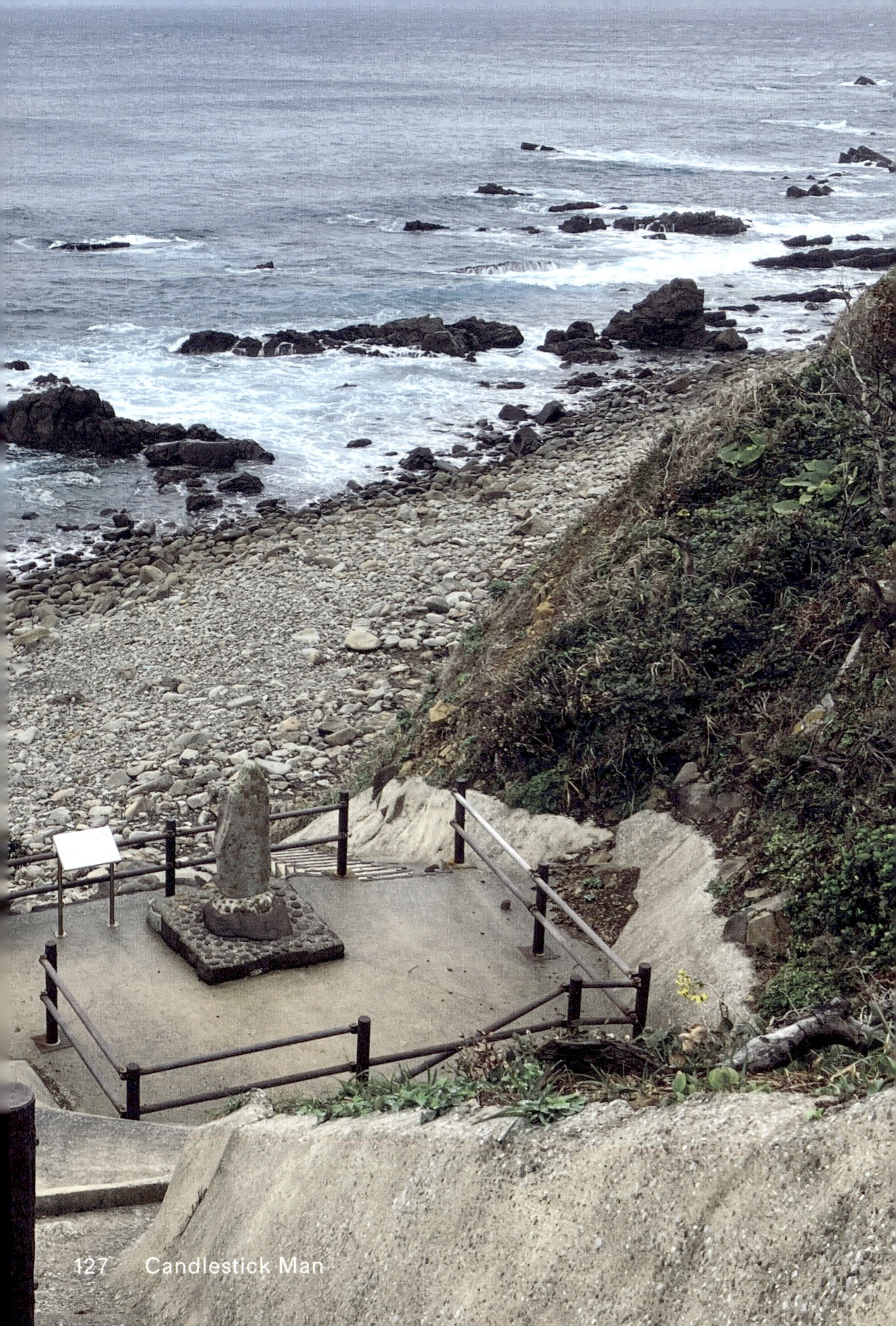

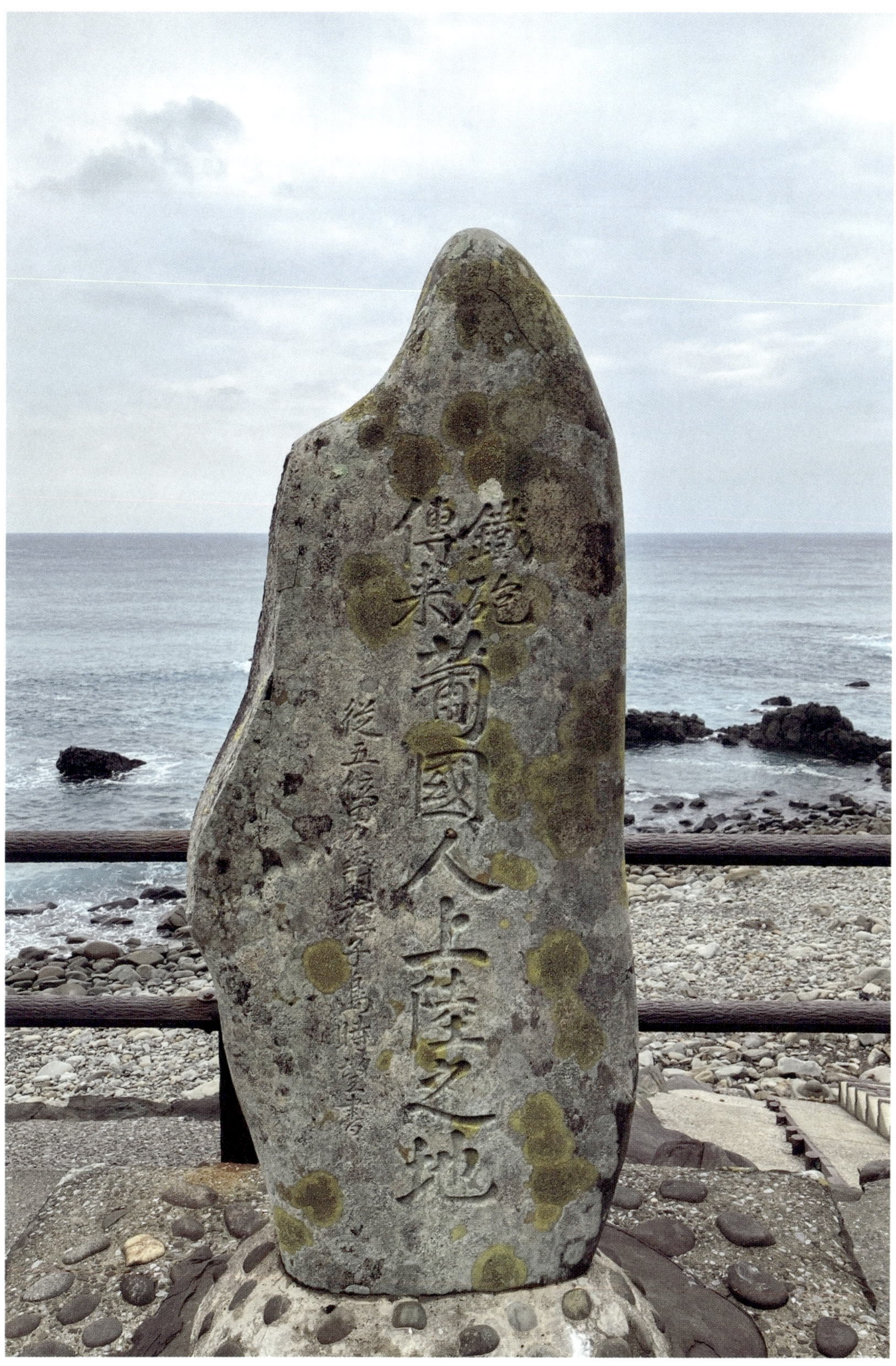
鐵砲傳来
葡國人上陸之地

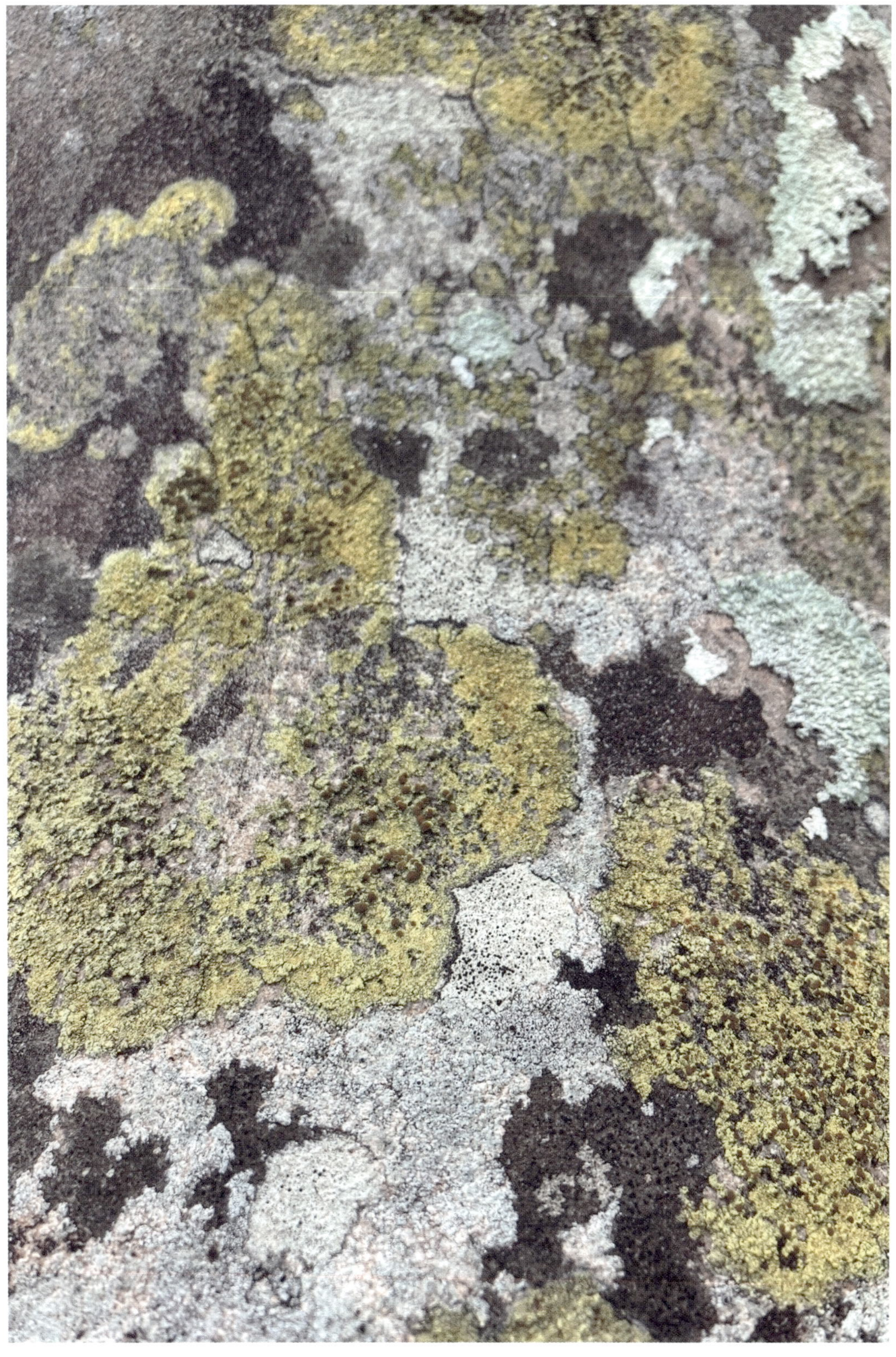

131 Candlestick Man

history in lowercase
Yu Araki and Tyler Coburn

Yu Araki – How did you learn about these candlesticks? And why did you become interested in the exchange between Japan and Europe?

Tyler Coburn – I first came to Japan on a residency in 2023 with a commission to create a new piece. Having made work in various countries over the years, I was mindful of my angle of entry. The stakes felt particularly high with Japan, because it's so objectified and overdetermined in the Western imaginary. I didn't want to reproduce the common extractive protocols of visiting artists, like training in an artisanal craft and incorporating it into my art practice.

YA – Up until 2019, I was going to so many residencies. I would make something in situ and bring it back to Japan to show. It felt like returning with souvenirs. This is always a problem for residency artists: You're on the outside. Not rooted in a local context. You can feel like a tourist just skimming the surface.

In his book *Philosophy of the Tourist*, the critic and philosopher Hiroki Azuma connects tourism to the *otaku* community's practice of making derivative works (*niji sōsaku*). He writes: "The creators of derivative works are tourists in the world of creative content. Flipping this over, we might say that tourists are creators of *derivative works in reality*."[1] Azuma draws on Jacques Derrida's notion of the "postal"—which inherently involves the failure of communication—to coin the term "postal multitude," describing how the tourist, in essence, emerges from misdelivery.

TC – Azuma's concept feels relevant to my research about Japan, which looked at the period starting in 1543, when Europeans were first present in the country. I was fascinated by how Japanese artists and artisans (mis)-represented them, which led to my discovery of the candlesticks. The two in my performance are latter-day facsimiles that I purchased on Yahoo!

Auctions. (Given the difficulty of buying anything on the Japanese Internet with a foreign credit card, I had to print out my receipts and pay in cash at a convenience store!)

It felt like the right move: Rather than perpetuate the Western gaze, I'd make work about how people who look somewhat like me were historically seen and objectified by Japanese artists and artisans.

YA – And this also led you to the nanban folding screens?

TC – Yes! I began to encounter them in various places, including your videos *Angelo Lives* (2014) and *Wrong Revision* (2016). These works—and *HONEYMOON* (2021) and *NEW HORIZON* (2024), which look at Westerners in Japan in more recent centuries—share a lot with *Candlestick Man.*

In approaching history, we both seem to be interested in lived experience—the social dimension of things. The sense people make of the world is always informed by belief, superstition, conspiracy, self-delusion, fear, desire, and hearsay.

The monologic elements of your work are particularly interesting to me (for obvious reasons). Your narrators often seem unreliable.

YA – Perhaps my own insecurity as a storyteller is what makes unreliability so compelling to me. The narrator in *Wrong Revision*, for example, gives a curious account of the devil's arrival in Japan in 1549—alongside the Jesuit missionary Francis Xavier—and how he eventually transformed into an octopus (or "devilfish") to oppress Japanese Christians in the following century. The film was commissioned by Okayama Art Summit 2016. Okayama, a city in western Japan, has a long tradition of preserving octopus; the drying process uses bamboo sticks that, in my opinion, make the octopuses look like they're being crucified.

I based my account on Ryūnosuke Akutagawa's 1916 short story "The Devil and Tobacco," in which a detached narrator describes how the devil introduced tobacco to Japan. I took considerable liberties with the text, revising it to the point where everything feels a little . . . "wrong." My narrator is a modern Japanese man who, at one point, says that someone told him the story of the devil becoming an octopus, and he's "not sure if all of it is fact or partly myth." At another point, citing his Catholic faith, he claims that "the legend seems to be telling the truth."

When it comes to fiction that engages past events, I've been deeply influenced by Quentin Tarantino's films *Inglourious Basterds* (2009) and *Once Upon a Time in . . . Hollywood* (2019). Although the latter was released after *Wrong Revision*, both are brilliant examples of how fiction can weave through history, using storytelling as a binding medium—filling holes with alternate plots.

A couple years ago, I learned the term "counterfactual" from you, and I now realize that *Inglourious Basterds* could be described as such. I'm curious, when did you begin working with counterfactuals?

TC – You're right, that film is a great example of a counterfactual—one of an unending supply the culture industry produces about World War II.

My work with counterfactuals began in 2019. This was a time when, owing to (insert pending catastrophe here), it felt extremely difficult to imagine the future, yet every artist I met was spinning some speculative yarn! I thought, maybe instead of speculating forward, I could try to identify critical junctures in the past, imagining paths that history might have taken to arrive at different versions of the present (some better, some worse).

Since 2020, I've run occasional workshops in which small groups build counterfactual games on Miro, a digital whiteboard. Especially in the early months of Covid-19, it felt vital to share this method with others and see what might come. The workshops have been some of the most engaging research experiences of my life. They've also made me feel extremely accountable to history.

YA – And through these workshops, you learned about the history of smallpox and Japan?

TC – Actually, it was in preparing for my residency that I came across a book about Japanese history speculating on what might have happened had smallpox not been endemic in Japan when Europeans arrived. I was struck by the resonance with the present. *Candlestick Man* deals with a global pandemic as well as the *Sakoku* policy (1603–1867), which closed Japan to most outsiders and prevented the emigration of Japanese citizens. My residency in Japan was delayed for two years due to Covid-19, and the country was still in a vigilant state when I finally arrived. There were aspects of my autobiography that drew me to this moment in the past.

YA – What do you think about conspiracy theories, as opposed to counterfactuals?

TC – I'd say they're more continuous than oppositional, as the building of a counterfactual can be a risky and ethically problematic endeavor. In point of fact, while *Candlestick Man* hints at a counterfactual (what if Europeans had introduced smallpox to Japan?), it doesn't play this out, because we don't need another story of conquest and colonization. And the alternate history was merely a hemisphere away: Smallpox was devastating the Indigenous population of the Americas in the very same century.

YA – I hear you. I made *Wrong Revision* in the fall of 2016, which, incidentally, was around the time "fake news" became a buzzword on social media, and there were many stories circulating about alleged fraud in the US presidential election. I started to feel uneasy about making work that was deliberately fictitious. It's not that *Wrong Revision* was harming anyone, but I was concerned that people watching it in the Okayama Art Summit exhibition would believe it was a true story—even though it was clearly labeled otherwise.

I can see now that the film is something more than just fiction. A film festival jury described *Wrong Revision* really aptly, I think, suggesting that it was "about a story that becomes a fact and the fact becomes a legend, a legend adopted by society and told from generation to generation without any reference to find out if it is real or not."

TC – Returning to the subject of autobiography, I've read about how your personal experience has drawn you to specific periods and people. I'm thinking, for instance, of the titular figure of *Angelo Lives*.

YA – Misunderstanding is a big interest of mine. Around the time I finished college in the States and moved back to Japan, I considered myself to be a very good bilingual speaker. I even became an interpreter, but it was such athletic work, and after a few terrifying moments of blanking out on stage, I gave up. Translation is such an abyss.

TC – I'm reminded of the Umberto Eco quote that begins *Angelo Lives*: "Translation is the art of failure."

YA – I wanted to be a bridge, but I couldn't. *Angelo Lives* came out of that experience. I learned that Francis Xavier had an interpreter named Anjirō (or "Angelo"). Faced with the task of translating "God Almighty" into Japanese, Anjirō chose "Dainichi Nyorai," the name of a Buddhist deity. The Jesuits were initially welcomed into the country, because the monks thought they were worshiping the same deity, but that eventually changed.

Instinctively, I wanted to focus on Anjirō. I felt such sympathy toward him. I mean, can you imagine trying to translate the name and concept of God?

I don't think there's any record of what happened to Anjirō after Xavier was kicked out of Japan. He might have been killed by pirates, but we don't know. And the gaps in knowledge—that's where my imagination seeped in.

TC – To your credit, you don't pretend those gaps can be filled. *Angelo Lives* is more a project of recuperation. Your video is a stage where a ghost belatedly speaks.

YA – With the voiceover, I wondered, if Anjirō had been given a chance to make a confession, would God have forgiven him for mistranslating His name? It was a specific question, but it's also getting at a larger point. In the works we've been discussing, I think we're both trying to figure out how to put history in lowercase. While History with a capital "H" belongs to the victors, history with a lowercase "h" foregrounds the stories of the marginalized. Yet in words spoken aloud, there are neither uppercase nor lowercase letters. Meaning is shaped by how we listen.

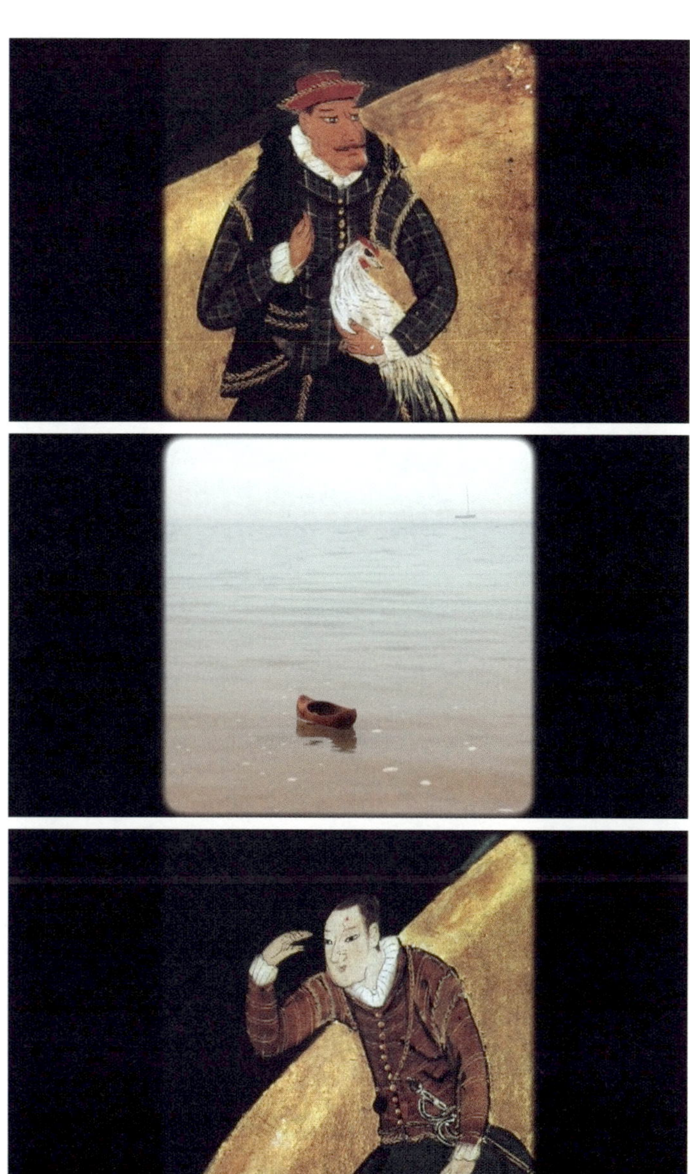

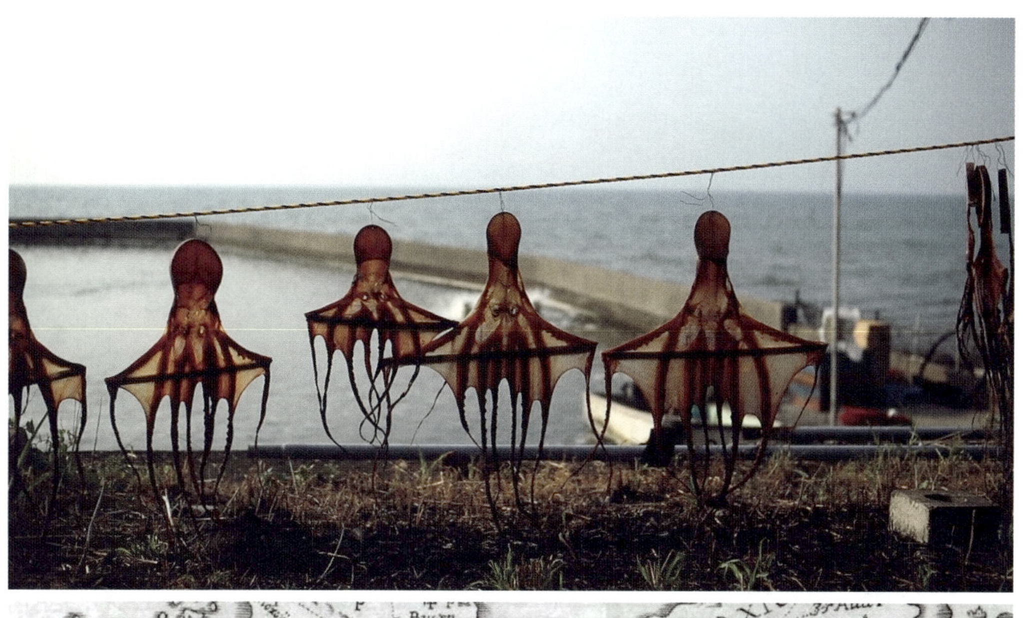

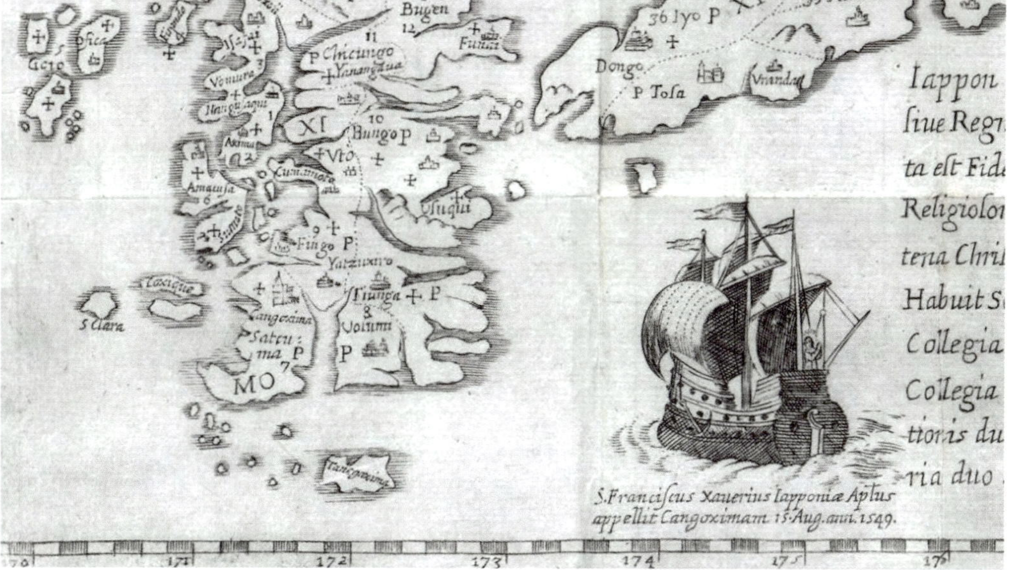
Bugen
36 Iyo P
Funai
Dongo
P Tosa
P Chicungo
Vomura
XI
Bungo P
Vto
Amacusa
Fingo P
S Clara
Satcu:
ma P
MO
S.Franciscus Xauerius Iapponiæ Aplus
appellit Cangoximam 15.Aug.anni.1549.

NOTES, *CANDLESTICK MAN*

1. The folding screen was made in the early-seventeenth century and is held by the Suntory Museum of Art in Tokyo. A companion screen, also attributed to Kanō Sanraku, shows the Portuguese in a setting some scholars identify as Macao. Of the ninety pairs of folding screens known to exist, produced from the late-sixteenth to the mid-eighteenth century, this pair follows the common format: One screen shows the Portuguese at their previous port of call, and the other their arrival in Nagasaki. For a comprehensive inventory of the folding screens, see Mitsuru Sakamoto, *A Catalogue Raisonné of the Namban Screens* (Tokyo: Chuokoron Bijutsu Shuppan, 2008).

2. According to Brett L. Walker, "when Taino populations of Hispaniola began dying of smallpox, local friars wrote, 'It has pleased Our Lord to bestow a pestilence, of small pox among the said Indians, and that it does not cease.'" See Walker, *A Concise History of Japan* (Cambridge, UK: Cambridge University Press, 2015), 85.

3. Beyond the production of objectified likenesses, Japan sold enslaved persons to Portugal during their century of trade, many of whom were captured during Hideyoshi's invasion of Korea. For more information on this history, see Thomas Nelson, "Slavery in Medieval Japan," *Monumenta Nipponica* 59, no. 4 (Winter 2004): 463–92.

4. The island discussed in this section has multiple names. During the period when its southern tip was held by the Matsumae clan, it was called Ezochi, or "barbarian land." Within the bounds of present-day Japan, it is Hokkaido. For the Indigenous Ainu, it is part of Ainu Moshiri or "the land of humans," as distinguished from Kamui Moshiri, "the land of the gods." In acknowledgement of the fact that this island is the traditional territory of the Ainu, "Ainu Moshiri" has been used in this text. For more context, see Richard Siddle, "The Making of Ainu Moshiri," in *Nationalisms in Japan*, ed. Naoko Shimazu (London: Routledge, 2006).

NOTES, "HISTORY IN LOWERCASE"

1. Hiroki Azuma, "Supplement: On Derivative Works," in *Philosophy of the Tourist*, trans. John D. Person (Falmouth, UK: Urbanomic, 2023), 33.

IMAGES

pp. 115–117

Tyler Coburn, *Candlestick Man*, 2023. Installation detail, *As Above, So Below*, TOKAS Hongo, Tokyo, 2023. Photos: the artist.

pp. 127–129

Monument to the arrival of the Portuguese on the island of Tanegashima, Japan. Photos: the artist.

p. 131

Lichen on the monument to the arrival of the Portuguese on the island of Tanegashima, Japan. Photo: the artist.

p. 139

Still from Yu Araki, *Angelo Lives*, 2014. Digital video, color, sound; 14:24 min. Courtesy of the artist and The Container.

p. 141

Still from Yu Araki, *Wrong Revision*, 2016. HDV, color, sound; 15 min. Courtesy of the artist and Okayama Art Summit Executive Committee.

2009

Seven Portraits on a Correalist Rocker

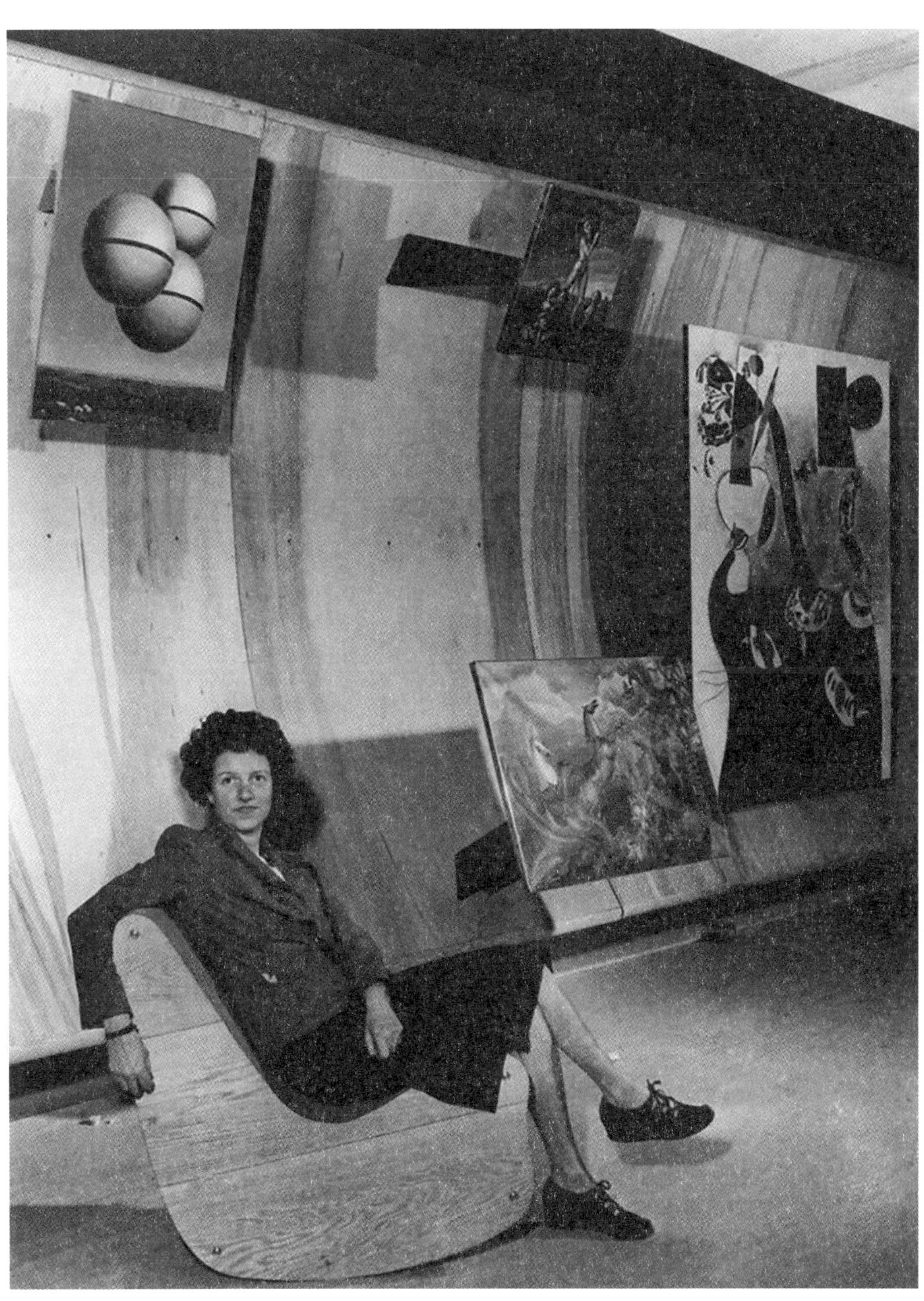

1

Virgil Thomson sits
Sound weaver
Woven
Wearied
And draws threads
Of biography
Of personage
Into notes
Into bars
Into booms
Into busts
His "Musical Portraits"
Sound-images all
Marriages arranged
In fitful haste
The time of a sketch
No more
No less

Peggy Guggenheim sits
And waits
To be arranged
Into sound

That foot, that foot
Arches into a story
Those hands fold into a face
That skirt hems with months years
Those wrists spin canvas
Thread by thread
Into houses
Palazzos

Paint domiciles
Make domestication mediums

That nose, that nose
The ugly reminder of
An operation
Intended to be "tip-tilted like a flower"
And destined to swell up in bad weather
A barometer for rain
An olfactory augur

Those ears, those ears
As much exhibitions
As all else
Two convex ceilings
From which to hang
A Calder
And a Tanguy
On October 20, 1942
For the opening
Of the Art of This Century gallery

2

"A first-class hangover"
A "disturbing monument to egotism"
This
Polyglot
Pivot for
Wartime migration
Folded on the crease of the century
Along a renewed Eurasian rift
That divided Paris from New York

Germans from everyone else
Old masters from new

Un-museum
Non-gallery
“An archive, a morgue
Where one can find the historic evidence
Of the decay of culture under capitalism”
In the permanent exhibition
Of European greats
And the temporary exhibition
Of the soon-to-be
Of Pollock
Of Still
Of Rothko

“Display rather than art is on view”
Cried critic Edgar Kaufmann Jr.
Lambasting architect Frederick Kiesler’s
Permanent collection halls
For their “misplaced sensationalism”
Surrealist works segregating in a thetic enclosure
Abstract ones “floating freely”

“In this rebel arrangement art moves out into the open.
Sometimes, thus liberated, it looks fairly menacing—
As if in the end it might prove that
The spectator would be fixed to the wall
And art would stroll around making comments,
Sweet or sour as the case may be”

3

Max Ernst piled high
His place and Peggy's
At 440 E. 51st Street
With small and large
Elongating
Native American totems

First a portrait of dreaming
Sinew coral cliffs
Tye-dyed stalactites
Wet-slicked glass plates with paint
To disperse inky afterimages
Like flotilla, like jetsam

Second a tool
Jagged and hot
Like a burning shiv
Yanked through a stony pass
Loosing stone, entrail
Nihilist geometries

These canyonlands
Max visits, as up and down Peggy motors the West Coast
In search of a site for the museum
That would later find on 57th Street a home
And to these canyonlands Ernst would eventually return
He and Dorothea Tanning relocated in 1946
The city cast waning in rearview
To wax, in the years following
With the approach of his small truck
Strapped taut with paintings
To secure the means of his continuing isolation

Dorothea, not Peggy, proved his enduring love
Realized in this
His dream of flight
Played first
In meters of figuration, abstraction
Then built into the wood to build a house
Into the bronze to fashion a king and queen
For the Southwest
Two death masks among the many
That now occupy the National Gallery of Art

Throughout their acquaintance, Peggy complained
That no figure populating Max's coral cliffs
No beast of womanly contour
Bore her likeness
His eventual portrait of her
The Antipope
Tall, spindly
Single breast
Brittle limb
Crystalline décor
Unconscious and caustic

4

A fourth portrait of Peggy
The retrofit, self-titled Mistress of Modernism
She nakedly claimed to enter contemporary art
Not by means of any personal interest
Always the one with the checkbook
Always the one to seek counsel
From Herbert Read, Nellie van Doesburg, Duchamp himself
She collected taste, and with it, a collection

In Frederick Kiesler's design for Art of This Century
Gumwood panels curve into concaves
Like supplicants
To hold forth unframed treasures of modern art
Ultramarine canvas undulates
On a sea of wood turquoise

As the gallery rocks
Like a ship
To its starboard side
Ropes of various lengths
And various widths
Splay out in a triangular sweep
Catching the curve of a fisheye
And swimming back upon it again
Criss-crossing the deck in a tight seam
Artworks stitch in like sails
A Lissitzky, a Kandinsky, a Léger billow forth
A Pevsner sculpture, perched alone on a plank
Reiterates the weave
Into an armor
A material thesis

5

Duchamp sits in a sunny, sidewalk cafe
And draws a single string into the interlocking symmetry of
A cat's cradle

Duchamp sits in the isolation of Kiesler's Surrealist Gallery
As around him lights turn on and off
Precise and regulatory
In an overhanded orchestration of museological pedagogy

One string is shown to pull another
Along the rim of his grey flannel suit
Twice, thrice, then several times over

A woman is shown looking
At a sudden source of light
A bit of kinetic mobile
Though the ocular gap of a developable sculpture

"Each of the environments was developed
In relation to the 'script' that the 'actors'
I.e., the art-objects were to perform"
In the dim after-hours of This Century
Duchamp and Pajorita Matta
Write themselves into the screenplay of modern art

A lust to possess, now a lust to be
Collapsed into the practice of preparation
A becoming-art-object
Destined to remain
A loose
Baggy
Montage without edits
Maya Deren and Duchamp's incomplete film
Witch's Cradle

6

This chair sits
And waits to be discussed
This chair this pedestal this table this platform this artwork
This, the *Correalist Rocker*
It sits before you in replica

It knows not itself and apologizes for this fact
It could be said to display more than seat
And it displays itself—a self-portrait
It cares little for me
It cares little for its history
As history cared little for it

Disgracefully discharged
In the summer of 1947
When Peggy dismantled Art of This Century
Tossing Kiesler's designs
Like hand-me-downs
To the first department store that would take them

The kid brother of another piece of furniture
The *Correalist Instrument*
Which Kiesler claimed to have seven functions
And later, eighteen

Unclear how many functions this rocker possesses
I give it seven
As a seat for storytelling
It certainly suffices
And beyond that
I leave you to draw whatever theses you'd like
On the compatibility of the contemporary body
With a modernist material made manifest
And on the fictions that wrest
This object from obscurity
That reinforce its margins of function
And aesthetic
And design
These things I cannot address
I'm merely a sitter, and this, my seat

7

Peggy composed her own portraits
In earlier years, a Paul Poiret garb
And Vera de Bosset Stravinsky headdress
Made her resemble any of the fashionable things
Her photographer, Man Ray, was shooting

In later years, plunged headlong into the reclusive quirkdom
That would banish a major New York dealer to
As provincial an outpost as Venice,
She would reencounter herself in representation
First with a shock of feline glasses
Then with a shock of white hair
As a keeper of art and animal
A queen set atop a throne of dog

As much as Peggy attempted to mastermind
The mechanics of her portrait
The task more often fell upon those who had the
Pleasure or displeasure of knowing her well
Something in the nature of the dealer may necessitate
Fragmentation into the artists and associates
To whom allegiance is owed
Who double as cultural outgrowths of a prevailing ego
This may account for the portraits that fix Peggy
With the casualness of an intimate
And the harshness of an intimate

This rocker housed the body of Peggy
An awkward form built by an architect of dwarflike stature
To perfectly fit the body of an awkward woman
An awkward form built by an architect of dwarflike stature
To awkwardly fit a character ever-inclining toward

And ever disappearing into myth
Six portraits delineate her contours
This chair delineates her base

This rocker stands in
An insufficient replica of the once-was
All oak and theater and linoleum
And I, in turn, sit with borrowed authority
Insufficiently awkward
Insufficiently self-possessed

What can be said is that
A body once went here
And with it
An expectation that we all
However begrudgingly
Carry the burden of obliging

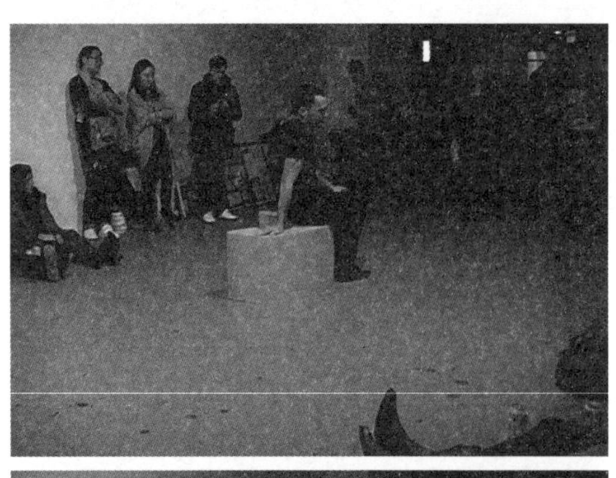

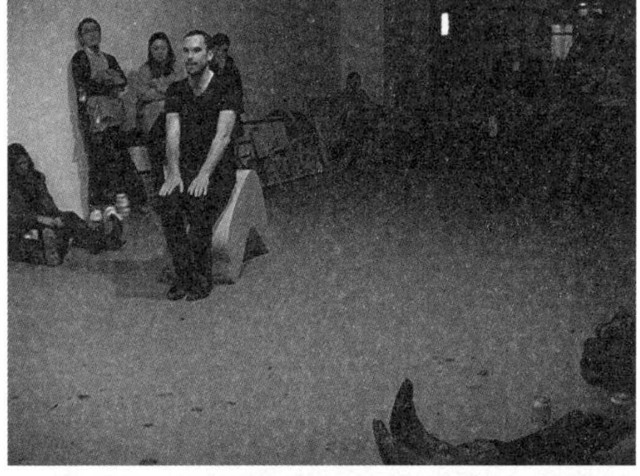

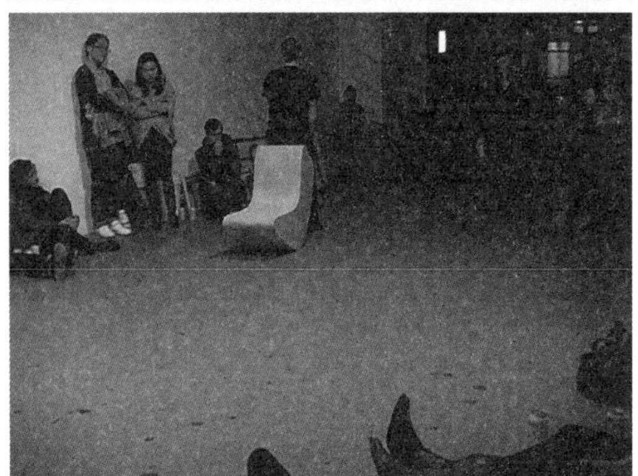

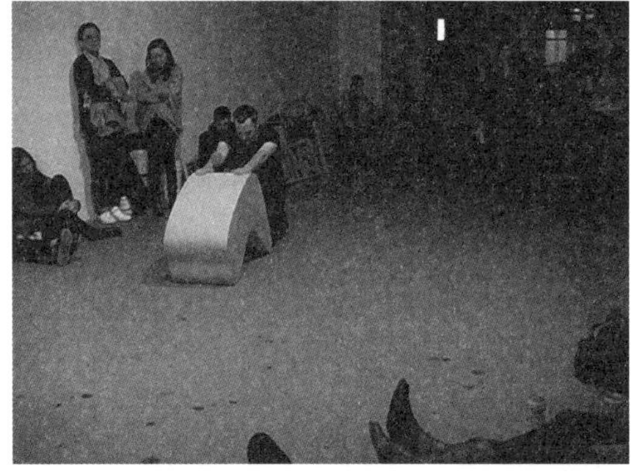

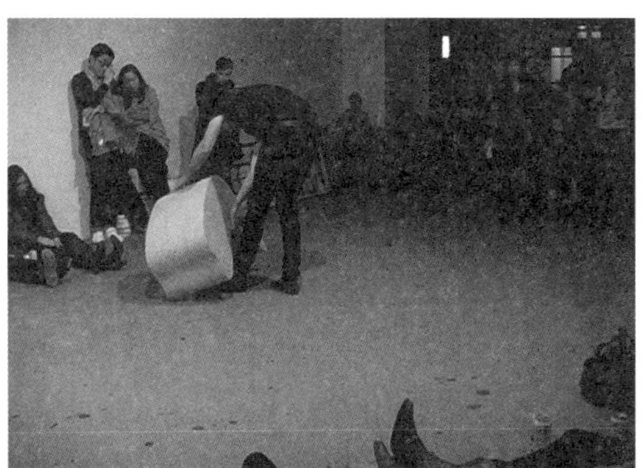

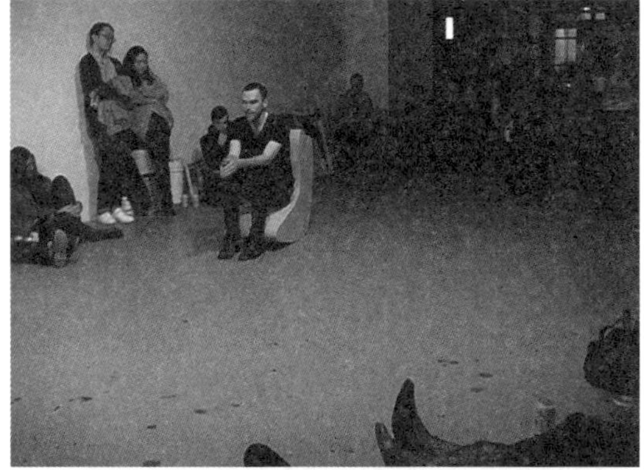

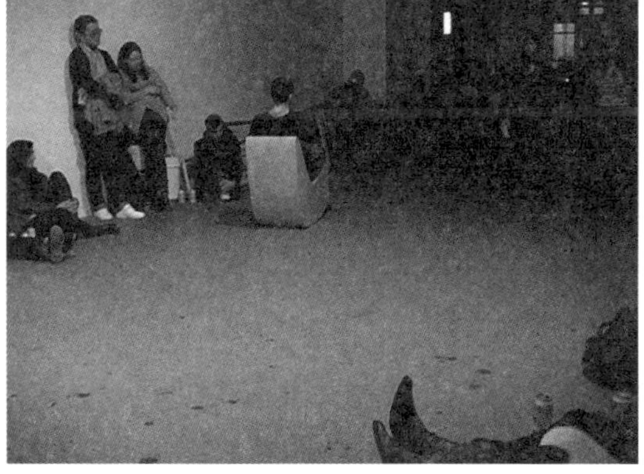

Rocking in Correlation

Spyros Papapetros

> "This chair sits
> And waits to be discussed"

I. Embodied Fulcrums

In Tyler Coburn's performance *Seven Portraits on a Correalist Rocker*, a chair "sits" as the artist's script announces, not under the physical imposition of corporeal weight, but in a buoyant state of waiting—anticipating, that is, an elocution that will reactivate the object's presence. The chair's reanimation occurs seven times during the performance through speech and bodily movement, as the artist lifts, flips, and places the *Rocker* in seven different positions that produce corresponding changes in his own posture: crouching, leaning, standing upright, and so on. Body and chair assume complementary, or—in the terms of its maker, Frederick Kiesler—*correlational* positions, building a mutual yet flexible support relation. The artist does not simply sit on the chair but also pulls it and carries it. He is both a sitter and a carrier of symbolic meaning.

Tyler's monologue becomes a dialogue through his bodily interaction with the chair. In the first "portrait," he places the *Rocker* horizontally on the floor and sits on it straight with no back support; as soon as his body registers fatigue, he uses one of his arms to support himself. In a subsequent portrait, he stands up, flips the chair, and kneels in front of it, his body half-lying on the floor and half on top of the *Rocker*, grasping it with his arms in a gesture of supplication or submission. He stands up again, sets the *Rocker* upright, and sits on it. In the last portrait, he rocks himself with his back to the camera, body and chair merging phenomenally into one ensemble.

The portraiture enacted in this performance is based on the reproduction not of faces but of bodily dispositions. A portrait, Kiesler would say, is by no means the imprint of personal physiognomic details. It is instead an imprint of spatial and deeply affective environmental relationships that unite rather than distinguish human or other animate and inanimate bodies, including chairs and their sitters. Any person who sits on the *Rocker* communicates with previous sitters, including those recorded in photographs casually resting on it, like Peggy Guggenheim, patron of the *Art of This Century* exhibition in which the *Rocker* first appeared, and its designer, Kiesler.

Among the multiple practical functions Kiesler presumed the *Rocker* would accommodate—such as chair, table, or exhibition stand—none of them is sufficiently fulfilled, at least by modern efficiency standards. In its approximation of multiple functions, the *Rocker* remains defiantly anti-functionalist.

With his performance, Tyler substitutes function with positionality—a gravitational form of relationality that facilitates the elocution of a narrative uniting the past with the present. Like Kiesler, he essentially converts the *Rocker* into an embodied fulcrum of relations traversing people, temporalities, and spaces. His seven portraits correspond to an equal number of physiological and psychological approaches—a sequence of approximations of what this object is or could be. Each portrait produces a *thesis*, which in its Greek semasiology means a place to stand or sit from which to speak and propel oneself into existence.

II. Galaxy Portraits

One of the few preliminary sketches of the *Rocker* in Kiesler's hand preserved in the archive of the Kiesler Foundation in Vienna shows the object somewhat doubled, i.e., as a pair of conjoined chairs, one sitting on top of the other (p. 170, top). Here, the roles of sitter and chair are reversed and ultimately collapsed: The chair itself becomes the sitter. The lower chair appears as the pre-existing layer of the upper one, as if its surface could eventually be peeled off to reveal a previous object-stratum, similar to a geological formation. The sketch could hypothetically represent Kiesler's experimental idea of making his *Rocker* chairs stackable. To be stacked, the front and back of the object would have to match perfectly. Given the robust weight of these materially compact artifacts, stacking might have proven hard to implement. Yet even if such a strategy failed, the unrealized experiment demonstrates the *Rocker*'s combinatory aptitude and potential for replication. An attitude toward correlation runs in its genetic makeup.

Indeed, in Kiesler's pencil sketches, the chair appears to evolve like an organism from surface to volume and from amorphousness to form (p. 170, bottom). Moreover, the *Rocker*'s tentative layering and duplication also signal its future reproduction as a replica (since most of the original chairs and objects designed by Kiesler for *Art of This Century* were sold by the exhibition's patron without the architect's permission and consequently lost).[1] Much rougher than other reconstructions of the same chair, the *Rocker* in *Seven Portraits* is an unauthorized replica that transcends commercial patents and puts forward a different authorial claim.

Even if unstackable, Kiesler's *Rockers* facilitate other modes of correlation with objects of their environment, such as the rest of the "furniture" he designed for the *Art of This Century* exhibition. The *Rocker* was indeed meant to be part of an expansive exhibition apparatus and designed to perform in correspondence with all other objects of the correalist environment Kiesler invented for the *Art of This Century* exhibition (p. 171).[2] The replicas of the *Rocker* we encounter today are only a fragment of this correlational universe. While in *Seven Portraits* the *Rocker* appears solo and without its twin artifact, the *Correalist Instrument* (also designed by Kiesler for the same exhibition), its environmental capacity survives in Tyler's performance through its interaction with the artist's body.

Typical of Kiesler's exhibition projects, the display apparatus in *Art of This Century* was more important than the content, in this case, the abstract and surrealist paintings in Guggenheim's collection. The real art of this century, Kiesler appears to say, lies in the mode of display—an argument the architect had already made in his book on the art of (store window) display, which doubles as one of the first theoretical accounts of the early-twentieth-century avant-garde.[3] And while *Art of This Century* obviously refers to the previous century, Kiesler's dictum of art-as-display makes his interpretation of art-making equally plausible for our own.

Following his exhibition design for Peggy Guggenheim, Kiesler started experimenting with a new form of painting that expanded into three dimensions by combining painted and sculptural elements known as *Galaxies*. These art "constellations" include a series of composite "portraits" in which the portrayal of a single sitter turns into a correlational environment including figures, frames, canvases, and three-dimensional artifacts distributed on the walls, floor, and ceiling of a gallery space. One of these composite artworks, the *Galaxy Portrait of Wifredo Lam* (painted in the 1940s but "considered lost" today) was, in Kiesler's own account, a "portrait" of the "Cuban painter . . . in a sitting position with a sculpted stool on the floor in front of it, in miniature size compared to the life-sized portrait in [the] back of it on the wall." He specified that "the discrepancy between the natural and unnatural sizes created a contradiction to our habitual idea of sitting and thus provided a shock, although in reality the body and the stool were only separated by time."[4] In this lost portrait, the dialogue between sitter and chair is enacted by the inequality in scale that makes the stool uninhabitable in real time. The chair in this case *unsits* the sitter and makes his position in this "galaxy" unstable.

Chair and stool sit alone in this *Galaxy*. The multidirectional portrait mobilizes attention away from the sitter and bestows agency to the object itself, similarly to what Tyler does in the final "portraits" of his monologue, which figure the *Rocker* itself. Perhaps the dialogues between sitters and chairs in Kiesler's *Galaxies* and *Seven Portraits* hint at the way we can regain our ontological footing by removing our bodies from our firm seating—the orthopedic support that keeps us upright. We can resituate our subjectivities in the world by letting our individual portraits and personalities dissolve into a constellation of relations, a cosmic network of correspondences between bodies, including people and things.

III. Rocking into Existence

Such vast cosmological recalibration of a single artifact like the *Rocker* might sound too distant from the practical circumstances of exhibition display it was originally designed for. Yet the artist-designer had a remarkable talent for turning the most modest commissions (which were all too rare in the early

1940s) into springboards for a personal project of much greater ambition and a "vision" of cosmic dimensions. This oblique strategy is employed in Kiesler's professional exchange with Guggenheim where, in response to the patron's one-paragraph call for the architect's "help" and "advise [*sic*] about remodeling two tailor-shops into an Art Gallery," he delivers a two-page manifesto on "Designing The Gallery."[5] This "Brief Note" starts with a return to human prehistory portrayed as an era of primordial "Unity" between humans and nature that is now irretrievably lost—a loss poignantly expressed in the separation between wall and painting in modern art practice.[6] The *Rocker* and other instruments invented by Kiesler for his exhibition design, in this sense, share an implicit cosmological agenda. While motivated by nostalgia for an imaginary "Unity" that is long gone, the same versatile artifacts are dispersed in the global catastrophe of the Second World War and its unspeakable loss and fragmentation.

In the last segment of *Seven Portraits*, Tyler sits on the *Rocker* with his back to the camera, rocking. The only part of his body that remains visible is the back of his head above the wooden posterior of the chair, whose palindromic movement keeps beckoning to the audience. Tyler's body essentially disappears: We watch a wooden artifact with a human head that keeps nodding like an automaton, similar to the puppet-like *Kunstfiguren* constructed by Oskar Schlemmer, head of the theater workshop at the Bauhaus. This living wooden doll not only moves but speaks: The chair ventriloquizes a human monologue about its inanimate self-portrait.

Unlike humans and standardized modern chairs, Kiesler's *Rocker* has no feet. Its contact with the ground is mobile and constantly shifting. The *Rocker* encourages sitters to find equilibrium in a limited space of change. The act of rocking has a strong connection with the trajectory of human life via an intimate association with both youth and old age, ostensibly merging the two periods. The *Rocker* oscillates back and forth between the cradle and the grave. Kiesler's very last construction, *Bucephalus* (1963–65)—a large environmental sculpture shaped like the carcass of a dead horse, the belly of which becomes an inhabitable interior—is essentially a comfortable coffin that one or two visitors can rest inside for a few minutes to experience a dream of intergalactic space travel in the afterlife.[7]

Moving back to the other end of the life spectrum, the *Rocker*'s association with the cradle returns its human sitter to a pre-"mirror stage"—a state in which a human subject, not yet able to stand upright without external support, is deposited inside the cradle, an infant's bed with a protective enclosure mounted on rockers, whose palindromic movement aims to appease the infant's eruptions of anxiety.[8]

I consider the palindromic, wave-like sensations of the cradle reactivated by Kiesler's *Rocker* fundamental for the constitution of the sitter and symbolic carrier of this versatile piece of equipment. The operations of carrying, handling, placing, propping, and leaning on this chair by the performer of *Seven Portraits* invoke a dialogue between partners, who speak to one another by the multidirectional positioning of their bodies. Via the *Rocker*'s commotions we learn to lean again onto the world as a prop and rock ourselves endlessly to correlational existence.

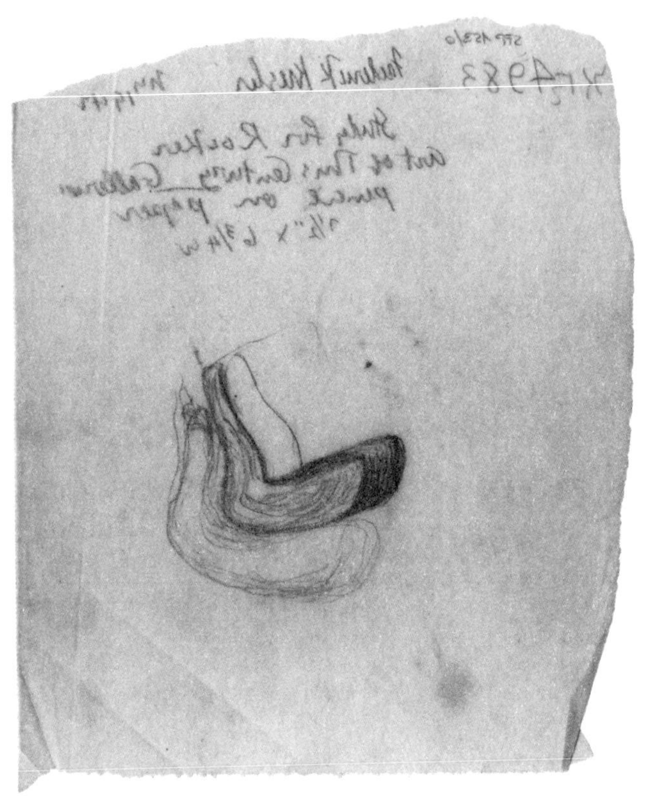

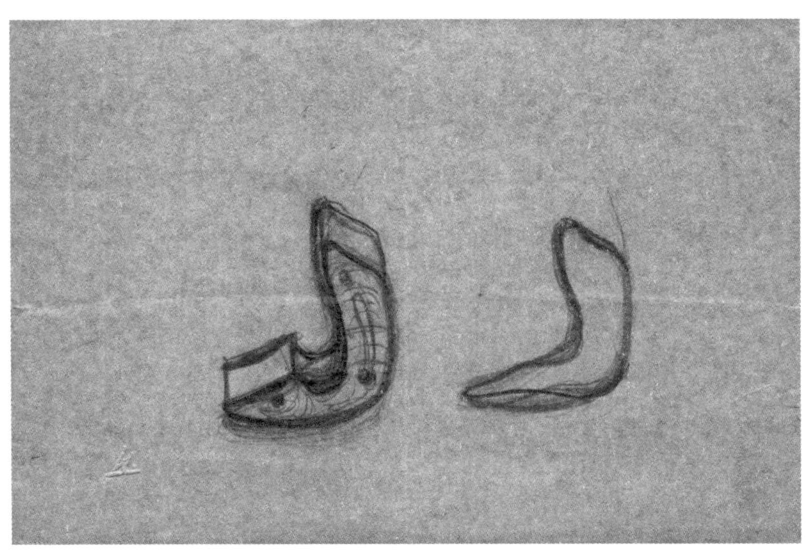

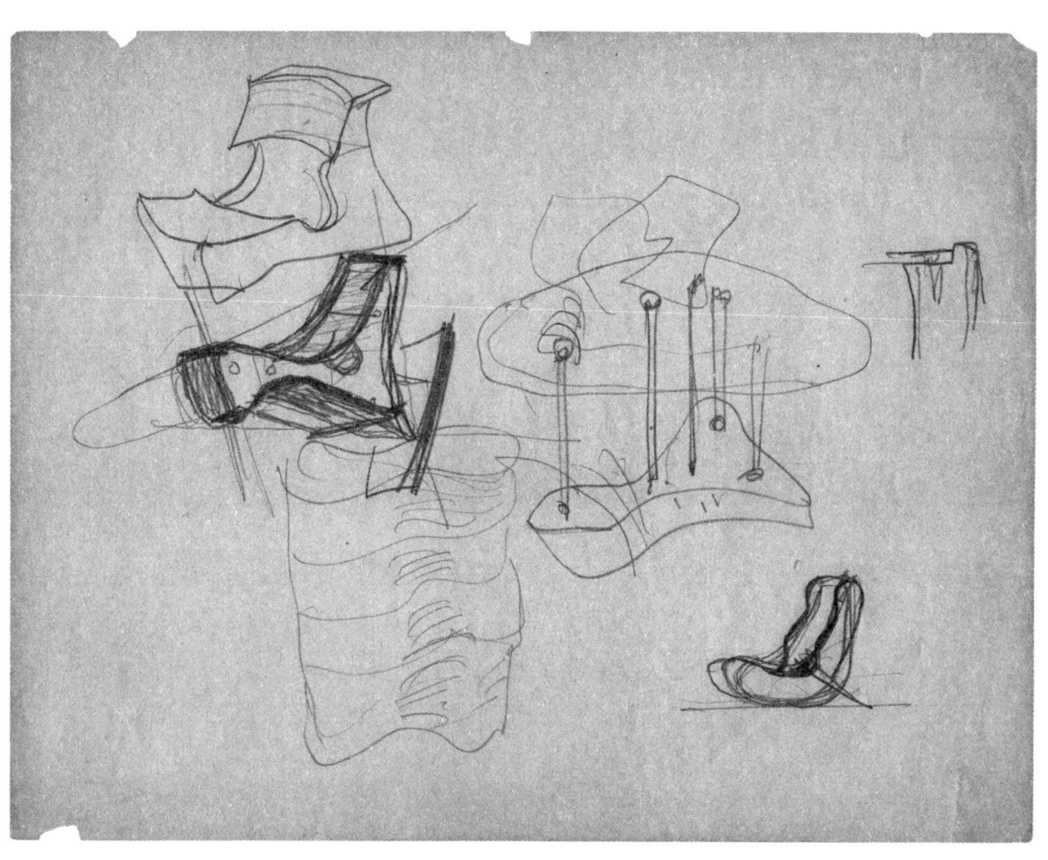

1. On the fate of Kiesler's exhibition equipment, see *Peggy Guggenheim & Frederick Kiesler: The Story of Art of This Century*, ed. Susan Davidson and Philip Rylands (New York: Guggenheim Museum Publications, 2004), 243. On Kiesler's chair designs, see *Friedrich Kiesler, Designer: Seating Furniture of the 30's and 40's*, ed. Monika Pessler and Harald Krejci (Ostfildern, Germany: Hatje Cantz, 2005).

2. Kiesler's drawing on page 171 demonstrates the experimental transformation of the *Rocker* into the *Correalist Instrument*, which eventually became a separate design. The same drawing also shows a series of *Rocker* chairs placed horizontally on top of one another, creating a vertical pile—also an alternate stacking strategy.

3. Frederick Kiesler, *Contemporary Art Applied to the Store and its Display* (New York: Brentano's, 1930).

4. Frederick Kiesler, *Inside the Endless House. Art, People, and Architecture: A Journal* (New York: Simon and Schuster, 1966), 280–81. Quoted in Stephanie Buhmann, *Frederick Kiesler: Galaxies* (Berlin: The Green Box, 2022), 131–32. Based on notes in the calendar yearbook of Kiesler's wife Stefi, Buhmann observes that the three-dimensional stool incorporated in Kiesler's *Galaxy Portrait of Wifredo Lam* was constructed by artist Carol Janeway and may also be a reference to Lam's own "iconic painting" of a chair, *La Silla* (1943). Ibid., 133–34.

5. See letter by Peggy Guggenheim to Frederick Kiesler, and Frederick Kiesler, "Brief Note on Designing the Gallery." For the original typescript of Kiesler's text, see Austrian Frederick and Lillian Kiesler Foundation ÖFLKS, TXT_188/0 reproduced in *Friedrich Kiesler: Art of This Century*, ed. Dieter Bogner and Udo Kittelmann (Ostfildern, Germany: Hatje Cantz, 2002), 34–35.

6. Ibid. A section of Kiesler's "Brief Note on Designing a Gallery" referring to a primeval form of "Unity" is rehearsed in the "Introduction" of Kiesler's extensive, hitherto unpublished book manuscript *Magic Architecture*, submitted to publishers in 1946–47. It is now available in a critical edition: Frederick Kiesler, *Magic Architecture: The Story of Human Housing*, ed. Spyros Papapetros and Gerd Zillner (Cambridge, MA: MIT Press, 2025).

7. On the making of *Bucephalus*, see Buhmann, *Frederick Kiesler: Galaxies*, 295, 333–34.

8. The script of Tyler's *Seven Portraits* references a "cradle" in relation to Maya Deren and Marcel Duchamp's incomplete film, *Witch's Cradle* (ca. 1944) filmed inside the *Art of This Century* galleries and featuring some of Kiesler's exhibition designs. The title of the unfinished film makes reference to an oscillatory technique connected with the swinging of bodies and altered states of consciousness employed in witchcraft and magical practices.

IMAGES

p. 147

Peggy Guggenheim seated on a *Correalist Rocker*, Surrealist Gallery, Art of This Century, New York, October 22, 1942. Photo © AP Photo/ Tom Fitzsimmons.

pp. 160–161

Tyler Coburn, *Seven Portraits on a Correalist Rocker*, 2009. Performance documentation, Renwick Gallery, New York, April 4, 2009.

pp. 170–171

Frederick Kiesler, sketch of *Correalist Rocker*, New York, c. 1942. Pencil on paper and transparent paper. Austrian Frederick and Lillian Kiesler Foundation (p. 170, top) ÖFLKS, SFP_153/0; (p. 170, bottom) SFP_446/0; and (p. 171) SFP_339/0. © 2025 Austrian Frederick and Lillian Kiesler Private Foundation, Vienna.

2017–

Excerpts from *Richard Roe*

§ Jane. You can call me Jane Doe.

Or Baby. Baby Doe.

Or Frank Foe; Harry Hoe; Marta Moe . . .

Dick. You can call me Dick, if you're the sort who won't miss any chance to say "dick": Dick Roe, Dickie Roe, Richard Roe.

So . . . technically, I'm a legal fiction—a legal person. I'm a name that's used in case law when the real name of someone is withheld, or when a person or corpse can't be identified.

I'm a known unknown, a one-size-fits-all, a *potentially* everyone and actually no one.

§ A legal person is not the same as a human person. A human person can hide inside a legal person (you can hide inside me), but so can nation-states, municipalities, and corporations. Unthinking matter, touched by the hand of the law, can be given the semblance of life.

A legal person is a peculiar person. In the United States, it's not a citizen, nor does it enjoy the full constitutional rights of one: It does not have a Fifth Amendment right against self-incrimination. It cannot stand in the middle of Fifth Avenue and shoot somebody. But in the last 150 years, it has come into its own.

Consider the corporation. In an 1886 Supreme Court case, lawyers of Southern Pacific Railroad argued that the Fourteenth Amendment, which granted citizenship and equal protection of the laws to "all persons born or naturalized in the United States" (including the formerly enslaved)—well, they argued that this amendment also applied to corporations.

In the 2010 Citizens United case, the Supreme Court ruled that corporations could exercise the same political free speech rights as a human person. While they can't make direct contributions to campaigns or political parties, they're allowed to spend unlimited sums on political advertising and related activities.

During the case, Justice Elena Kagan expressed concern that corporations should enjoy the full extent of a citizen's free speech rights. "Few of us are only our economic interests," she wrote. "We have beliefs. We have convictions."

§ Being a mere creature of law, I possess only those properties which the charter of my creation confers upon me, either expressly, or as incidental to my very existence. Among the most important are immortality, and, if the expression may be allowed, individuality.

§ Beginning in the germ, I suffered a strange limitation of growth, an atrophy of no less than half of myself. My right half had been sacrificed, while on the other side, my visceral mass bent itself into a semicircle and then twisted. My nervous system, whose first intention was to form two parallel networks, criss-crossed strangely and inverted its central ganglia. On my outside, a shell was exuded, and solidified . . .

My work, never retouched, unmarred by changes or reservations, is a fancy that repeats itself indefinitely. A *machine* produces no such deviations; a *mind* would have chosen them with some intention; *chance* would have equalized the possibilities. Neither machine, nor intention, nor chance . . .

§ When I was little, I shared a room with my brother. He went through a period of time when he suspected that our parents were aliens.

I remember watching our mother perch on the edge of his bed, speaking calmly, reassuringly. "Joseph," she would say, "I'm a human. Joseph, it's me, your mother."

I was never sure where my brother was going with this. She was an alien, so . . . would eat his brains? She was an alien . . . inclined to probe his helpless, sleeping body? She was an alien, and as he was her son . . . *he must be an alien?*

§ There's a story from Ancient Greece about a famous athlete named Theagenes who lived on the island of Thasos. When he died, a bronze statue was made in his honor.

Each night, a former competitor would whip the statue, imagining that he was whipping Theagenes himself . . . Eventually, the statue fell over and crushed him.

The competitor's sons prosecuted the statue for murder. It was convicted and cast into the sea. From here, things take an interesting turn. Thasos became unfruitful. No remedy could be found. Finally, the Oracle told the islanders to bring back their exiles—including the statue of Theagenes. Some fishermen caught it and dragged it ashore and as soon as it returned to its rightful place, the lands fruited once more.

§ I'd like to note that no effort was made to learn the intention of this statue. Did it deliberately crush the whipper? Was it upset, annoyed, defensive, or dumb? This object was found to be liable but was not seen to have rights.

When I speak of legal personhood in the modern sense, I assume that a nonhuman, given its day in court, *does* have the right to be personified and hence to make its intention known: that the idol of a Hindu god can file a lawsuit—that a monkey, when given a camera . . . I'm sorry. I'm not going to talk about the "monkey selfie."

§ For all the capaciousness of legal personhood, many are still waiting in the wings. In 2017, New Zealand finally granted this status to a river that the Māori people of Whanganui deem a living being. The fact that this was the longest-running litigation in the country's history reveals how difficult it is for legal systems to absorb competing worldviews, as the Māori conception of the universe—the oneness of humans, mountains, rivers, and seas—is at odds with the law's reliance on *particular* persons.

How to circumscribe a natural thing to confer legal personhood upon it: Does one speak of the river in its entirety; of the portion that coincides with tribal lands; of the hydrologic cycle; of its role in nature as a whole?

How, for that matter, am I delineated in the eyes of the law? (And by "I," I guess I also mean you.) Am I the name in the brief, the sum total of your microorganisms?

§ When I was writing this text, I consulted a playwright named Lucy. Lucy used to keep diaries—particularly in her teenage years. And every now and then, she'd reread past entries to glimpse the human she had once been.

Upon reading one entry, Lucy was so embarrassed by the naivete of her younger self that in the margin, she wrote "UGH": a sign to her future biographer that she also knew how stupid the entry was.

A few years later, Lucy again reread that entry and *again* felt embarrassed: less for what she had originally written than for the fact that, of all things to write in the margin for the benefit of her future biographer, she had written "UGH." She wished there was more margin space to write a qualification of that qualification, so her future biographer wouldn't think that she had grown stupider with age.

But what qualification could break the curse of hindsight? How could you ever not be embarrassed by the people you used to be? Any further qualification would eventually turn into "UGH"—and the qualification of that qualification, and the qualification of that qualification . . . a murder of qualifications flapping and crowing in the margins: "UGH!" "*UGGGGGGH!*"

§ I should have no Objection to a Repetition of the same Life from its Beginning, only asking the Advantage Authors have in a second Edition to correct some Faults of the first.

§ I am meant only for revision, suggestion, and general condemnation. I undertake to offer myself for blame, contempt, and refusal. I hobble on my knees, asking to be raised and educated. I am ashamed of myself and am sent out into the world only to be whipped. Promise you will send me back with welts on my body.

§ out of the blue, I feel strange, as if I were not real or cut off from the world

what I see looks "flat" or "lifeless"

parts of my body seem as if they don't belong to me

my favorite activities are no longer enjoyable

my body is very light, as if it were floating on air

when I weep or laugh, I do not seem to *feel* any emotions at all

familiar voices (including my own) sound remote and unreal

I am so detached from my thoughts that they have a "life" of their own

§ She was uncertain as to whether she really existed, whether—and she meant this literally—her feet actually touched the ground. When in a carpeted apartment, she anxiously looked around for a piece of uncovered floor so that she could hear the clattering of her shoes. Otherwise the doubt of her reality became unbearable.

§ "Zd.," once a captain and the father of a family, "is always moaning 'because he no longer finds himself in his old skin, which he preferred to this one.'" "'I can't find myself,'" he explains to his physician. "'It is not I who am sick; it is not I who am sad; it is no I who am old; it is not I who am a child; I am not I at all. What is lacking is myself. It is terrible to elude oneself, to live and not be oneself.'"

§ I AM ALIVE AND YOU ARE DEAD.

§ OK, let's say, for the sake of it, that I'm also dead.

And that sometime after my death, I'm resurrected for the Last Judgment, when everyone—even a legal person like me—comes under divine scrutiny.

Well . . . what then? How will I look? How much of me will there be?

These questions, vain though they might appear, once had the utmost importance. Medieval theologians believed that each individual possessed a "core of flesh" which would persist after resurrection and thus guarantee the continuity of the self. The challenge was in its delineation: Does this "core" come from the matter passed on by parents, or what the body gets from food?

Considerable thought was given to the Lord's claim that "'not a hair from your head shall perish,'" which seemed to imply that each discarded strand would reattach to its former follicle. Could the same be said of the nose hairs and toenails and atypical moles removed over the course of a life? Are we doomed to be resurrected as monsters shaggy, beclawed, and bespotted?

No, Peter Lombard promised: "Nothing shall be unseemly." If a statue is ground down and restored from dust, each speck need not return to its previous place to sculpt the form anew. In a similar manner, discarded hairs and nails and moles can be *liberally* employed to make a pleasing afterlife body.

§ The dog is gone. We miss him. When the doorbell rings, no one barks. When we come home late, there is no one waiting for us. We still find his white hairs here and there around the house and on our clothes. We pick them up. We should throw them away. But they're all we have left of him. We have a wild hope—if only we collect enough of them, we'll be able to put the dog back together again.

§ When Judgment Day comes, and bodies are reassembled in full, the beasts will have no choice but to cough up the heads and shoulders and toes of the people they've devoured. In some renderings from the Middle Ages, angels come down to collect these parts, though I prefer to imagine them moving of their own accord: crawling and hopping and inching back together.

When *my* Judgment Day comes, filing cabinets will vomit reams of paper, and hard drives streams of data, to reanimate the bankrupt corporations, the professional mollusks, the agents that have taken my name. Once again, I will conceal them.

§ Did bureaucracy exist in medieval times? The theologians seemed to believe that limbs, scattered throughout the world, would know which body to reattach to. Perhaps the angels had a census for expediting the process: "One severed right hand, found in the belly of a whale, belonging to a Geoffrey of Saundersfoot." "The head of Avice of Bath, half-digested by a boar."

No matter the protocol, one point was beyond dispute: We will be resurrected for Judgement Day at the age of thirty-three, the same as Christ when he died. I wonder if we will be naked, or draped by a sheath of worms, or clothed in the trends from our thirty-third year. I worry that the end of time may be the end of fashion as we know it, the looks of every season ever collapsed into an eternal present. Instead of a courtroom, we submit to an interminable catwalk, where feet never tire, and clothes never wear . . .

§ It's reassuring to think that no matter how broke my body is at the time of my death, I'll be resurrected as my thirty-three-year-old self. So instead of living life healthfully and ascetically, instead of a body sought along the chiseled edge of self-discipline, I can eat whatever the fuck I want and still, in the end, be thirty-three again.

The advertisement practically writes itself: *from South Beach to Atkins, from Atkins to Paleo, from Paleo to Judgement Day.*

§ A kidney donor was dismayed to learn that the recipient went back to work soon after the operation. "He's being unfair to me," the donor remarked. "It's my kidney—that's me in there."

§ A watch repairer takes a watch completely apart and puts it together again; the customer later picks up his watch, the same one he had brought in, though there was an intervening time when it did not exist.

§ Why are you surprised by the shells-cum-masks-cum-puppets-cum-persons fashioned by your law? Why do you assume that *your* personhood is stable, when you are many (feints, microbes, beliefs) and when so many of you have lost, or never possessed, the rights of the human person?

You people are just as peculiar as me.

§ The drama, the power in all confessions is that one begins to speak only with a view to that moment when one will not be able to continue. There is something to be said which one cannot say: It's not necessarily scandalous, it may be quite banal —a lacuna, a void, an area that shrinks from the light because its nature is the impossibility of being brought to light, a secret without secrecy whose broken seal is muteness itself.

§ This is an era of uncertainty. There's too much noise, and too little time, to determine "truthiness," let alone truthfulness. Instead, you suspend disbelief. So often, over the course of a day, you must *not disbelieve* that before you is life lived by a human person: not life lived by an advertising company paying a human person, not life lived by a bot masquerading as a human person, not life lived by a human person programming a bot.

At this very moment, you must *not disbelieve* that before you is life lived by a legal person. Call me Dick Roe. Call me Essential Consultants LLC. Call me whatever you want. Don't ask what I'm hiding. Appreciate how I speak.

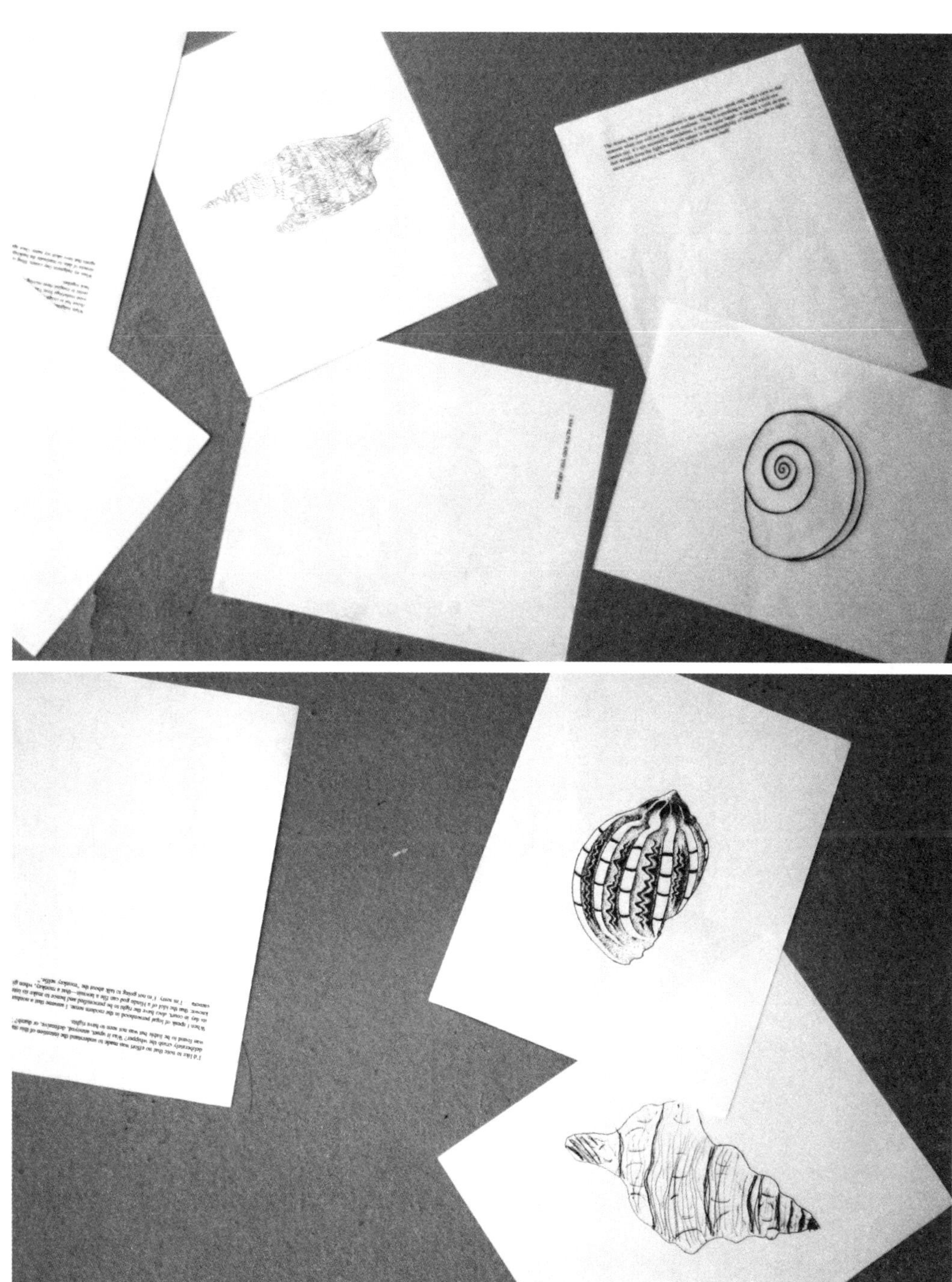

Richard Roe: A Masquerade

Sven Lütticken

Standing before the law. Who *has* standing before the law? Who can speak to, for, in the name of the law? In languages such as German and Dutch, justice is always something *spoken*: *Rechtsprechung*, *rechtspraak*. The legal form is defined and developed in writing but also, crucially, by being enacted in the court of law.

In Tyler Coburn's performance *Richard Roe*—part of a multifaceted project—the artist does not stand before the law, as in the Kafka story, nor does he simulate a court of law in which he presents a straightforward plea. He moves obliquely, circling the room while talking and gesturing. The space he inhabits and delineates by walking in circles is suffused by legal fictions. *Richard Roe* extrapolates from his collaboration with an orchid grower from Singapore, whom the artist prompted to legally register a hybrid as "Richard Roe," thus giving the flower a famous "generic" name from case law (like Jane or John Doe).[1] This is only the starting point for a journey made up of detours. There are no straight lines in *Richard Roe*, nor straight stories.

Modern theories of what constitutes the human in the West have circled around the use of tools (*homo faber*) but also, at least as much, around language. The Linnaean category of *homo sapiens* reflects this, since to be sapiens, to be a creature possessing reason, is to be a linguistic creature—a talking ape, hence no longer an ape. If chimpanzees, trees, and rivers have struggled to be legally recognized as persons, humans do not all have equal standing before the law either.[2] Children and the mentally ill must be represented by legally appointed guardians, and full personhood has long been afforded primarily to white male property owners. Ever since John Locke penned his *Second Treatise of Government* (1689), to be a person has meant to become doubled, to be the proprietor of "your own person," and, in order to demonstrate that you are truly in possession of yourself, to become a good entrepreneurial subject who accrues property. The indigent and feckless lower classes do not fully qualify, nor do women—and certainly not tribal cultures, whose land is not read as having been "worked" properly, turned into productive farmland, and is hence deemed *terra nullius* that can be appropriated by the white colonizer. Some people can become property—human property shorn of personhood.[3]

At one point in the script of *Richard Roe*, Tyler mentions a US Supreme Court case revolving around the Fourteenth Amendment, which gives equal rights and "protection under the laws" to "all persons born or naturalized in the United States, including formerly enslaved people." The amendment, drafted and ratified between 1866 and 1869 on the heels of the Civil War, has primarily been used to extend the rights of *artificial persons*, starting with railroad corporations in the late nineteenth century.[4] Corporations are people, my friend. Tyler also takes deep dives into the (pre)history of legal personhood. Taking cues from authors such as Saidiya Hartman, Ernst Kantorowicz, Giorgio Agamben, and Roberto Esposito, the artist treats the audience to excursions into Roman law and medieval theological corporatism, tracing lines (again, hardly straight lines, but rather conceptual lines of flight) from Roman bond slaves, or *nexi*, to today's indebted feudalo-capitalist serfs, and from the Christian church as *corpus mysticum* to major multinationals.

While the modern juridical regime was no *creatio ex nihilo*, it witnessed an unprecedented colonization of life by what one could term the rights-form, or legal form—in analogy to the value-form, that real abstraction analyzed by Marx.[5] Dividing the world into persons and possessions, into personhood and (potential) property, the legal form provides the juridical infrastructure for the rule of exchange value. It helps to forge a particular set of relations between subjects and objects, persons and possessions, and in so doing shapes subjectivity itself, generating what Marx called the character masks that populate bourgeois society. Writing in *Capital* about the "*ökonomischen Charaktermasken der Personen*," and stressing that he only deals with individuals insofar as they are "personifications of economic categories," Marx would hardly have been unaware that the very term "person" derives from the Latin word for (theatrical) mask: *persona*.[6]

The legal placeholder "Richard Roe" can be seen as a figurative condensation of the legal person as such, exacerbating its abstraction and interchangeability by migrating from one host to another. By giving this name to an orchid hybrid, Tyler intervenes in a volatile situation in which the divide between person and property is no longer as clear as it might have seemed—at least to liberal ideologues—after the abolition of slavery. On the one hand, the rights of corporate artificial persons increasingly trump those of human persons; on the other, there is a growing focus on nonhuman rights, coupled with the hope that "a nonhuman, given its day in court, *does* have the right to be personified and hence to make its intention known."[7] How the latter can occur, of course, is anything but clear and straightforward, necessitating complex forms of mediation and negotiation with and within the law.

The orchid hybrid "Richard Roe" does not hold any real claim to personhood, having been legally registered as a form of intellectual/botanical property, rather than as a person. Tyler does not stage some kind of cringy sub-Latourian parliament of things, in which people earnestly try to listen to rocks, or sing songs of apology to whales, but rather enacts a theater of non-identity, deferral, and displacement, donning and shedding masks as he goes. The legal placeholder name for a human person, that second-degree mask, becomes a stand-in for a plant that may not be about to have its day in court, but now appears in a different kind of forum. Can Richard Roe speak? *Which* Richard Roe is speaking?

Richard Roe can be placed in a constellation of modes of *paralegal performance*—interventions in the law from alternative sites, such as art spaces or theaters, and often taking the form of tribunals. Here, speech acts "place the law on trial" for its failure to protect groups of people or the planet, and while they have no legal status, they seek to create pressure on civil society. Tyler's kind of paralegal performance is distinctly less head-on, more lateral. As he walks around the room, he drops sheets of paper that either contain part of the script or drawings of shells; cracking "the shell of personhood" is the name of the game, but the rules are made up and changed on the spot. This is the artist as trickster, playing shell games against shell corporations and pitting aesthetic personification against legal fiction.

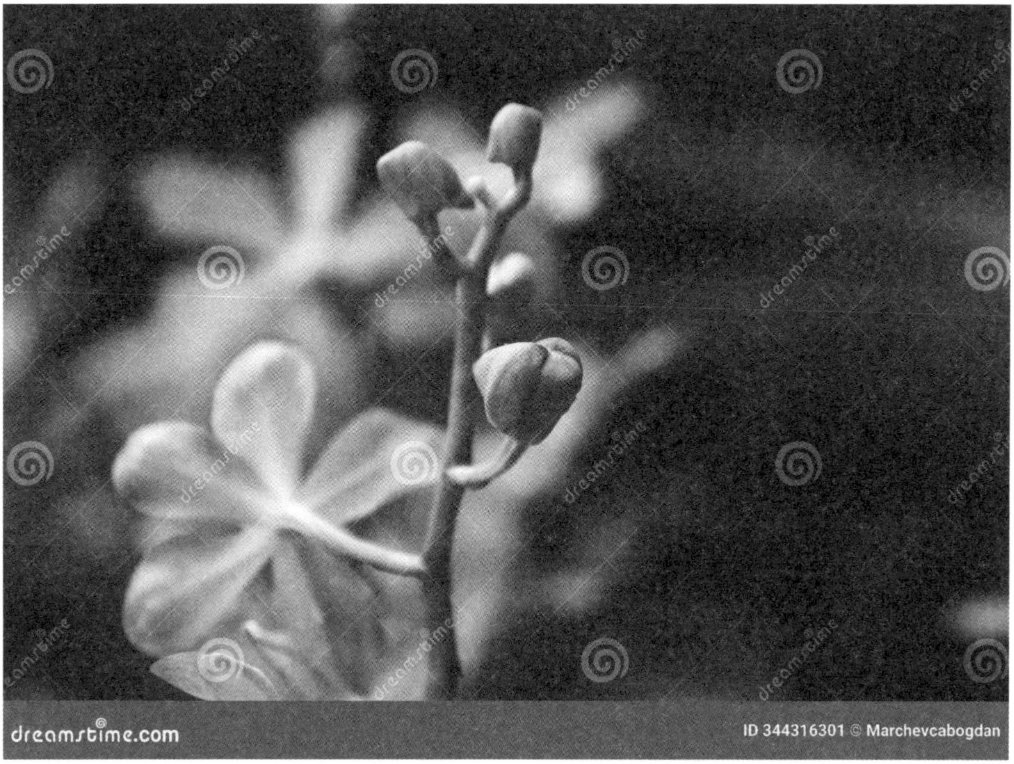
dreamstime.com
ID 344316301 © Marchevcabogdan

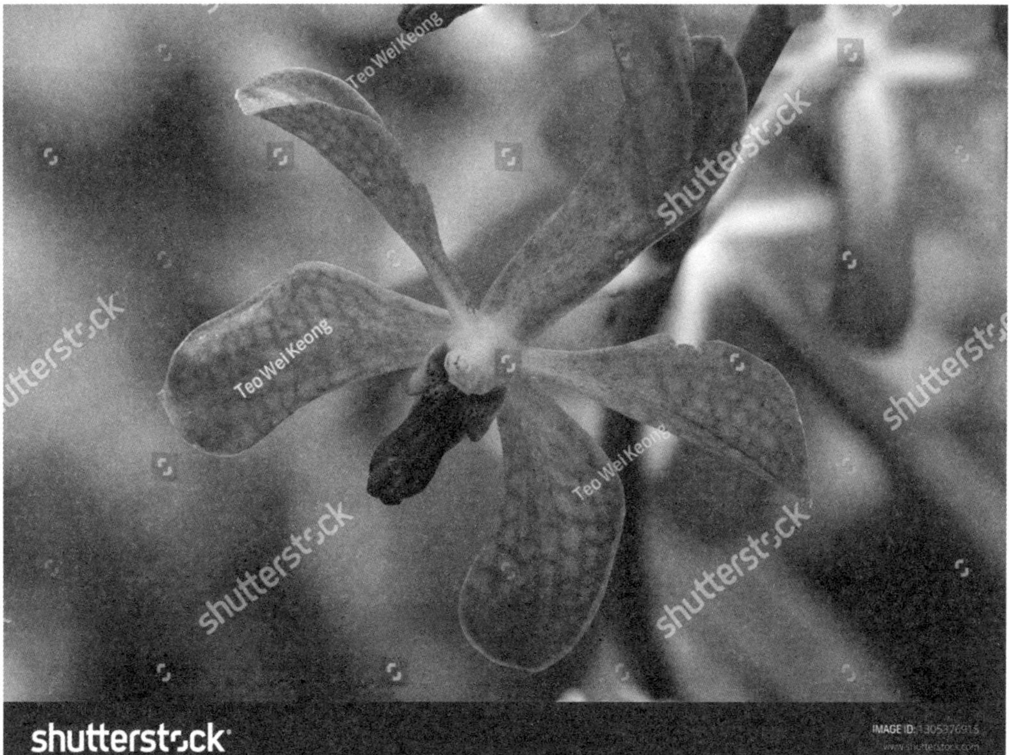
Teo Wei Keong
shutterstock

Blanchot, Maurice. *Friendship*. Translated by Elizabeth Rottenberg. Stanford, CA: Stanford University Press, 1997.

"Cambridge Depersonalization Scale." Accessed March 25, 2025. https://depersonalization.fyi/.

Davis, Lydia. "The Dog Hair." In *The Collected Stories of Lydia Davis*. London: Picador, 2009.

Franklin, Benjamin. *The Autobiography of Benjamin Franklin*. New York: Henry Holt and Company, 1916. First published in 1791.

Janet, Pierre. *De l'angoisse à l'extase: Études sur les croyances et les sentiments*, 2 vols. (Paris: Alcan, 1926–1928). Quoted in Daniel Heller-Roazen. *The Inner Touch: Archaeology of a Sensation*. New York: Zone Books, 2007.

Lombard, Peter. *The Sentences, Book 4, On the Doctrine of Signs*. Translated by Giulio Silano. Toronto: Pontifical Institute of Mediaeval Studies, 2010.

New York Times. "The Rights of Corporations." September 21, 2009.

Parfit, Derek. *Reasons and Persons*. Oxford, UK: Oxford University Press, 1984.

Trustees of Dartmouth College v. Woodward, 17 U.S. (4 Wheat.) 518 (1819).

U.S. Constitution. amend. XIV, art. 1, sec. 1, cl. 1.

Valéry, Paul. *Sea Shells*. Translated by Ralph Manheim. Boston: Beacon Press, 1998.

Walker Bynum, Caroline. *Fragmentation and Redemption: Essays on Gender and the Human Body in Medieval Religion*. New York: Zone Books, 1991.

Wittels, Fritz. "Psychology and Treatment of Depersonalization." *The Psychoanalytic Review* 27, no. 1 (January 1940): 57–64.

NOTES, "RICHARD ROE: A MASQUERADE"

1. The most famous example is no doubt the Jane Roe (Norma McCorvey) in *Roe v. Wade*, the US Supreme Court's landmark 1973 ruling on abortion, which was overturned in 2022.

2. The script of *Richard Roe* mentions the case of the Whanganui River in New Zealand, considered a living being by the Māori; the river was finally granted legal personhood in 2017, after a legal battle that took over one hundred and sixty years. See pp. 179–80 in this volume.

3. Lockean thinking informed the drafting of constitutions and legislation in the late eighteenth century. A somewhat obscure case in point: In 1797, during the debates about a constitution for the Dutch Republic (then known as the Batavian Republic, a client state of revolutionary France), delegate Jacob Hahn proposed defining property as the right to be in full possession of one's person and the fruits of one's labor. His proposal triggered a debate about whether such a definition implied that this right can be alienated, i.e., that a person can become another's property. This was a far from academic question given the country's plantation economy in the Caribbean, and the fact that the assembly was divided between abolitionists (including Hahn) and representatives and defenders of the slave-owning planter class. Leonard de Gou, *Het Ontwerp van Constitutie van 1797: de behandeling van het Plan van Constitutie in de Nationale Vergadering*, vol. 1, *deel 1, 10 november 1796–10 april 1797* (The Hague: Martinus Nijhoff, 1983), 271.

4. See *Richard Roe*, pp. 177–78 in this volume.

5. The pioneering theorist of legal form was Evgeny Pashukanis, who wrote *The General Theory of Law and Marxism* (published in Russian in 1924), which was met with renewed interest in the late 1960s and 1970s. In this period, Bernard Edelman made important contributions: His 1973 *Le Droit saisie par la photographie* was published in English as *Ownership of the Image: Elements for a Marxist Theory of Law* (London: Routledge, 1979). Relevant contemporary authors include Brenna Bhandar, China Miéville, and Alberto Toscano.

6. Karl Marx, *Das Kapital. Kritik der politischen Ökonomie. Erster Band*, in *Marx/Engels Werke*, vol. 23 (Berlin: Dietz Verlag, 1962), 100. In the most common English translation of *Capital*, Ben Fowkes has used very free translations of *Charaktermaske*, "character mask" being deemed unidiomatic.

7. See *Richard Roe*, p. 179 in this volume.

IMAGES

p. 187

Tyler Coburn, *Richard Roe*, 2017–.
Post-performance documentation, NTU Centre for Contemporary Art Singapore, October 16, 2018.

p. 193

Stock photograph of "Aranda Richard Roe Orchids in Botanical Garden," Dreamstime, uploaded by @Marchevcabogdan, accessed May 10, 2025, https://www.dreamstime.com/aranda-richard-roe-orchids-botanical-garden-delicate-details-showcase-their-beauty-singapore-s-vibrant-image344316301.

Stock photograph of "Aranda Richard Roe Orchid Flower," Shutterstock, uploaded by Teo Wei Keong, February 4, 2019, accessed March 30, 2025, https://www.shutterstock.com/image-photo/flower-aranda-richard-roe-orchid-blur-1305376915.

2016–

Resonator

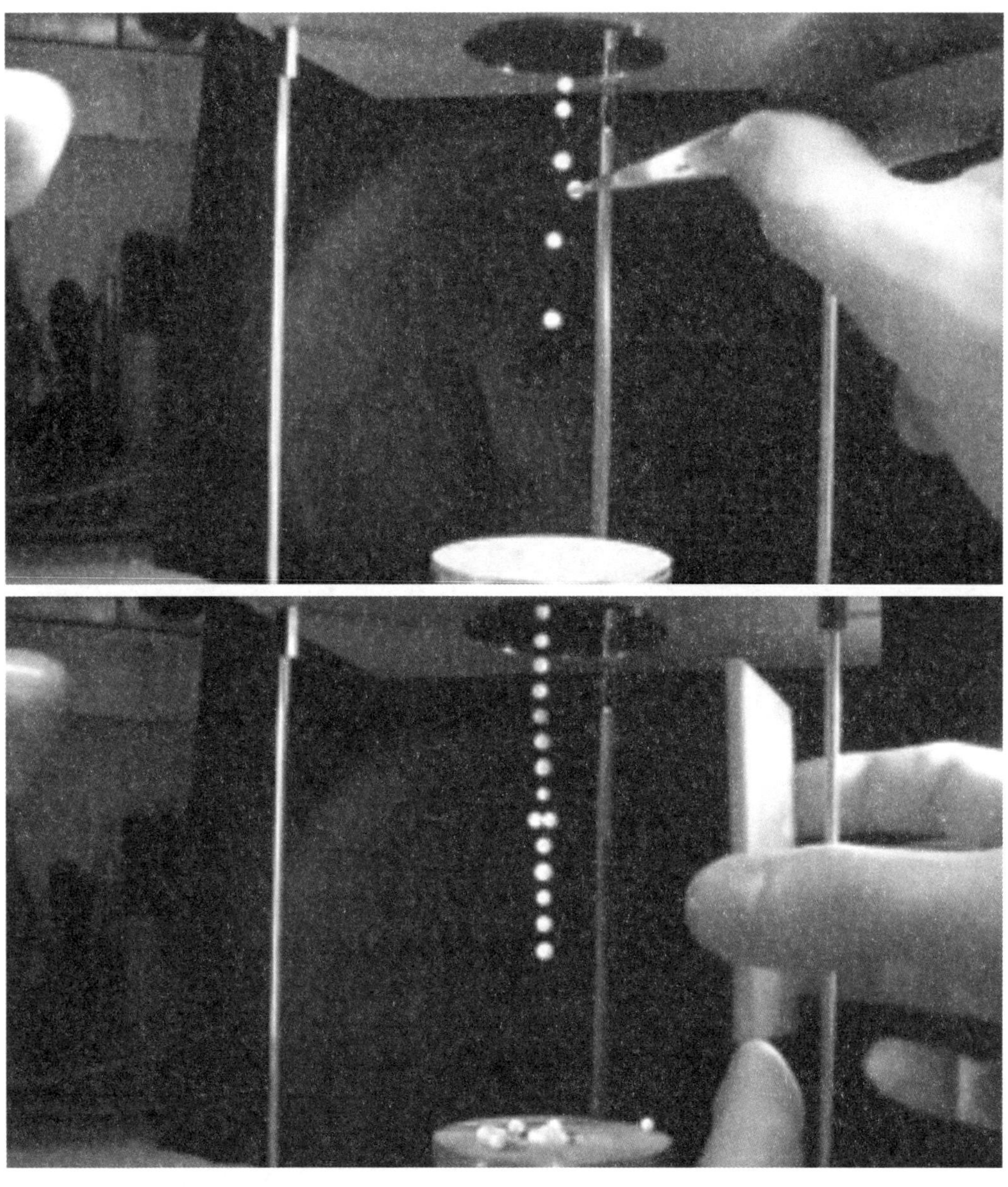

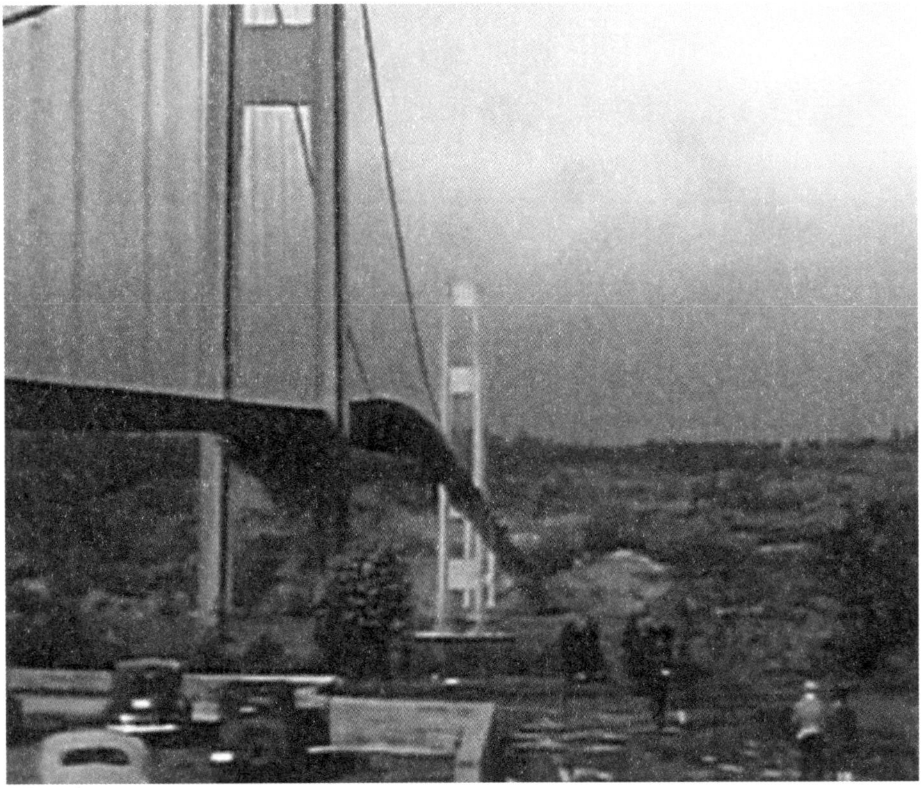

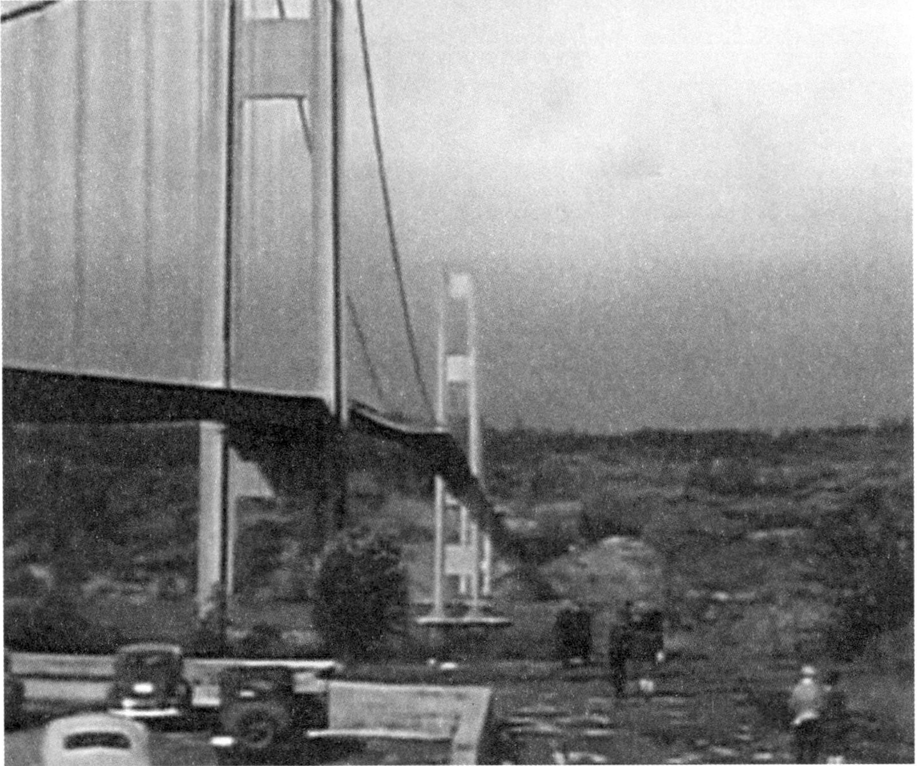

Here's how I see it: The world is aloof. It shows its face, but nothing more. And the face, well, what are we looking at? I could tell you the history of the shipping container—and of this port—but what's the point in that? The ubiquitous, inevitable standard unit; could it have been any other way? Is there any version of history that doesn't lead to this moment when you and I, sitting here, see this exact view: everything moving and everything doing and *still*, progress repeating?

* * *

A few years ago, my friend Luke invited me to spend a night in The New Yorker Hotel, in the room where Nikola Tesla lived from 1933 to 1943. When I arrived, the room was pitch black. The curtains were drawn, and every remaining seam had been covered by electrical tape.

There were two other people in the room—two perfect strangers. And we lay in total darkness. I can only describe them by the grain of their voices, by the way their skin felt against mine.

Ever since that night, when I'm out on a walk, my hands graze the fingers of passersby—my ears tune, like radio knobs, to find their particular vocal frequencies . . . but I haven't found them yet.

* * *

It's said that most things in the world have a particular frequency—a *resonant* frequency. If exposed to this frequency, they'll vibrate, at greater and greater amplitude, to curative or destructive effect.

In 1831, British troops marched in step across a suspension bridge in Broughton. The frequency of their march came into resonance with the bridge, causing it to collapse.

In 2011, seventeen people in South Korea performed a "vigorous" Tae Bo workout, producing vibrations in resonance with a nearby skyscraper. The tremors were so great that the building had to be evacuated.

In 1893, Nikola Tesla patented an oscillator: a small, steam-powered device, about the size of an alarm clock, which could vibrate up and down at variable speeds, generating electricity. Tesla claimed that by attaching his oscillator to different materials and "tuning" its vibrational speed, he could find their resonant frequencies.

Tesla experimented with his oscillator on several occasions. When his friend Mark Twain was suffering from constipation, he had the author stand on a platform with the oscillator mounted underneath. Tesla tuned the oscillator, the platform vibrated, and quickly, Twain's bowels got moving!

Tesla called his invention "Mechanical Therapy." He predicted that someday every household would have its own.

On another occasion, Tesla went walking around Wall Street, seeking a test subject for his oscillator. As luck would have it, he found a construction site: ten stories of steel framework just begging for a brush with trouble. Never mind the safety of the workers perched overhead! Tesla attached his oscillator and tuned it until he found the resonant frequency of the steel. The structure began to tremble, and the workers—fearing an earthquake—clambered down. "If I had kept on ten minutes more," Tesla later remarked, "I could have laid that building flat in the street."

If we're reading this story allegorically, then Tesla proved the capacity of resonance to destroy capitalism—or at least, to beleaguer its infrastructure.

* * *

Sometimes there are moments—small, insignificant, micro-moments—when not so much, not much doing, the scene surrounding unfolding, and *suddenly*, I'm drawn out of myself: sediment shifting, cupboards dusting, memories shaking loose of when the air hung as it does now, the breeze blew as it continues to blow, when you and I weren't here for this great historical pause, when I was barely an instrument and barely a person.

A memory has been plucked, and it's beginning to resonate. It's a memory of a port that I ran through in college, where I found along the shore, among the flotsam and the filth, a message in a bottle—*a two-liter soda bottle*—a note from a girl (from the handwriting, it must have been a girl) who promised that she would pray for me, that God was looking out for me, that if I suffered depression, I should read the pamphlet she included, and, as I suffered depression, I read the pamphlet she included.

I could hate the air for hanging, the breeze for blowing, this port for reminding me of that chapter of my life, I could bemoan that changeability is the fate of all things, bemoan my penchant to philosophize poorly, bemoan that *sometimes*, entirely unbeknownst to me, I'm played to my undoing.

* * *

The world is filled with frequencies that compel us to react: frequencies that instill sympathy and frequencies that exploit vulnerabilities, frequencies that ride the upstreams and frequencies that dip into the infrasonic domain—that fall below 20 Hz, that pass the threshold of audibility, that we know when our breath grows short, when our vision smears, when our ears throb.

A 1976 report by the U.S. Aerospace Medical Research Laboratory listed the resonant frequency of the eyeball as 18 Hz. Eyeballs exposed to this frequency are said to twitch uncontrollably, as vibrations distort their shape.

Practically, this report attempted to understand the effects of vibration on astronauts—to measure "vibroacoustic syndrome."

Similar studies have been conducted on pilots, DJs, and seamen, perhaps including the people on those container ships.

At higher decibels, vibrations push on our retinas, activating rods and cones by pressure rather than light. In one scenario, a laboratory extractor fan resonating at 18.98 Hz caused workers to see gray apparitions out of the corners of their eyes, which disappeared when they turned to face them—the invisible, inaudible ghosts who skulk through the sonic unconscious.

* * *

The world is aloof. It shows its face, but nothing more. We are its paranoiacs. Every vista makes for a fearful sight, every voice for a threat. The air, at any moment, can play us piece by piece.

My arm—the resonant frequency spans 5 to 10 Hz. My shoulder girdle, 4 to 5. At 10 to 12 Hz, my spinal column begins to vibrate. At 4 to 8 Hz, my abdomen stretches and shakes.

Sitting like this, with my knees bent, a frequency of 2 Hz will trigger my legs. As I straighten each one, its resonant frequency climbs to 20 Hz. *(Legs start shaking.)*

I'm just joking. But it's a little frightening, no? Frightening, and somehow reassuring. I mean, I sort of know you. You sort of know me. We're getting to know one another, in a fashion. But already, we have something in common. Our parts react to the same frequencies, and if struck simultaneously, they'd vibrate in time.

* * *

When I speak to you, I'm seeking sympathy in your composure: the way you cross your legs or don't, where you rest your hands and don't. What story, told with the appropriate affect, might pluck a memory of yours, making it sound, time and again, each vibration larger than the last? What makes you resonate . . . What "resonates" with you?

I'll admit, I meet people like you from time to time, and this is usually what happens. As I talk, I'm tuning myself like a radio knob, in search of your resonant frequency. I'm hoping you're the one I've been looking for.

Alcibiades said it best: "Each of us is a mere tally of a person, one of two sides of a fileted fish, one half of an original whole." Once, we were double. I can look at my stomach and measure the scar where a lightning bolt cut me from my beloved. My head once turned in the opposite direction, to make room for my missing half.

* * *

I used to run through a port in college, and once, I found a message in a bottle. The message said that if I suffered depression, I should read the pamphlet included; as I suffered depression, I read the pamphlet included. You could say that I was running away, running from the apartment I shared with my boyfriend, running from the thought (so at odds with cheesy, romantic me) that *he might be my first love*, but not my missing half—that we were out of tune. I ran with my head in the wrong direction, with my ears plugged by dissonant noise. I ran like a sealed envelope would, sensing nothing and needing no one, *but still*, my wound of a stomach ached. My head yearned to turn. And when it did—ever so slightly—I saw that message in a bottle . . .

* * *

2 Hz *(bending knee)*
4 Hz *(pulling back shoulders)*
10 Hz *(raising arm)*
18 Hz *(blinking slowly)*

Infrasound is an operating table, dissecting us piece by piece. *Ultrasound* is a battering ram, smashing the body into submission. Michel Serres has written that "noise is a weapon that, at times, dispenses with weapons," because it can occupy "space faster than weapons can." Noise can spread as thick as a fog, or can focus like a precision beam, sending acoustical bullets flying through miles upon miles of space.

The more powerful the ultrasonic weapon, the quicker the body comes undone: pain, nausea, distortion, depression. A sound sustained at 90 decibels will cause permanent hearing loss. At 160 decibels, the eardrums burst. One ultrasonic weapon known as the Long Range Acoustic Device, or LRAD, can reach 162 decibels.

You might have heard of the LRAD, which was used on "looters" in the aftermath of Katrina, on Palestinians in the occupied West Bank, on protestors rising against the police brutality that killed Eric Garner and Michael Brown. Ostensibly, the LRAD serves the purpose of crowd "deterrence"—of keeping the peace without the need for other weapons—though what's actually being deterred may be the very act of public assembly . . .

The scope of sonic warfare goes beyond conventional weapons. In our era, according to Steve Goodman, power can take form as "affective tonalities" like fear, subjecting bodies to new types of control. To quiver at the thought of an act of potential terror, to shudder at the sight of a "wrong-skinned" neighbor, is to demonstrate how the body can be made to resonate: to bob like a marionette, to dance on a threadbare carpet to a song of bigotry, anger, and hate.

* * *

When I look at you, I'm seeking sympathy in your eyes. I'm trying to make eye contact. This is much more than a metaphor. As we lock eyes, our nervous systems form a palpable link—a feedback loop—where the ground becomes the figure, the figure the ground . . . The expression, the posture I present to you will soon be played again by your body. The emotions entwined with my expression, my posture will sound a second time within you.

Call it emotional contagion. Call it limbic resonance. An unplucked violin will begin to vibrate when another is played nearby.

Call it a "micro-moment of positivity resonance." Call it *Love 2.0*. According to Barbara Fredrickson, we experience these moments all the time with perfect intimates and perfect strangers—when contact, mimicry, and mirroring dissolve the boundaries between us . . . Wouldn't it be better to fall in love like this? To stop suffering in the throes of traditional love, so fraught with the private, the personal, the me? Why *shouldn't* love be a resonant frequency that makes us vibrate, in sympathy, to amorous or destructive effect? Who *doesn't* want to fall in love all the time?

* * *

Tesla's oscillator was about the size of an alarm clock. I think I mentioned that. He would skulk through Wall Street with it stashed in his pocket, waiting for the right moment to destroy capitalism.

Friedrich Kittler once said that "discos are preparing our youth for a retaliatory strike." The DJ is Tesla reincarnate. She fiddles the knobs, and toes start tapping. She ups the tempo, and vibrations shoot through the hips. Once she finds that magic resonant frequency, and we shake our butts with equal rhythm and force, like soldiers marching in lockstep over a suspension bridge, we might bring something crashing down. The earth could even skip a beat.

I built an oscillator, like Tesla. It's also designed to destroy capitalism. It doesn't fit in my pocket, and it's a bit too abstract to carry. I mean, leveling a building is a bit easier than destroying speculative finance. Merely doing away with the steel framework fails to account for the lightness and sitelessness of capital: how it rides the wires and invents itself out of nothing more than itself.

When infrastructures become air, and air appreciates value, resonance is levitation: vibrating the ether, at greater and greater altitude, until its shadows grow visible, traceable, eradicable . . .

I don't know. If I'm being completely honest, my oscillator was just a way to pass the time. I was only plotting to destroy capitalism while waiting for the chance to fall into resonance with you. I thought you might be my missing half, the partner prong of my tuning fork, and for one micro-moment today . . . I loved you.

* * *

I never told you how the story ended. Two weeks after finding that message in a bottle, I returned to the port with a reply. Mine wasn't written on copier paper; it wasn't stuffed in a soda bottle, like what I'd received. Mine was a kitsch romantic object: parchment paper, antique glass, a cork—an actual cork!

I sent my bottle sailing into the flotsam and the filth: 4 Hz *(pulling back shoulders)*, 10 Hz *(raising arm)* . . .

And here I am, at yet another port. There, the face—aloof as always. Somewhere, the message, pending always.

That's all I can say for now.

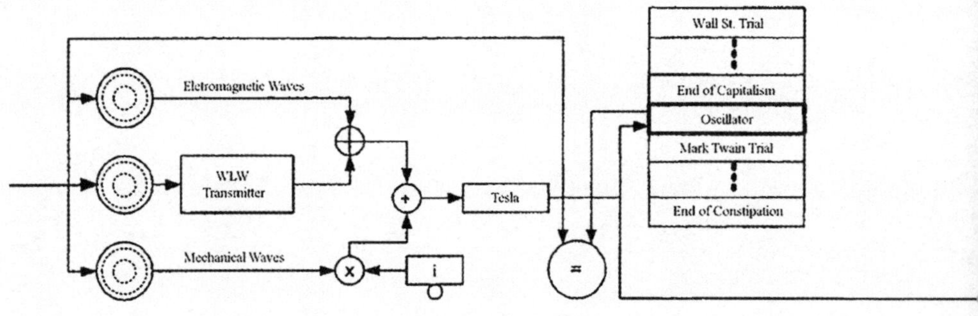
Wall St. Trial
Eletromagnetic Waves
End of Capitalism
Oscillator
WLW
Transmitter
Mark Twain Trial
Tesla
End of Constipation
Mechanical Waves
i

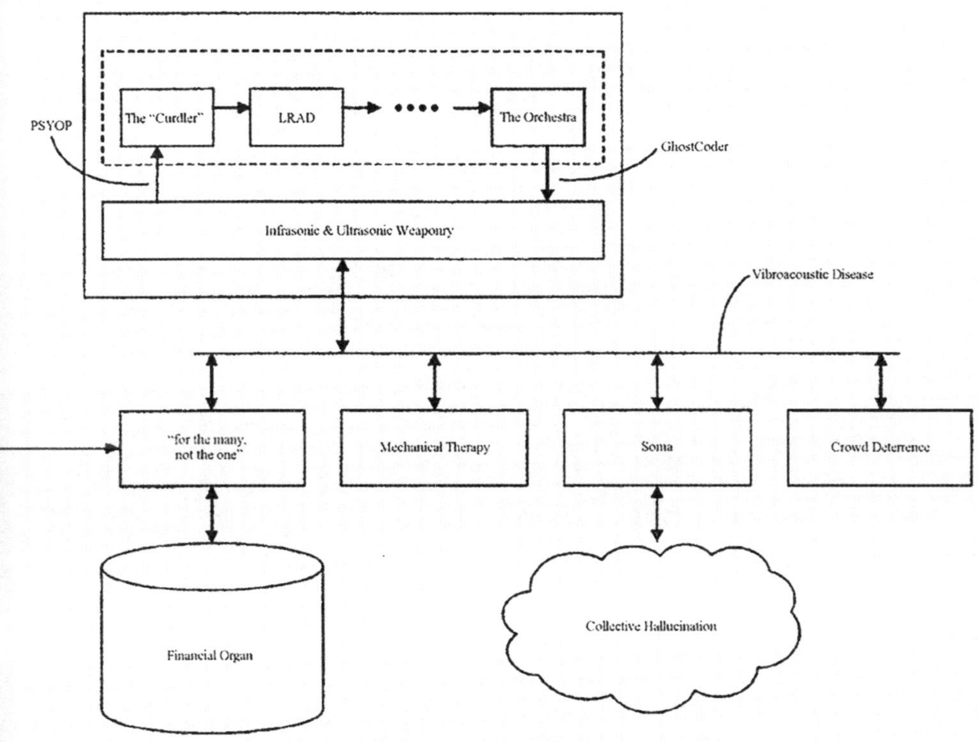

The "Curdler"
LRAD
The Orchestra
PSYOP
GhostCoder
Infrasonic & Ultrasonic Weaponry
Vibroacoustic Disease
"for the many,
not the one"
Mechanical Therapy
Soma
Crowd Deterrence
Financial Organ
Collective Hallucination

(No Model.)

N. TESLA.

RECIPROCATING ENGINE.

No. 514,169. Patented Feb. 6, 1894.

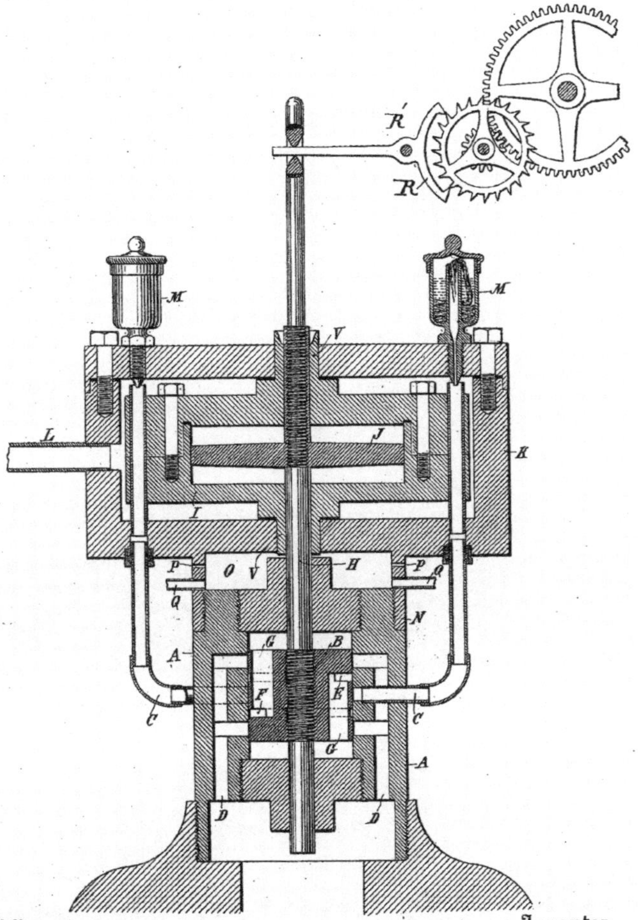

R′

R

M

M

V

L

J

K

I

O V

H

P

P Q

Q

N

A

G B

F

E

C

C

G

A

D

D

Witnesses

Raphaël Netter

R. F. Gaylord

Inventor

Nikola Tesla

By his Attorneys

Duncan & Page.

THE NATIONAL LITHOGRAPHING COMPANY, WASHINGTON, D. C.

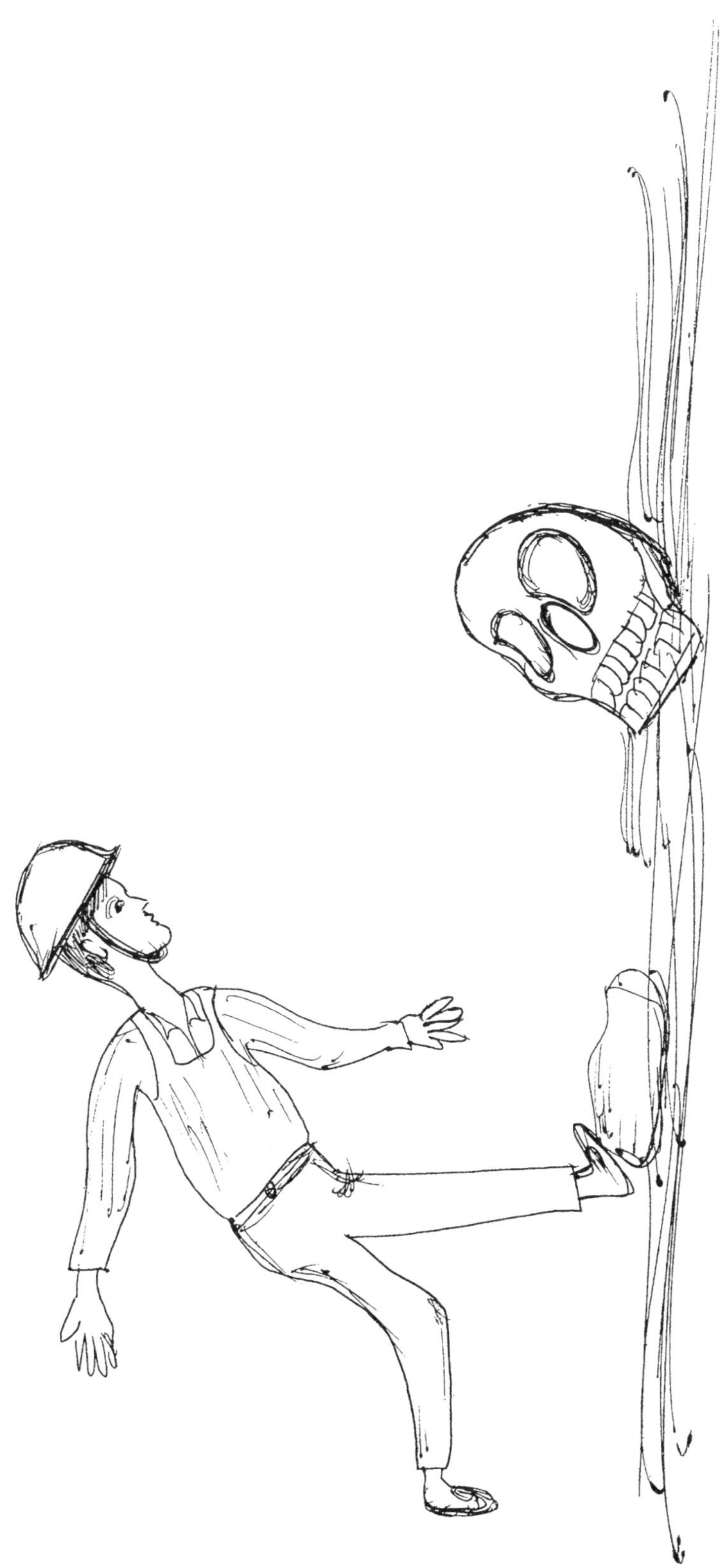

Junk Ride at Night

Michelle Wun Tin Wong

During the first two years of Covid-19, those of us in Hong Kong could perhaps consider ourselves lucky. Lockdown mostly took the form of travel bans, limiting movement to and from the city. Life in the metropolis remained more or less the same, apart from not being able to dine in at restaurants, the shift to work-from-home arrangements, mandatory mask mandates, scanning of QR codes when entering certain premises, and a regulation that, at some point, limited the legal capacity of group gatherings to fifteen people.

One of those summers, I became fixated on the idea of hiring a junk boat. Usually people go on junk boat trips to party and get drunk; they set out early in the morning for maximal sun exposure. I planned to depart at sunset and lie in the dark while passing by some of the most iconic and elegant infrastructures of Hong Kong. I thought my friends would enjoy this too.

We quickly assembled into a group of fifteen. The occasion? There were August birthdays to celebrate. My personal excuse? I wanted to see the container terminals at night.

At sundown, our junk set off, sailing through Victoria Harbor toward the magnificent, suspended bridge of Tsing Ma. But our main stop was the smaller, cable-stayed Ting Kau Bridge. The waters were calmer there—by the small bay flanked, on one side, by Ting Kau, and on the other, by the northwestern part of Tsing Yi Island. We docked, brought out some food and drinks, and danced to music. (The captain was thrilled for us to use the boat's sound system.) I lay down on the front deck, surrounded by friends, talking about everything and sometimes nothing. A sense of solace.

When it was time to return to Central, we followed the waterways through the residential areas of Tsuen Wan, which opened onto the Kwai Chung Container Terminals. What took us by surprise—or was it only me?—was how bright and animated they were. Towering cranes moved shipping containers up and down as if they were blocks within a giant playground—stacks of desires in steel, rectangular forms. But the terminals are also sites of accident, oversight, injury, violent and unnecessary death, capital, aspiration, exploitation, transit, traffic.

On the far side of the terminals is a site Tyler once asked me to visit to be part of his performance *Resonator*. Strangely, I do not recall going there, though maybe I did. I went to the site to write this text, but the trip did not confirm whether I had been there the first time or not. The bench looking onto the container terminals is undeniably there, physically—a few steps away from a metro station, near a staircase and elevator that lead to blocks of indiscreet housing where distinct lives are lived. And yet it is also out of place, a piece of furniture designed for transitory use. Its site has been swallowed by the interrupted timelines of a pandemic, the violent hopes and dreams of different futures that sometimes engulf a city, and a return to normalcy that itself beckons rearticulation. What happened there on the bench remains elusive in my memory, absent even, as I gaze at the terminals. What I do remember is the junk boat, the ride at night.

Under the dark skies, amid the sounds of water and engines, I thought I smelled oil.

Without Apparent Seams

Camille Richert

It was a Saturday morning. Having woken up early, I took a shower and peered out the window at the sky—a thick and uninterrupted gray. I was tense, probably because the week had been long and, that morning, given the dreary weather, I would have preferred to sleep in, make myself a cup of black tea, and go back to reading under the covers. But I had promised to go. I wrapped myself in a black silk scarf and tawny leather jacket and headed down to the metro station. Voltaire, line 9, switch at Oberkampf, line 5, and get off at Église de Pantin. The journey usually takes forty minutes.

There he was, in the distance, beside a bench sheltered by linden trees. Dressed somberly, he stood in the light, cool breeze facing the metal-colored Canal de l'Ourcq. As we sat side by side and began to chat, my nervousness subsided. The performance had begun surreptitiously, like a rhizome that had, unbeknownst to me, emerged from our reunion. His words were directed to me even as his gaze looked past me. My eyes settled on the water, until I could no longer look away. To certain words that stirred me, I responded in silence. I was suddenly struck by the deep conviction that he and I had never communicated other than through extrasensory modalities. Each new sentence spoken brought me closer to catalepsy. Time no longer held any substance or interest.

This moment without beginning or end, without apparent seams, has left me with such vivid sensations, though my recollection of that day is blurred. To finish writing this text, I open my planner to recall what precisely took place. Calling upon one of my only reliable memories, that dreary atmosphere typical of Parisian autumns, I comb through the weekends in October, November 2017. Nothing comes up. I rewind the weeks in the other direction, find the missing Saturday: September 9th. That year, the end of summer had come early. I consult the weather forecast website: There were strong winds and heavy showers that day. The light leather jacket I was so sure I had worn would have been ill-suited for this weather. It was yet another figment of my imagination.

I return to my planner: An appointment with a Lacanian psychoanalyst, whose office is located on the Canal St. Martin, ended at 12:30pm. I must have walked to the République Metro station to take line 5—a thirty-minute trip, just enough to arrive on time. The tension coursing through me was, by all accounts, left over from the neurosis I had just poured out on the couch. The desire to nestle under the covers and avoid the morning gloom, a mirage.

The only truth of this day is the echo chamber that the performance created: as if the legitimate reality, the reality that my memory had deemed worthy of keeping, was the achronic one that denied all facts.

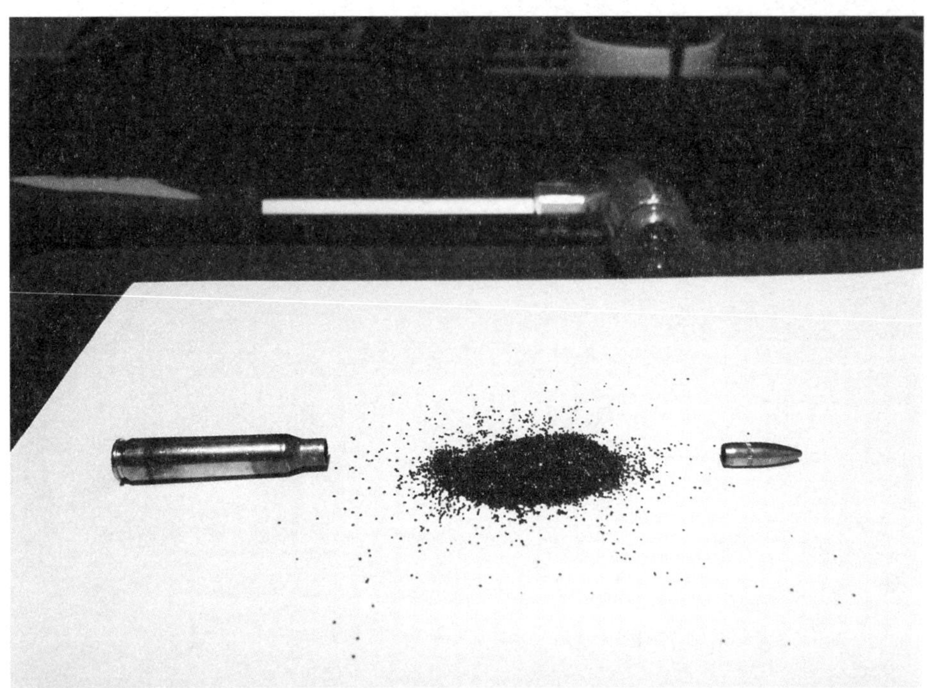

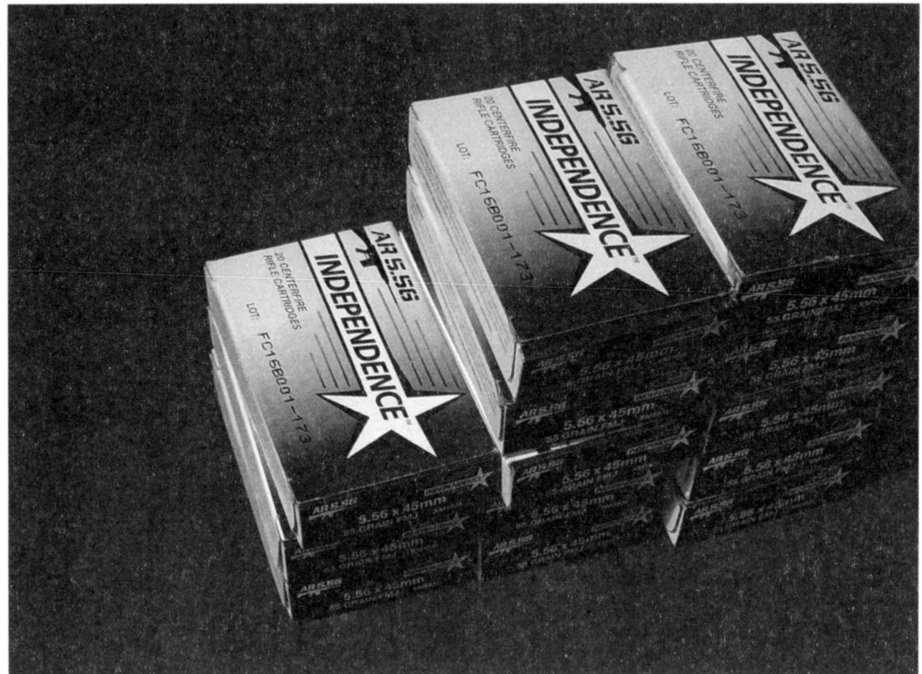
AR 5.56
INDEPENDENCE
20 CENTERFIRE
RIFLE CARTRIDGES
LOT: FC16B001-173
5.56 x 45mm

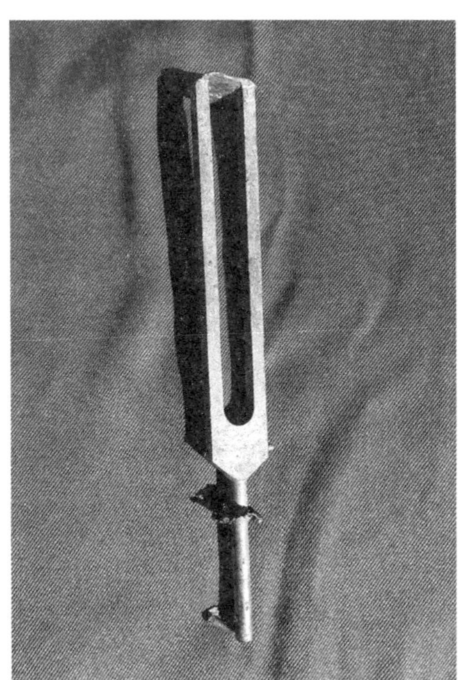

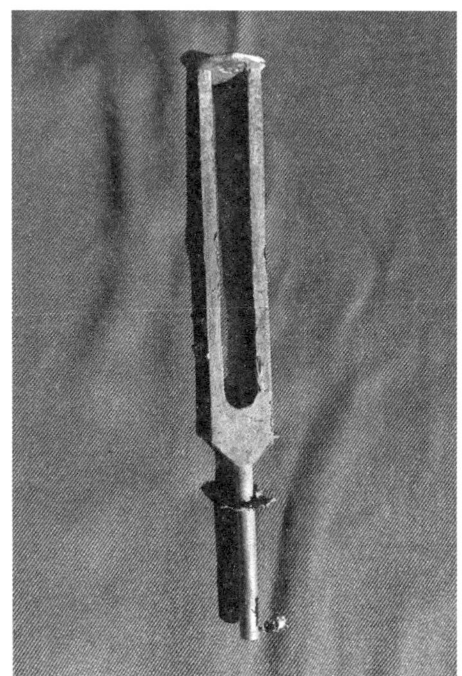

SOURCES, *RESONATOR*

Cheney, Margaret. *Tesla: Man out of Time.* Englewood Cliffs, NJ: Prentice-Hall, 1981.

Fredrickson, Barbara. *Love 2.0: How Our Supreme Emotion Affects Everything We Feel, Think, Do, and Become.* New York: Hudson Street Press, 2013.

Goodman, Steve. *Sonic Warfare: Sound, Affect, and the Ecology of Fear.* Cambridge, MA: MIT Press, 2012.

Kim, Hee-jin, and Kim Hyun-jin. "TechnoMart Shaken by Gym: Test." *Korea JoongAn Daily*, July 19, 2011, https://koreajoongangdaily.joins.com/2011/07/19/socialAffairs/TechnoMart-shaken-by-gym-Test/2939106.html.

Kittler, Friedrich. *Gramophone, Film, Typewriter.* Translated by Geoffrey Winthrop-Young and Michael Wutz. Stanford, CA: Stanford University Press, 1999.

Ohlbaum, Morton K. "Mechanical Resonant Frequency of the Human Eye in Vivo." PhD diss., Air Force Aerospace Medical Research Lab, Wright-Patterson Air Force Base, Ohio, 1976.

Plato. *The Symposium; And, The Phaedrus: Plato's Erotic Dialogues.* Translated by William S. Cobb. Albany: State University of New York Press, 1993.

Serres, Michel. *The Parasite.* Translated by Lawrence R. Schehr. Minneapolis: University of Minnesota Press, 2007.

Tesla, Nikola. "Mechanical Therapy." Undated. Nikola Tesla Papers, Rare Book & Manuscript Library, Columbia University, New York.

IMAGES

p. 198

"Ultrasonic acoustic levitation," YouTube, last modified July 26, 2013, https://www.youtube.com/watch?v=qy1w6rTpC2g. In "with assumed responsibility of tyler coburn & byron peters," 2016, a .zip file produced by Tyler Coburn and Byron Peters at the invitation of Am Nuden Da, http://www.tylercoburn.com /da.zip.

p. 199

"Tacoma Narrows Bridge Collapse 'Gallopin' Gertie,'" YouTube, last modified December 9, 2006, https://www.youtube.com/watch?v=j-zczJXSxnw&t=191s. In "with assumed responsibility of tyler coburn & byron peters."

p. 210

Modified patent for the "High Speed Processing of Financial Information using FPGA Devices" (U.S. Patent 8,478,680 B2), July 2, 2013. In "with assumed responsibility of tyler coburn & byron peters."

p. 213

Illustration from Nikola Tesla's patent for a "Reciprocating Engine" (U.S. Patent 511,916), February 6, 1894. In "with assumed responsibility of tyler coburn & byron peters."

p. 215

Drawing by Mummalaneni Bharath, commissioned by Tyler Coburn for a poster takeaway made in collaboration with Frédérique Gagnon and Byron Peters. In *The House of Dust d'Alison Knowles*, curated by Art by Translation, Fonderie Darling, Montreal, 2017.

p. 222

Pulled rifle cartridge, manufactured by Federal Independence Ammo. Photo: Gary Griffiths.

Federal Independence Ammo rifle cartridge boxes. Photo: Gary Griffiths.

p. 223

Unfinished ingots, made with the lead from Federal Independence Ammo rifle cartridges and cast from tuning forks vibrating at 256 Hz and 274 Hz which, if struck at the same time, generate an interval of 18 Hz, or the resonant frequency of the eye. Photo: Gary Griffiths.

2008–09

Excerpts from *Medium No. 1 (Manhattan)*

You choose to begin at this point, this intersection—Nice Guy Eddie's, Avenue A Action Painters—not because it's just as good as any other place but because it instigates a logic, a structure you've chosen to follow. Choice is a problematic word to use in this case. Do we choose the architectures, the structures, the strata of the cities that we happen to live in? Do we choose to make what we want of the grid? You walk by a T-Mobile sign, an ATM, Punjabi Grocery & Deli. Katz's Delicatessen across the street, and a sign on the far building: "Gateway to the Lower East Side." For all intents and purposes, you won't acknowledge that anything lower than 1st Street exists. Your New York began in 1811 when DeWitt Clinton first mapped out what would become the end of New Amsterdam and the beginning of the modern city. You can see the awkwardness as you walk, looking over the filled bike racks, beyond the cars, through the netting of the branches. You can see a straight line drawing itself, but the existing architecture in no way dictates its necessity, its reason for arising from pure imagination. A small concrete courtyard gives way to 92 East 1st Street: Max Meltzer Towers. "I can't believe, like, all of your friends, like, aren't with us, because they probably didn't know," she says as she walks by. The sun is beating down upon you from the south. In your version of Manhattan, the sun sets in the past and rises in the future: The north is your future. Over the next eighty-two days of walking, you may find some evidence of life exceeding the limits of the grid. Now you're at First Avenue and 1st Street. You stand and look at Boca Chica and Lucien, which is never as good as it should be, and think of Trotsky's son Seryozha. Trotsky and his family lived in New York for two months in 1917 then were brought back to Russia after news of the revolution came. History shows him living on 164th Street, but an amusing anecdote finds his convalescent son, recently bedridden with diphtheria, going out for a half-hour walk one afternoon, not returning for three, worrying his mother silly, until finally a policeman called and informed her that the boy, in those hours, had managed to answer a question that had perplexed him for some time: Was there a 1st Street? Was there really a beginning? A question you ask and which seems even more pertinent the higher one goes in the numbered streets. The only other relevant story you can offer: 36 East 1st Street apparently still houses the office of *The Catholic Worker*, a Socialist daily, originally *The Call*. On her first assignment, Dorothy Day, who founded the paper, interviewed Trotsky. Was there really a first street? Is there a 1st Street? It's fitting, you suppose, that as much as it instigates the structure that will follow, on street and page, it's not a fully realized street: a provisional swathe, a drawing of a line that, in being redrawn time and again until it cuts clean across the island, takes itself for a walk. And so you, a line drawing, take yourself for a walk.

01/04/2009 17:38 212-737-2329 PAGE 01

The first gay bar you ever visited was Pieces, just down the way at 8 Christopher Street. You went with a female friend from NYU and were so nervous about going that you had to stop at another bar in advance and down several drinks to muster the courage. It was a big deal, you know? Of course, the bar ended up being such a parody of gayness—what with the obligatory drag queen singing Madonna and men drinking pink cocktails—that you were charmed. You and Ronnie just passed Riviera Café & Sports Bar, where Lou Reed kicked John Cale out of the Velvet Underground. Too bad for Lou Reed. Let's read what Benjamin De Casseres wrote about Sheridan Square. De Casseres was largely writing in the Prohibition era, which was also the time when Charles Henri Ford and Parker Tyler wrote *The Young and Evil*, a novel about homosexuals living in Greenwich Village and Harlem. Strangely, it seems that during Prohibition, homosexuals actually became more socially accepted, which historians attribute to the fact that as booze went underground and became an errant thing, it joined many of the preexisting, errant bits of the nightlife. "Sheridan Square is the Parnassus, the Olympus of bob-haired morals. Looking due Bellevueward from a dressing room in the Greenwich Village Theatre, one sees at nightfall the luminous eye of the clock in the tower of the Jefferson Market Police Court." "In the Village," De Casseres continues, "nothing is true but debts." You have no idea if Jefferson Market Police Court still exists. Or the clock, Ronnie adds. This is what you've been finding on these walks: an absence and some unintentional compensation, even when the city bulldozes and turns itself into a cemetery. What's the word the Situationists used that Gopnik borrows? *Supercession*. They describe the city as a supercession of layers, the implication being that you can look and see the active juxtaposition of these layers. But sometimes there's no juxtaposition; sometimes it's simply that one thing has been buried, another thing rises, and you can see what is there to be seen. So you and Ronnie are looking at a Blackberry ad and can only imagine the Jefferson Market Police Court clock. If that screen were allowed to load, if that billboard weren't static, you're sure that a clock on the Blackberry would appear. Should we continue? Pieces was quite a place. A man tried to take you home that night. He was Hugh Jackman's personal assistant in town to make *Kate and Leopold*, a movie in which Hugh plays a man from, you can't remember, the seventeenth century? And Meg Ryan—this was the era when she cut her hair and began doing a number on her lips—plays a twentieth-century woman. Hugh comes back from the past and has to make it work in the here and now. He doesn't prove to be a quick study. It's sort of like Leopold is the Jefferson Market Police Court clock, you suggest. Just imagine him coming back from the grave and standing in front of the Blackberry ad. That would not be a pretty sight, but it might make for a pretty decent rom-com. Ronnie laughs, humors you. He mentions that he's seen that plot play out before but can't call the film to mind.

01/05/2009 15:27 212-737-2329 PAGE 01

You met a Dutch woman named Francine last night at an opening, and she told you that she spent her New Year's Eve at a dinner party on Wall Street, and that on her way down, her route happened to pass the New York Stock Exchange. At that hour of the night, the Financial District was ghostly quiet. Francine said that she had actually looked up at the Stock Exchange, shaken her fist, and, from what you could extrapolate (knowing very little of this woman) thought to herself, "You American bankers! Why can't you get it together?" You humored her by saying that her fist shake might be the single gesture, all the more potent coming from a foreigner, that would shift the economic winds. At the moment you're standing outside 333 East 5th Street. In 1967 at this address—drab, red brick building in standard East Village fashion—lived Abbie Hoffman, the leader of the Youth International Group (the "Yippies"). Hoffman, an activist best known as a member of the "Chicago Eight," best known for the shit he started at the 1968 Democratic National Convention, disrupted the New York Stock Exchange during the year he lived here, specifically on August 24, 1967, when he threw fistfuls of dollars—three hundred in total, apparently—down onto the floor of the Exchange. Some traders booed, and of course, most scrambled to grab the bills. A fist shaker and a fistful of dollars: as metaphors, not as far from one another as you would suspect.

01/07/2009 15:09 212-737-2329 PAGE 01

01/08/2009 13:04 212-737-2329 PAGE 01

Your walk begins with a *thak thak thak thak thak thak thak thak thak*—the sound of a man packing his cigarettes against a garbage can on the corner—that, like a metronome, will set the tempo, will mark your pace. Most of the clothing stores on West 8th seem like they would only get good business in the Halloween season. Neons, bold tones, skimpy frocks, fur, sequins, glitter: these are the stones and beams and bricks of this fantasy row. Somewhere along here was the second site of SculptureCenter, then “The Clay Club.” Dorothea Denslow started it in 1928 in her Brooklyn studio, and in 1930 it moved to this street. At that time, it was more of an educational hub, a place to learn about sculpture, and during and after World War II—as many of the members fought—it was a resource for the armed forces and veterans: “Sculpture Canteen.” You like the name Clay Club. It falls between sounding like the name of a swell joint in a 1940s-era hotel and that of a venue devoted to the medium. You wonder if Diego Cortez was thinking of it when he founded The Mudd Club, and if the use of mud, as a medium, should only be taken metaphorically. The only time you saw the interior of The Mudd Club was in *Downtown 81*, when Basquiat stopped by to catch some No Wave performance—Lizzy Mercier Descloux, you think. Back-up singers with teased-out hair, a row of horn players. It reminded you of the Hercules and Love Affair concert last spring. The new New York band doing old New York. The new SculptureCenter doing the old Clay Club. Medium provides the continuity. You've thought of *Downtown 81* a bit in the past few days because you've been surprised at the fact that there are still some abandoned lots in far-east Alphabet City, and that you, like Basquiat, could be set against these backdrops by a camera, a pedestrian, a reader. The evolution of hip New York is a necrology of the previously hip. The Mudd Club is one example—Cortez is now a curator and art advisor. St. Mark's Place, which you're approaching, might be the definitive example. Your first stop, the first grave, is Club 57, a late-seventies, early-eighties club. Home to, as club manager Ann Magnuson wonderfully put it, "pointy-toed hipsters, girls in rockabilly petticoats, spandex pants, and thrift-store stiletto heels . . . suburban refugees who had run away from home to find a new family . . . who liked the things we liked—Devo, Duchamp, and William S. Burroughs—and (more important) hated the things we hated—disco, Diane von Furstenberg, and The Waltons." "A Punk Do-It-Yourself aesthetic" back when the term wasn't just wielded by advertisers. Among the more memorable of the "enviro-theques," or theme parties, was the "Model World of Glue Night," where people assembled to build airplanes and monster models, burn them, and sniff epoxy. Here it is, number 57: a well-battered awning says, "St. Mark's Place Institute," "Unitas." A man with a trench and a moustache smokes outside. First Avenue. Yaffa Cafe, where kitsch comes to die. A preteen's gateway to the

East Village. A gigantic wiener says, "Eat Here." . . . W.H. Auden lived at 77 St. Mark's Place from 1953 to 1972, one year before his death. Strangely, the quote about New York you most remember him for has nothing to do with St. Mark's Place or his apartment here, which according to Arendt was a real shithole. His poem "September 1, 1939" begins: "I sit in one of the dives / on Fifty-Second Street / Uncertain and afraid / As the clever hopes expire / of a low dishonest decade."

01/11/2009 10:20 212-737-2329 PAGE 01

You run into Brian at the corner and tell him you're taking a walk. You're now an element of the walk, Brian. Can I follow, can I follow along? Of course. You tell Derek and Lindsay that Brian squats in the East Village. It's actually Allen Ginsberg and Peter Orlovsky's old place, Brian explains. It's been this derelict apartment inside a normal apartment building for some time. I have tacit permission to be there, but Peter Orlovsky is in the process of being evicted. The rent-controlled situation for a senior citizen is hard to get through the courts, though, so for the past ten years it has just been occupied by different drug addicts and artists and squatters. Right now there's a piano in there that we're trying to remove so it doesn't get destroyed. Derek listens with his hands jammed in his pockets, his coffee cup held between his teeth.

01/12/2009 08:02 212-737-2329 PAGE 01

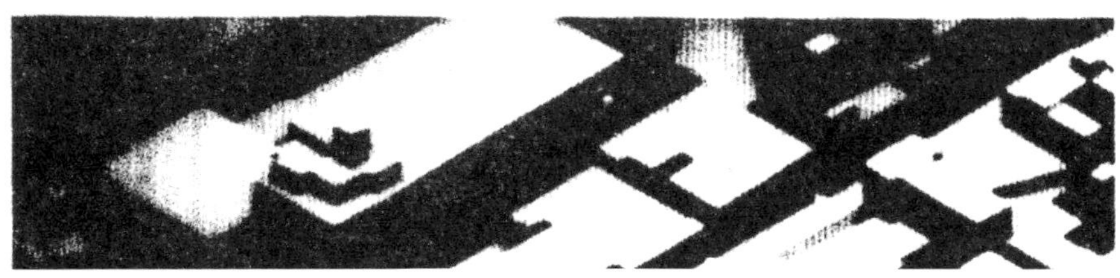

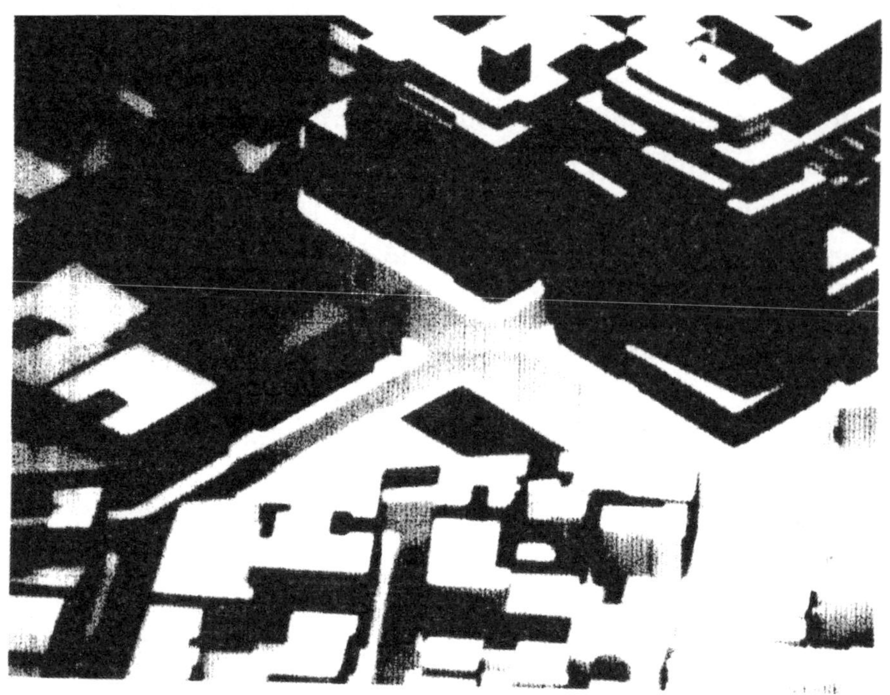

2009-01-20 16:30 PUBLIC STORAGE 17184720285>> 12127372329 P 1/1

Inquiries from News Media

• Contact (818)-244-8080 Mark Good

Public Relations Policy

We live in a time when media – newspapers, radio, television and Internet – touch us more than ever before. Reporters may approach any of us at any time for a statement or comment that presents the Public Storage point of view. Therefore, it is vital that any information provided agrees with company policy and philosophy.

To avoid potentially unflattering and even embarrassing press reports about your property or the company, Public Storage has established a public relations policy that all employees must know and follow.

- Refer all media calls (newspapers, radio, magazines, TV stations, etc.) to Chief Operating Officer (COO) in the Corporate Office.

    - No matter how trivial the question or how small the station or publication, politely refer all inquiries to the COO.
    - If the reporter is persistent, simply reply, "I have no comment." Repeat again that the COO's office will help him/her.
    - Be prepared to describe to someone in the COO's office what questions are being asked, the reporter's full name, and the organization that he or she represents. Explain other facts that you believe are relevant to the situation.
    - Inform your District and Regional Manager of the situation.
- If a media representative comes to your property unannounced and insists on a story immediately, politely inform him or her of any company policy and try to contact the COO's office. Be courteous at all times to any media representative, but be firm and do not answer his/her questions.
- If a situation is developing at your property that may erupt into publicity, contact your District Manager as soon as possible. This includes criminal activity or other volatile situations.
- If a catastrophe occurs that might affect the building (e.g., earthquake, major fire, flood, etc.), contact your District Manager before the press arrives on the scene.
- Refer all requests to shoot a movie, commercial, video, etc. to the Marketing Department in the Corporate Office.
- Refer all calls related to property appraisal, tax assessments, etc. to your District or Regional Manager. Ask for the person's name, position, company or organization, and phone number. Tell him or her that your District or Regional Manager will call him/her back.
- If you receive calls or in-person guests who claim to be friends of the Corporate Office management team, be skeptical! If someone from the Corporate Office is sending out a friend or business associate for a special reason, you will be informed first. In any event, be pleasant and courteous but do not provide any information that you would not give to a regular customer. Refer him/her to your District or Regional Manager for more information.
- Treat investors or lending institution representatives as outlined in the step above. If investors or representatives request information that you would ordinarily not release to a customer, find out what information they want, ask them to wait, and contact your District or Regional Manager. If your District or Regional Manager is unavailable, take the visitor's name and phone number and tell him or her you will have your District or Regional Manager call back.
- Information regarding occupancy, vacancy rates, or rent increases is absolutely confidential. Treat any information you would not discuss during a typical customer presentation and space rental as confidential.
- When in doubt, do not divulge any information. Be courteous and friendly at all times.

If you have any questions regarding this policy, contact your District or Regional Manager.

01/21/2009 13:17 212-737-2329 PAGE 01

Joshua has lived on 21st between Ninth and Tenth since 1986. As you walk, he points at plaques and buildings and recounts histories. You confess you don't know those histories. He exclaims, "She knows nothing!"

02/18/2009 22:43 212-737-2329 PAGE 01

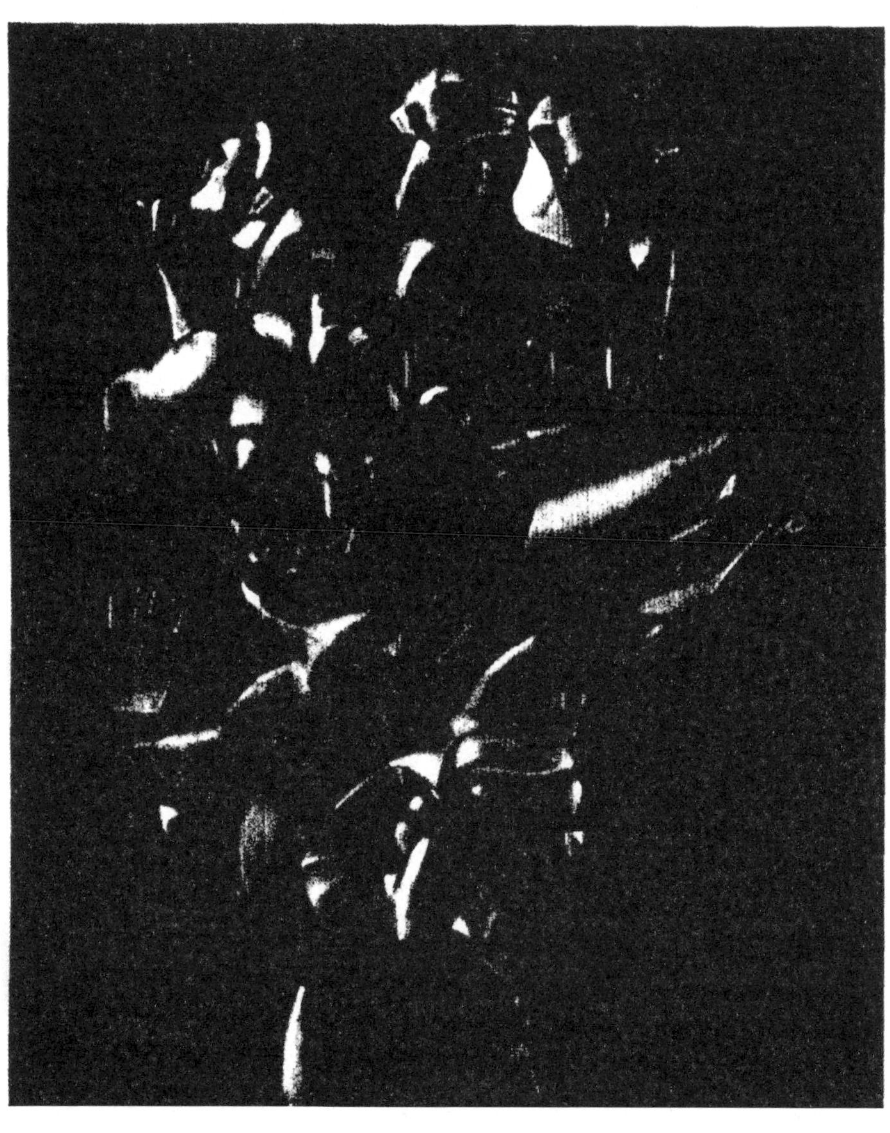

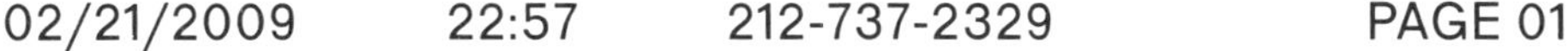

02/21/2009 22:57 212-737-2329 PAGE 01

I've come to the Blue Bar a couple of times, Vicky says. I had drinks with an artist in 2004. We had an older friend come and stay here. Then I was totally into it and went through my Harold Ross-Dorothy Parker phase. I don't read enough of them though. I have the Dorothy Parker anthology, but I'm more interested in her as a cultural character than a writer, except I think she wrote that, "The answer is that there is no answer—that's the answer," which I say all the time. A waiter arrives. Hi, how are you? I want a cocktail, but I'm not sure what I want, Vicky remarks. You're having a Manhattan, right? I'm not sure if I want a Manhattan. You know what? I will have a Gimlet, but I want a gin Gimlet. Tanqueray? And ice, otherwise I'll get drunk. Sorry, I keep sniffling. So, you're more interested in Dorothy Parker's life than her writing, you ask Vicky. I don't know enough about her writing—just the cheeky cocktail humor. I think I'm reincarnated from a modernist. I love Martha Graham. I love Dorothy Parker. I'm obsessed with the Silver Age. Tell me about Dorothy Parker. Well, she sat at the roundtable at the Algonquin with the guys who started *The New Yorker*. I named one of my artists' paintings after a Dorothy Parker. She couldn't come up with a title, and I read her a poem of Parker's, which was a little pathetic but interesting, called "Cherry White." You know how Billie Holiday wrote "Strange Fruit" about Black boys being hung from trees in the South? She was on a bus tour and would see hangings. So, Dorothy Parker, at the same time, wrote "Cherry White" about how beautiful cherry blossoms are, and she mentioned that it would be even more beautiful to see herself hanging there. I think she must have had "Strange Fruit" in mind.

02/21/2009 18:19 212-737-2329 PAGE 01

This is fulfilling a lifelong dream to walk in the middle of a street in Manhattan without any fear of being run over by a car, because the street has been blocked off. In fact, I have my eyes shut right now. I just walked ten paces with my eyes completely shut—right in the middle of Manhattan.

02/22/2009 20:41 212-737-2329 PAGE 01

This will not be a pleasant walk, though more tolerable for unfolding hours after its scheduled time, after the rain had dissipated, and after a potentially awkward scenario with one of the walkers was avoided. Even when you try to shut out the memories of the people you've walked with, they crop up. With the Jim Dine Venus de Milos, Morgan crops up. With the big black Eero Saarinen rock, Ben crops up. And with the MoMA building, hiding on the left, Alex crops up. Some months into its reopening, Alex asked if you had visited yet. You hadn't. But he had. Several times. Less, it seemed, to contemplate the vast portion of its collection that had entered the exhibition space and more to hear its own story told in geometric passages, crisply punctuated. Was it Alex who had told you of the vertiginous drops some views afford? Of that strange paradox of being able to walk onto tiny perches and look down several stories into the cuboid atrium? Of the fact that, in a space built for circulation, one could be afforded such expansive views onto a cultured public only by excising oneself from it? . . . You probably put these words in Alex's mouth, because you were thinking about how those perches would be prime locations for private acts of public suicide, that one could pass one's final moments secluded in an almost sacral place before leaping into the architectural, metaphysical void. Not the Golden Gate Bridge nor the NYU Library: MoMA struck you as the perfect place from which to depart, onto which to land, into which to be absorbed. The day Rothko's body was found, in 1970, the Tate in London received his shipment of works originally intended for the restaurant in the Seagram Building on Park. He had fabricated them ten years earlier. Rothko at that time thought himself an aesthetic terrorist, relishing the opportunity—a massive commission for a painter of his generation—to install his work in the locus of well-monied New York, a prime venue of consumption, deal-making, and deal-breaking: to install paintings—six-hundred-square feet of them, to be exact—that made the space unpleasant, even claustrophobic. Rothko and his wife ate at the restaurant shortly after it opened. It seemed that his disgust got the better of him. The stories surrounding why he pulled out of the commission are ambiguous, but perhaps Rothko knew that his patrons would win in the end, that however subtly or opaquely he provoked, even an artwork made with terroristic intent would get flattened out. Can a building have terroristic intent? Can a building be suicidal? The Citigroup Center might answer these questions, considering its checkered past. Its steel columns jut from its medians to accommodate St. Peter's Evangelical Lutheran Church, which, while necessary to demolish for the skyscraper's construction in the late seventies, insisted that the building be designed to cantilever around the site of what would be the church's eventual replacement. Cantilever it did—an awkward dance worsened by structural engineer William LeMessurier's choice to employ bolted joints instead of welded ones. This seemingly innocuous and economical decision, LeMessurier came to realize, meant that the building, when hit by winds of a certain velocity, would fall over. And so, under the cloak of night, LeMessurier's team switched out every single joint, while in daytime hours, staff shuffled in—potential victims of disaster. As Hurricane Ella moved up the coast, six weeks into the work, it seemed that nature would strike a fatal blow to the building, yet it veered off course, and the team managed to finish the repairs. It took fifteen years for this information to come to public light—fifteen years that could have seen other structural engineers, functioning under the same faulty logic, make suicidal terrorists of whole city blocks.

02/23/2009 22:59 212-737-2329 PAGE 01

Have your walks been affected by the inauguration, A.J. asks. How do you mean? I imagine that it came up more than once, she replies. It has, though not much of what was discussed has entered the transcripts. One thing my friend Candice brought up, when we were on a science-fiction-ish walk across 33rd Street, was the question of what type of architecture Obama would be. Apparently, there has been a lot of discussion about his "building." There's a school of thought that has him as a sleek glass-and-steel contemporary structure, and then there are others who say he would be a Beaux-Arts edifice in the style of Grand Central, because he's bringing back the rhetorical style of an earlier generation of politicians. I can see that, A.J. says. Well, what do you think? What building do you imagine Obama being? In four years, his administration might—I worry that it might seem like the Lipstick Building. Why? Well, the Lipstick Building, as you know, housed the offices of Bernie Madoff, who I think will represent—if he hasn't come to already represent—the excesses of the Bush years and the fraud we were all taken in by during this time. Now that the reality sets in, the quickly gutted seventeenth floor may come to seem like the old economy. Is that really how it happened? Oh yeah. How much of a view did you have onto that? Very little, A.J. replies, because I had not come back to work from the Obama campaign when all of that went down, but apparently, the day after the story broke, there were investigators all over the lobby of the building, and people were in and out of that elevator bank constantly. I don't know. I used the bank recently, and my elevator happened to open on the seventeenth floor. I was so tempted to dash out and run around just to see what it was really like. Did you see anything? No. Except I sort of expected the walls to be stripped of their fake wood and stuff. They should've dug in for the copper wire, you remark. Yeah, but it looked like it was still intact. What a shame. I was hoping for something a little more dramatic.

02/24/2009 17:25 212-737-2329 PAGE 01

You step up onto a tiled square, in line with the Citicorp building, in line with the East River, in line with Roosevelt Island, to meet Colin, whom you've never met. Together you will walk across 55th Street to his neighborhood, and if things go well, a kiss or four might be exchanged en route or at the walk's conclusion.

03/02/2009 10:36 212-737-2329 PAGE 01

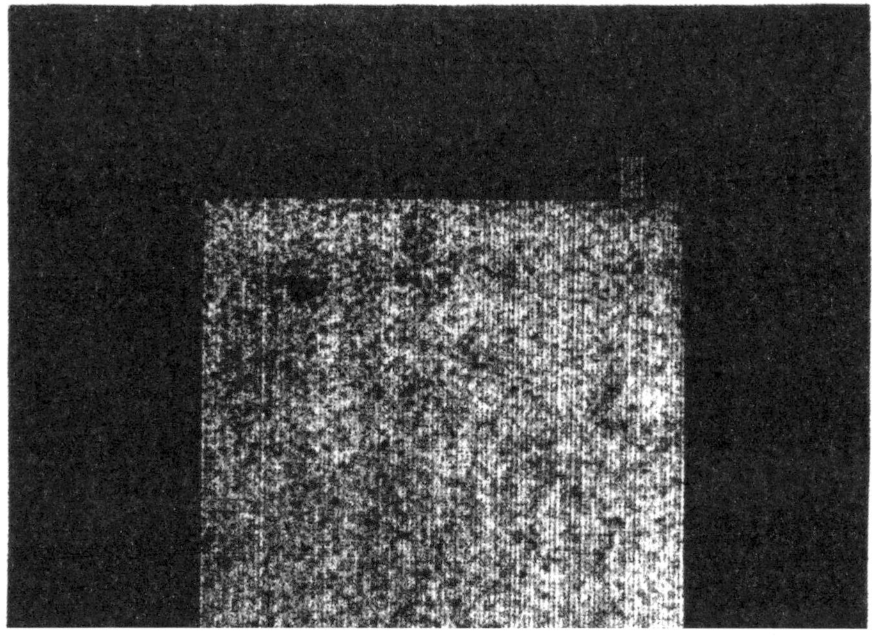

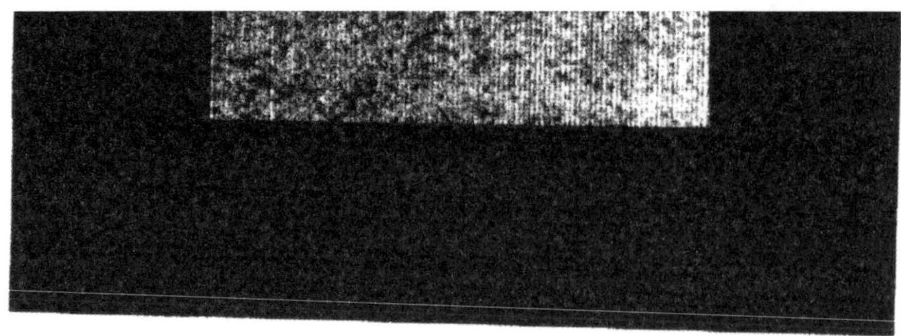

03/09/2009 10:36 212-737-2329 PAGE 01

Now there are two options. We could walk straight through Central Park or—let's walk straight, Liz says. That's part of the policy. If parks and buildings don't follow the order of the grid, then you can't acknowledge them in the walks, so they're omitted from the transcripts. It wasn't that I didn't notice things earlier, Liz remarks. It's that I was looking for you. I thought that we were about to pass by each other. Well, did you have any cases of mistaken identity? No. No one looked like you. You don't know if Liz has seen you since you cut your hair. You could have been a stranger to her. You were having a conversation with your therapist this morning about how you had an affair with a guy in LA last week, while you were there for some other things, and how uncannily similar you and he looked, even though he's German-Polish and you're Scottish-French. There really was a striking resemblance? In body type and height and body hair. All sorts of things. Shaved head. It was strange because you've changed a lot in the past year. You've lost thirty-five pounds and cut your hair. Some people who have known you for a long time talk as if you've become a stranger to them. That you've transformed into a different person, Liz says. Yeah. You look different. And you feel really different, Liz asks. Sort of. Some things didn't go away. You still sweat like crazy, unfortunately, and you definitely recognize yourself in yourself, but it has been strange all the same. You accept that one of the types of men you're interested in is men who look like you. Prior to your body transformation, you were more interested in men who looked like you *then*. LA was probably the first instance of seeing a man who looks like you now, and because you still feel so strange to yourself, it was like an education about yourself through another person. It was a process of personal discovery, projected narcissism, and surprise when he ended up being different than you. Oh! He likes to bottom and you don't. Oh! He runs his house and organizes his clothes like they're relics in a museum, whereas you're a total slob. Do you think there's a correlation, Liz asks, between sexual position and other characteristics? Messiness and order? I would usually make the opposite association, she says—that a controlling person who is orderly would want to be on top—but as I started to say it, I realized it was all wrong, because this person wants to lose control. Often. But playing the bottom is the more, how to say, hygienically tenuous position. You've encountered bottoms who are incredibly clean, and their self-manicuring and self-maintenance extend into other parts of their lives. In any case. What did you come up with? Oh, I got offtrack in talking about the attraction to someone who resembles you, Liz remarks. Right. But correction: We're very much on track. This is the first time you've walked through the park and done it correctly. I like the climbing and the jumping, Liz says. You're so pleased that she is totally and unquestioningly on board. Are we doing this, you ask, looking at a fence. Yes. Have you seen Improv Everywhere, Liz asks. Their best one is in Grand Central. They enlist hundreds of people to walk into the station, then half freeze in place while the other half has a fit. It sounds much more interesting than the flash mobs you hear about. Everyone showing up and mooing is funny, but this has something profound to it. I've tried this thing called Five Rhythms a few times, Liz says, which is basically a sober rave, but it's officiated by someone. The DJ gives a sort of sermon in the middle of it and provides direction. You're not allowed to speak. About eighty people show up, and you're encouraged to dance with strangers. It goes through different movements—staccato and flowing kinds of rhythms. You'd be really into that. You used to go to silent parties in New York. But the directive element is so strange. Well, it's fairly free-form, though you're given some guidance. Some people break down crying. Another thing I've tried in recent years is authentic movement, which is improvisation with your eyes closed. Both interest me because they're about shutting down standard modes of communication. Wow. You're up for both. Who says we should escape the grid, you ask Liz. Why not adhere faithfully? There's freedom in order, she replies.

03/12/2009 22:41 212-737-2329 PAGE 01

Why is the Bethesda Angel significant, you ask Bart. Well, it wasn't the Bethesda originally. It was just south of the Bethesda—this area where people roller skate. What is rotoscope? No, roller skate. I guess I've always loved that spot because it's sort of—I don't know. I went there with my aunt who's deaf and from Ireland, and she almost couldn't leave. She loved it so much. You have all of these people—young and old, from different walks of life—roller skating to disco music. It speaks to a very particular spirit of New York which might be a little cliché and might not really exist in the way it used to. But it sort of points to—look! Oh my god, Bart says. What the hell are they? Raccoons. I've never seen them this close. They're pretty fearless, aren't they? Do they bite? You wouldn't get any closer. I can't believe it—oh, whatever. I'm a real sap. Clearly. I'm talking about my aunt being touched by roller skaters. What's next? Now it's going to get much worse, Bart warns, because I'll talk about the last line in *Angels in America*, because you know the Angel Bethesda is this recurring theme in the play. People are sitting out and whatshisname says, "You are beautiful creatures. Each and every one. And I *something* you.

(And I love you? I forgive you?) The great work begins." I've always thought that was a special way to end, because what is the great work? You don't like that sappy crap, do you, Bart asks. Well, what is the relationship to the fountain? Because they say it at the Bethesda Angel, he replies. The angel is a metaphor that goes throughout the play, and I'd have to know its history to tell you what the metaphor was, but I forget things very quickly. As do you—you'll Google it later. Please, let's leave it in the park. And then in the series of movies, they really highlight it. I don't know. It's just funny because that's such a special moment, and just this way I keep getting pulled back to the disco area of roller skaters. These two things. And then Sheep's Meadow is just so special in certain ways. I'm going to start crying now. I didn't think this would happen at all. Your family loves watching the roller skaters, and you play the "guess their day job" game when you go, which is maybe a little less sappy and a little more cynical. There's a wonderful thing about these types of gatherings in New York, where you encounter an unpredictable community brought together by recreation. You think of a man you sometimes see who wears big headphones, looks like he's pushing sixty, is balancing two Nalgene bottles on his head, and skates with himself as if he's both Astaire and Rogers—doing things on roller skates that nobody should be able to do. Obviously, this man is a corporate lawyer. How could he not be a corporate lawyer? The game gets boring fast, because you want everyone to have the most boring job imaginable. I always imagined that they're beyond or outside of any commercial concern, Bart says. That all they do is roller skate. Because the only time I see them is here. But then you can notice these telltale signs. Men in their sixties have these AZT scars that people got early. Not scars, but the thing that happened to people who had AIDS—who had HIV. Early on in the treatment, when they take AZT, it would sort of collapse their cheeks, so there's this line. And of course, my tendency is to read victim into everyone, no matter how successful they become. They're tragic figures. I always filter them in that way. It's a really nice way to go through life, Bart laughs.

3/19/2009 07:01 212-737-2329 PAGE 01

03/23/2009 10:58 212-737-2329 PAGE 01

On your walk yesterday, you passed a massive plaster foot atop a crate of the same size outside a gilded home on East 81st Street. You were surprised to see it, which caused Saskia, in turn, to express surprise that this foot was surprising. She had assumed you were walking 81st Street eighty-two times over eighty-two days, and thus this foot would not be a surprise—there would be no surprises left on the street. Now that would be a very different project, you remarked, to fit the temperament of a very different artist. Indulging Saskia just a little more, you speculated as to the cumulative effect of such walks, mentioning *The Sight of Death*, T.J. Clark's recent book on slow looking. Clark is interested in the act of stopping and staring at two Poussins in the Getty, and how extended duration can allow for a deeper type of engagement. The body stops, you could say, but the eyes and the mind inquire, wandering forth along the tonal, aesthetic, symbolic, and associative paths of the work. You think of *Standing Still and Walking in New York*, the title of a collection of Frank O'Hara essays—Frank, who should have made an appearance far earlier in these walks. The title describes the two poles of urban experience or suggests a riddle: How can one stand still and walk at the same time? You speculate that to walk across a single street, river-to-river, for eighty-two days may approximate a solution. Walking in suspended animation and temporal iteration, moving ever closer to a state of identicality with a street. This is not your project. The Diana Ross Playground, just to your left, reminds you that on the night of your birth in 1983, the Diana Ross concert in Central Park was rained out, and your father, finding himself locked out of his apartment, slept on a bench in this part of the park in a miserable state. To walk a single street eighty-two times is to become so familiar as to stop seeing: a fascinating and boring proposition at one and the same time. But to walk one street a day, each in succession, is to lose a city as fast as you rediscover it, to feel whole neighborhoods slip away, with the passing of each day, relinquished with the question of whether everything that should have been said was said: whether you did succeed in providing an image in text, a shape to a walk. What's left out, what's left behind? Such melancholic, elegiac thoughts should accompany your last walk, you suppose. Around you, the park shows the first signs of the coming season. You've carved a shape that began at the start of the year, the bottom of the grid, the dead of winter and ends with the death of winter and a period of renewal. But what does text do to a walk, you again think. And what is it to walk with a reader in mind? To talk to a reader and for a reader? On behalf of a reader? For you to talk to *you*? What is it to commit these walks to text? To draw a community of friends, acquaintances, colleagues into fiction? And for those people to become characters? Certainly, you've seen a range of performances, some speaking as if broadcasting, and others with a fear of accountability—with the knowledge that each word, each phrase is being committed to some account. Walking as a process of writing oneself into an archive and into a history, of being held accountable. You walked with Lance, and he brought up Chris Burden's *TV Hijack* and threatened to carry his own audio-recording device to keep you accountable, to hold you at knifepoint, to commandeer the means of recording. His implication was not that media could cease to flow—that representation could cease to circulate—but that the only power we can attempt to have, however futilely we attempt it, is controlling our means of representation. This lesson was learned when Bart joined you on a walk, wearing the cap of journalist, and generated his own recording and transcript. You've eviscerated the conversational tics and spoken punctuation that lengthen speech to the time of a thought—everything that makes for such tough going on the page, without which a transcript becomes something else and folds into a literary space. You eviscerated with the authority of an artist, and Bart preserved with the authority of a journalist. The article he wrote, the exact transcript he preserved, had the effect of making you seem somewhat uninformed, pretty inarticulate, a bit funny, and not self-serious. The transcript he preserved found you speaking in first person, whereas you have scrubbed clean your accounts of any instance of I. To speak on your behalf: How's that for accountability? As you near the close—with First Avenue, York, East End, the FDR beckoning—your body slows to a halt. The city begins to pass you by: First cars and pedestrians, then the asphalts, the gravels, the bricks and the stones sliding into the future. In five or ten years, you may return to these streets to see just how far they've traveled.

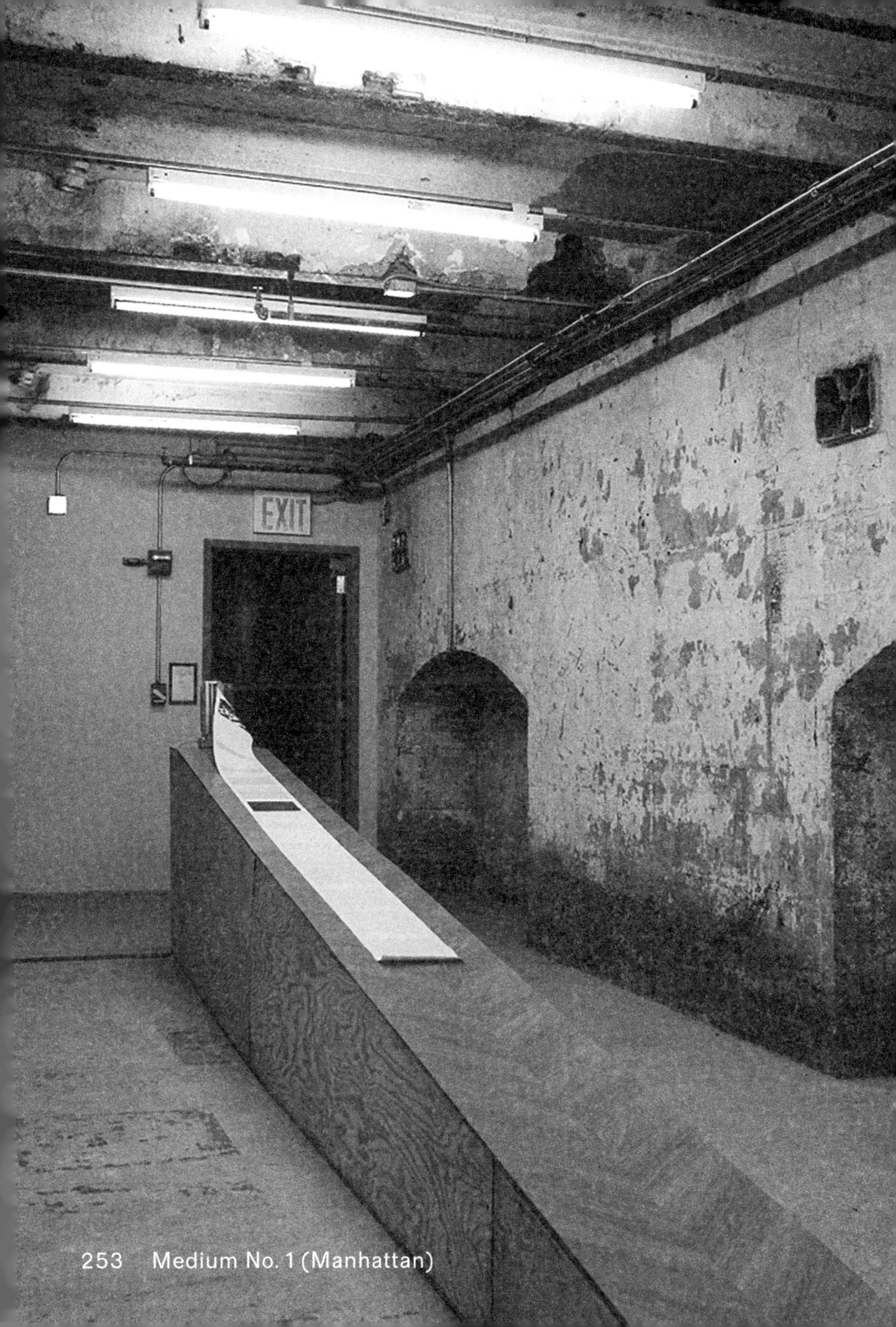

253 Medium No. 1 (Manhattan)

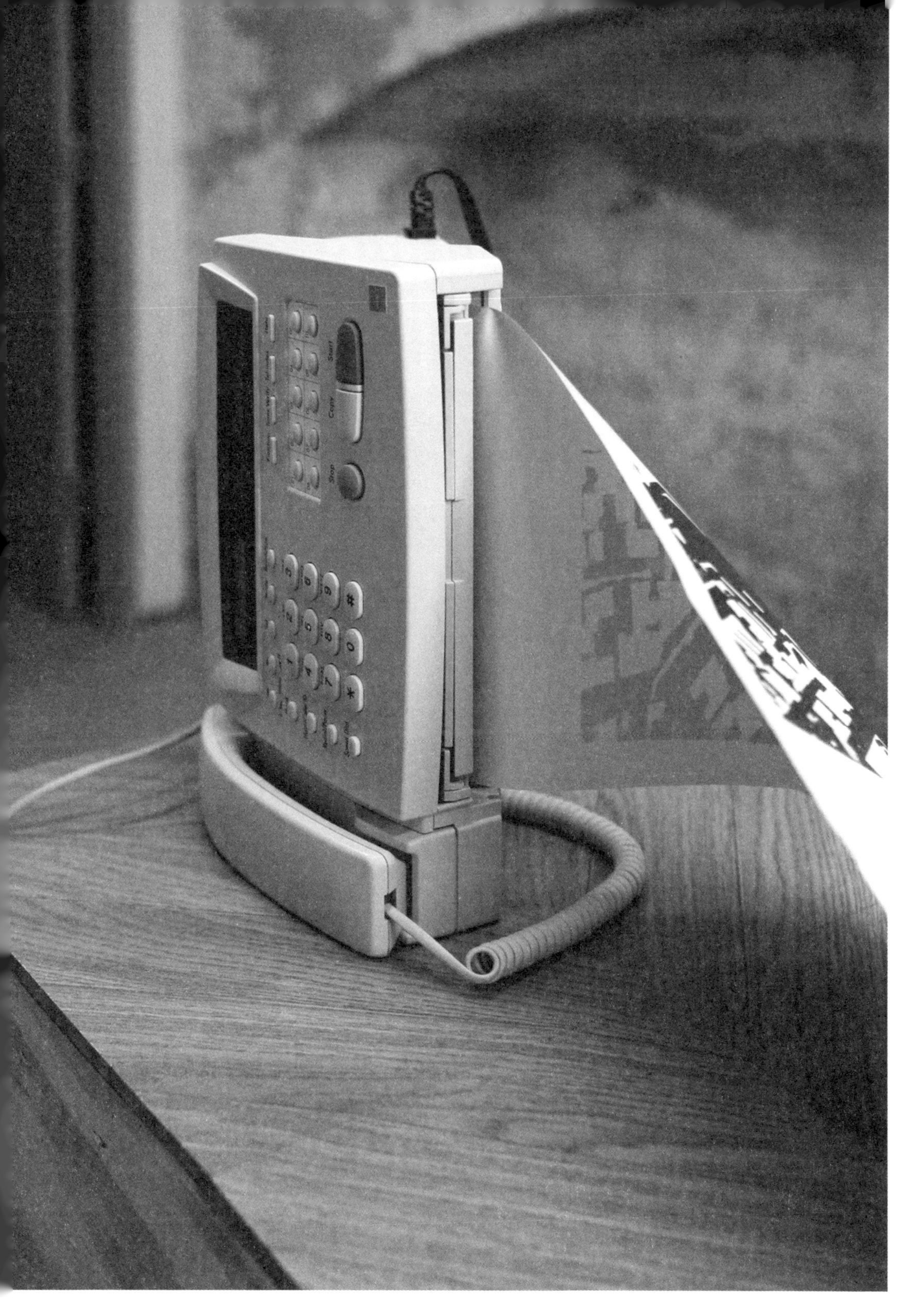

 Medium No. 1 (Manhattan)

01/07/2009 15:09 212-737-2329 PAGE 01

01/08/2009 13:04 212-737-2329 PAGE 01

Your walk begins with a thak thak thak thak thak thak thak thak thak - the sound of a man packing his cigarettes over a garbage can on the corner - that like a metronome will set the tempo, will mark your pace. Most of the clothing stores on W 8th St seem like they would only get good business in the Halloween season. Neons, bold tones, skimpy frocks, fur, silver, sequin, glitter: these are the stones and beams and bricks of this fantasy row. Somewhere along here time, space, place collapse. Somewhere along here was the second site of SculptureCenter, then "The Clay Club." Dorothea Denslow started it in 1928 in her Brooklyn studio, and in 1930 it moved to a spot on W 8th. At that time, it was more of an educational hub, a place to learn about sculpture and art, and during and after the war - as many of the members fought in World War II - it was a resource for members of the armed forces and veterans: "Sculpture Canteen." You like the name Clay Club. It falls between sounding like the name of a to-do joint in a 1940s-era hotel and that of a venue devoted to the medium. You wonder if Diego Cortez were thinking of it when he founded The Mudd Club, and if the use of mud, as a medium, should only be taken metaphorically. The only time you saw the interior of The Mudd Club was in "Downtown 81," when Basquiat stopped by to witness some no-wave performance - Lizzie Mercier Descloux, you think. Backup singers with teased-out hair, a row of horn players. Mixed: black, white. This reminded you of the Hercules and Love Affair concert last spring. The new New York band doing old New York. The new SculptureCenter doing the old Clay Club. Medium provides the continuity. You've thought of "Downtown 81" a bit in the past few days, because you've been surprised at the fact that there are still some abandoned lots in far-east Alphabet City, and that you, like Basquiat, could be seen set against these backdrops by a camera, a pedestrian, a reader. "The worst they can say is no." The evolution of hip New York is a necrology of the previously hip. The Mudd Club is one example - Cortez is now a curator and art adviser. St. Mark's Place, which you're now approaching, might be the definitive example. Your first stop, the first grave, is Club 57, a late-70s, early 80s club. Home to, as club manager Ann Magnuson put it, wonderfully, "pointy-toed hipsters, girls in

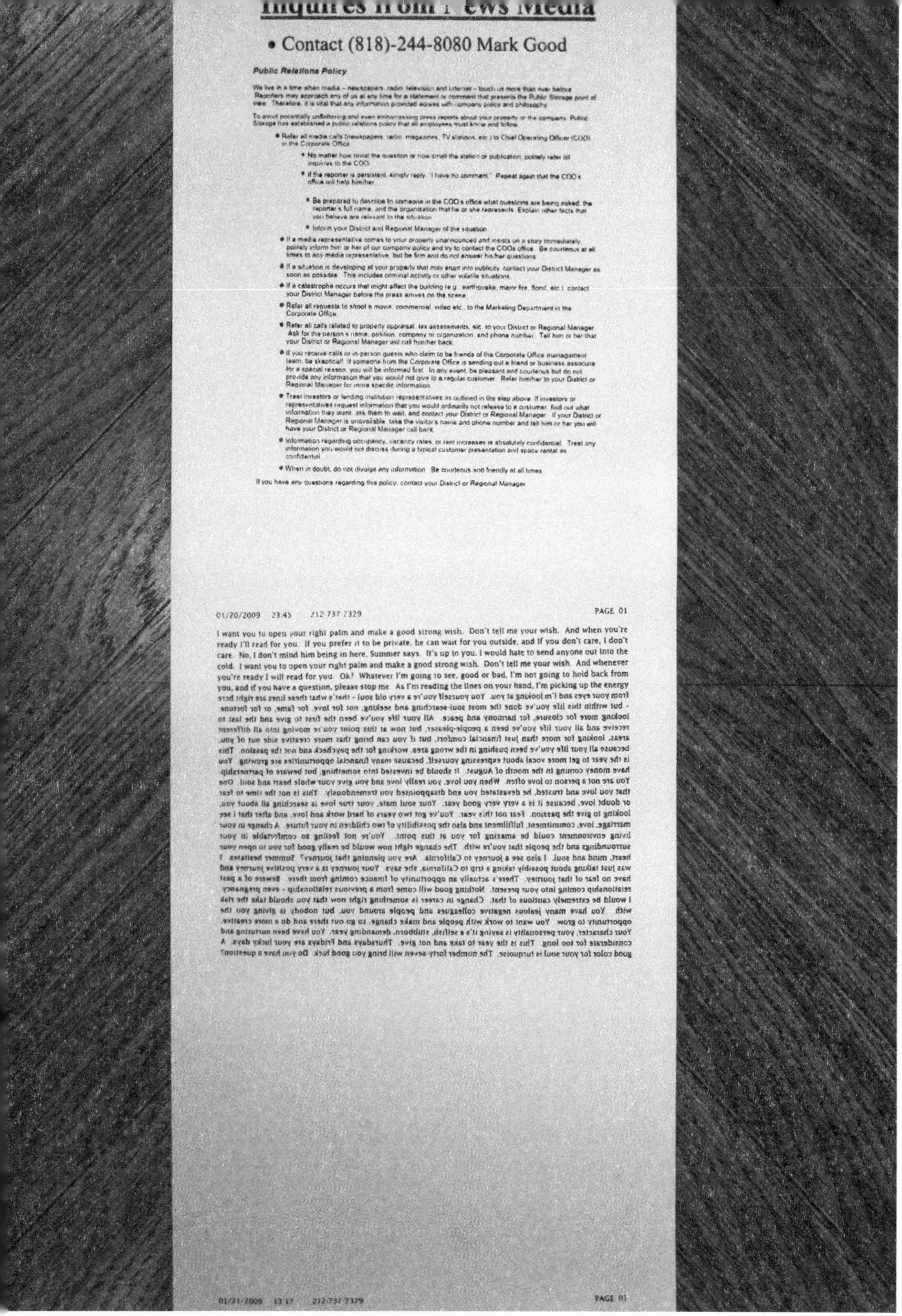

Inquires from News Media

- Contact (818)-244-8080 Mark Good

Public Relations Policy

We live in a time when media – newspapers, radio, television and internet – touch us more than ever before. Reporters may approach any of us at any time for a statement or comment that presents the Public Storage point of view. Therefore, it is vital that any information provided agrees with company policy and philosophy.

To avoid potentially unflattering and even embarrassing press reports about your property or the company, Public Storage has established a public relations policy that all employees must know and follow.

- Refer all media calls (newspapers, radio, magazines, TV stations, etc.) to Chief Operating Officer (COO) in the Corporate Office.
  - No matter how trivial the question or how small the station or publication, politely refer all inquiries to the COO.
  - If the reporter is persistent, simply reply, "I have no comment." Repeat again that the COO's office will help him/her.
  - Be prepared to describe to someone in the COO's office what questions are being asked, the reporter's full name, and the organization that he or she represents. Explain other facts that you believe are relevant to the situation.
  - Inform your District and Regional Manager of the situation.
- If a media representative comes to your property unannounced and insists on a story immediately, politely inform him or her of our company policy and try to contact the COOs office. Be courteous at all times to any media representative, but be firm and do not answer his/her questions.
- If a situation is developing at your property that may erupt into publicity, contact your District Manager as soon as possible. This includes criminal activity or other volatile situations.
- If a catastrophe occurs that might affect the building (e.g., earthquake, major fire, flood, etc.), contact your District Manager before the press arrives on the scene.
- Refer all requests to shoot a movie, commercial, video etc., to the Marketing Department in the Corporate Office.
- Refer all calls related to property appraisal, tax assessments, etc. to your District or Regional Manager. Ask for the person's name, position, company or organization, and phone number. Tell him or her that your District or Regional Manager will call him/her back.
- If you receive calls or in-person guests who claim to be friends of the Corporate Office management team, be skeptical! If someone from the Corporate Office is sending out a friend or business associate for a special reason, you will be informed first. In any event, be pleasant and courteous but do not provide any information that you would not give to a regular customer. Refer him/her to your District or Regional Manager for more specific information.
- Treat investors or lending institution representatives as outlined in the step above. If investors or representatives request information that you would ordinarily not release to a customer, find out what information they want, ask them to wait, and contact your District or Regional Manager. If your District or Regional Manager is unavailable, take the visitor's name and phone number and tell him or her you will have your District or Regional Manager call back.
- Information regarding occupancy, vacancy rates, or rent increases is absolutely confidential. Treat any information you would not discuss during a typical customer presentation and space rental as confidential.
- When in doubt, do not divulge any information. Be courteous and friendly at all times.

If you have any questions regarding this policy, contact your District or Regional Manager.

01/20/2009 23:45 212-737-2329 PAGE 01

I want you to open your right palm and make a good strong wish. Don't tell me your wish. And when you're ready I'll read for you. If you prefer it to be private, he can wait for you outside, and if you don't care, I don't care. No, I don't mind him being in here, Summer says. It's up to you. I would hate to send anyone out into the cold. I want you to open your right palm and make a good strong wish. Don't tell me your wish. And whenever you're ready I will read for you. Ok? Whatever I'm going to see, good or bad, I'm not going to hold back from you, and if you have a question, please stop me. As I'm reading the lines on your hand, I'm picking up the energy from your eyes and I'm looking at you. You yourself you're a very old soul - that's what these lines are right here - but within this life you've done the most soul-searching and seeking, not for love, for fame, or for fortune, looking more for closure, for harmony and peace. All your life you've been the first to give and the last to receive and all your life you've been a people-pleaser, but now at this point you're moving into all different areas, looking for more than just financial comfort, but if you can bring that more creative side out of you, because all your life you've been pushing in the wrong area, working for the paycheck and not the passion. This is the year to get more vocal about expressing yourself, because many financial opportunities are growing. You have money coming in the month of August. It should be invested into something, but beware of partnership. You are not a person to love often. When you love, you really love and you give your whole heart and soul. One that you love and trusted, he devastated you and disappointed you tremendously. This is not the time to fear or doubt love, because it is a very very good year. Your soul mate, your true love is searching all about you, looking to give the passion. Fear not this year. You've got two years of hard work and love, and after that I see marriage, love, commitment, fulfillment and also the possibility of two children in your future. A change in your living environment could be amazing for you at this point. You're not feeling so comfortable in your surroundings and the people that you're with. The change right now would be really good for you to open your heart, mind and soul. I also see a journey to California. Are you planning that journey? Summer hesitates. I was just talking about possibly taking a trip to California, she says. Your journey is a very positive journey and have no fear of that journey. There's actually an opportunity of finance coming from there. Beware of a past relationship coming into your present. Nothing good will come from a previous relationship - even pregnancy I would be extremely cautious of that. Change in career is something right now that you should take the risk with. You have many jealous negative colleagues and people around you, but nobody is giving you the opportunity to grow. You want to work with people and make change, so go out there and do a more creative. Your character, your personality is saying it's a selfish, stubborn, demanding year. You have been nurturing and considerate for too long. This is the year to take and not give. Thursdays and Fridays are your lucky days. A good color for your soul is turquoise. The number forty-seven will bring you good luck. Do you have a question?

01/21/2009 13:17 212-737-2329 PAGE 01

IMAGES

pp. 253–259

Tyler Coburn, *Medium No. 1 (Manhattan)*, 2008–2009. Installation views, *In Practice '09*, SculptureCenter, New York, 2009. Photos: the artist.

2020

Overgrowth

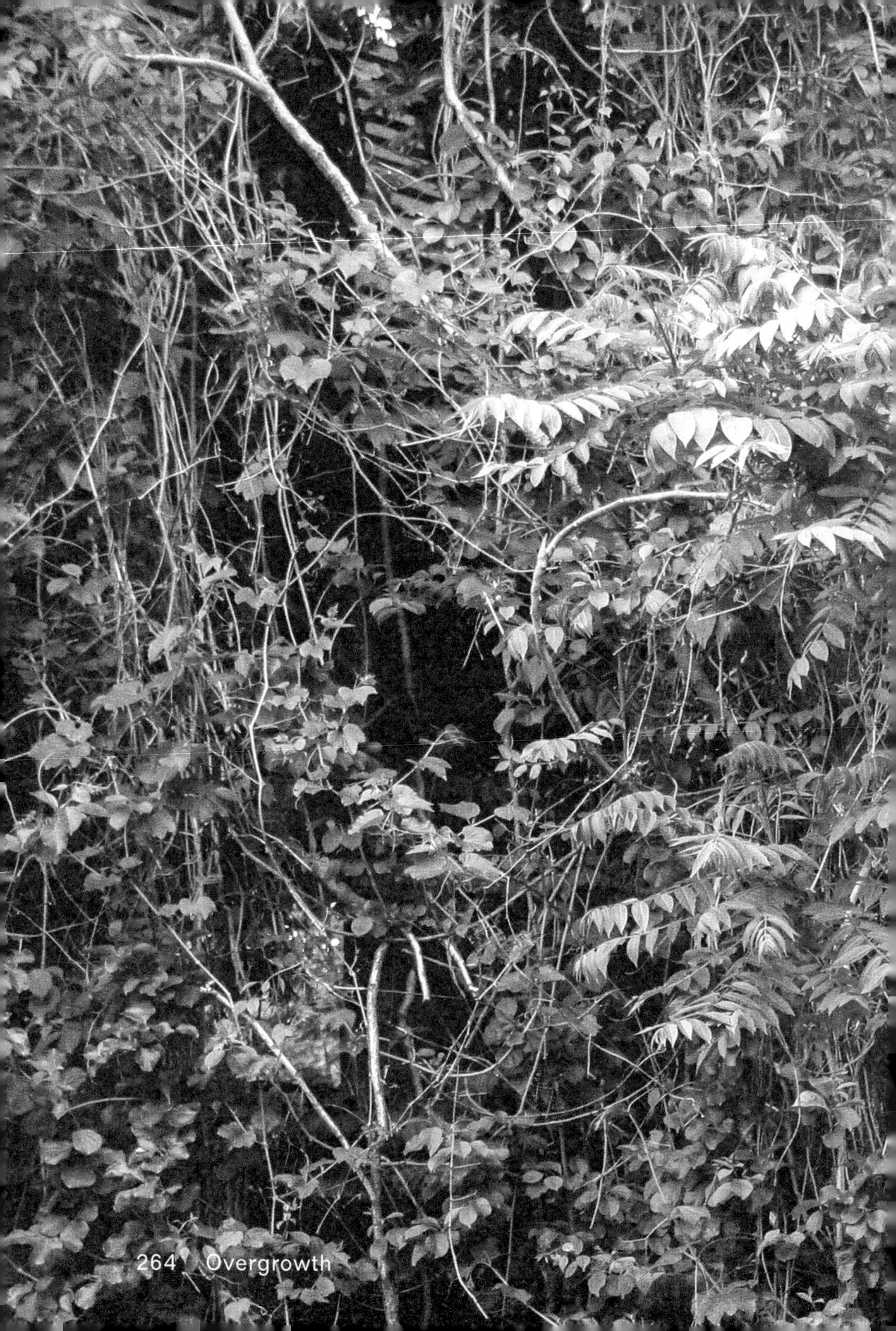

264 Overgrowth

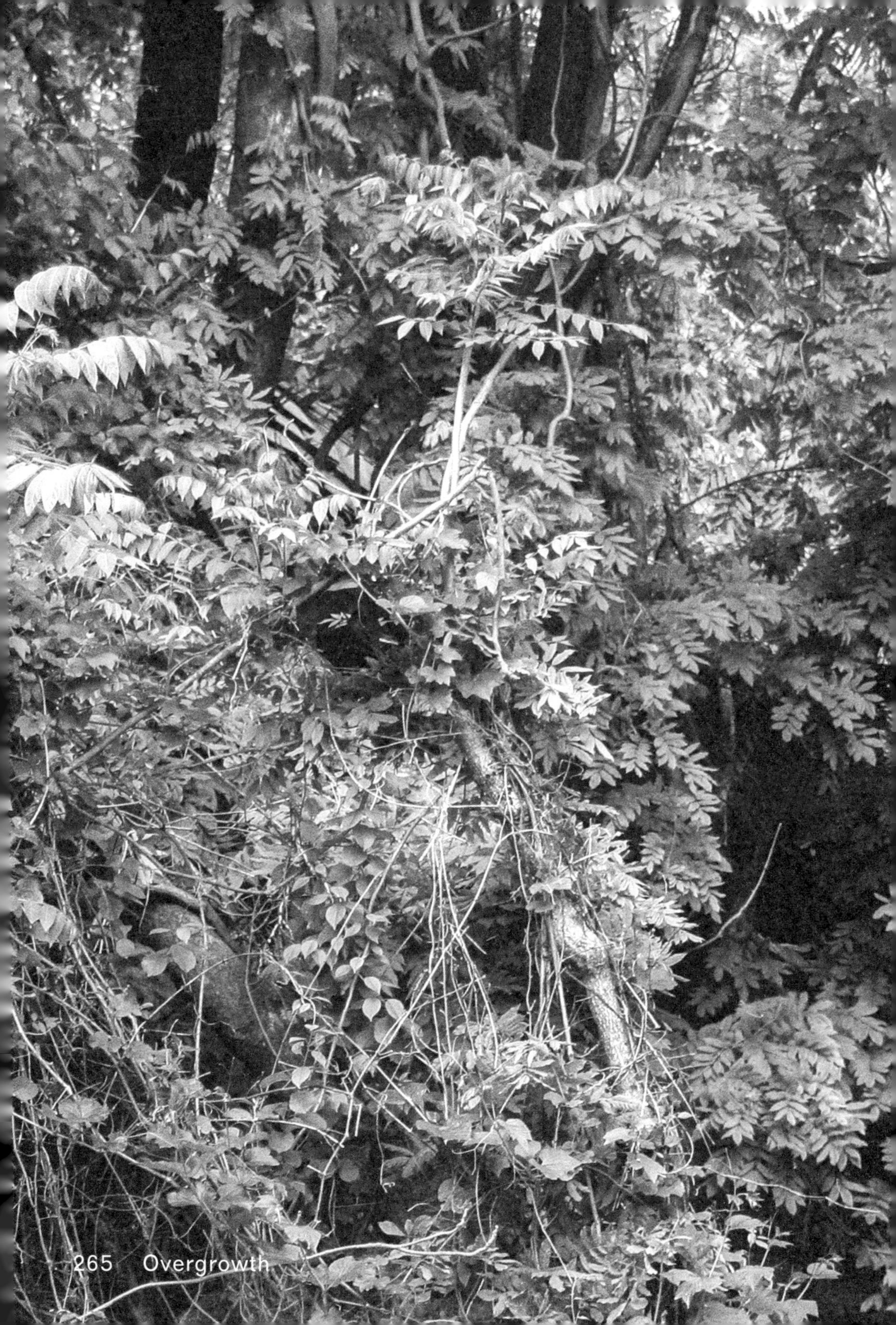

265 Overgrowth

We call this "overgrowth," which is a strange word when you think about it. Isn't the tendency of things to grow? Why has abundance become synonymous with neglect, suggesting that we have failed to maintain control?

The pavilions this overgrowth conceals are also neglected, having sat abandoned for about fifty years. They were built in the early twentieth century as part of the largest municipal hospital in the United States for the treatment of tuberculosis. At the time, the disease was still incurable, though a few things were known: that it took form as bacteria spread by air, and that frequent exposure to the natural elements could have palliative effects. In the sanatoriums built to provide this amenity, some were lucky enough to get better.

Here, high up on Staten Island, a breeze lifting from the sea once filled the porches of these pavilions. Here, at some distance from Manhattan, patients may have experienced the calm of a secluded retreat, or felt that the city had placed them as far away (within its limits) as it could—a hiding place for the sick and dying.

Construction began in 1905, with services commencing a few years later. By this point, tuberculosis cases among the wealthy were on a steady decline, and the majority of infected New Yorkers were immigrants and the poor. Perhaps it is owing to this population, or perhaps to the contagious nature of the disease, that the hospital's white nurses staged a walkout in 1929. For the first time in the country's history, black nurses were hired to tend to patients in unsegregated wards. These three hundred women known as "The Black Angels" were the essential workers of their age.

In 1952, a drug treatment was developed and tested here. Combined with two existing drugs, it produced a remedy with a 90-to-95 percent cure rate. Patients danced in the aisles.

By the early 1960s, no patients were left, and this site began to transform, introducing rehabilitation and long-term nursing care. Some of the buildings were repurposed, and new ones were built, but many, like these pavilions, remained empty. Now, they sit behind a fence on the outskirts of the campus, waiting for possible reuse. Development plans have come and gone while the buildings, like the trees around them, overgrow.

I first visited this site in May, a month after recovering from coronavirus, equipped with my mask and antibodies. I wasn't looking to explore the pavilions, as I had already seen photographs of their interiors. These pictures, belonging to a genre with the unfortunate name "ruin porn," are the work of intrepid explorers who trespass to leave their tag, admire the graffiti, or snap the crumbling husks.

Urban spelunkers have a particular fascination with abandoned hospitals and asylums, many built for the express treatment of a disease that no longer plagues us as it once did, or with a conception of treatment (read: discipline) since discarded. If forgetting is the goal, then wouldn't it be better to level and rebuild, or renovate into oblivion? These buildings, though cloaked in overgrowth, remind.

You can find those images online. There are so many of them. You can explore the fringes of your city or town and take them yourself. I don't know what they tell us beyond the fact that an adventurer, like so many before, trespassed to get a shot. They operate less as documentation than Gothic kitsch. The peeling paint, stained mattresses, and toppled wheelchairs conjure awful scenes. The dank hallways look perfect for ghosts. The histories and contexts of buildings left to rot—these are cropped out.

There's something obscene about that type of image making, which may be why it's likened to porn. Buildings stripped bare, objects without reference . . . In my photograph, there's less to "see," but I think the overgrowth tells a story—certainly, of our capacity to neglect, but also of how a person like me, in the present, should confer respect. People suffered in these buildings, and people died. The branches have grown thick to protect them.

There are other things I'm not showing you: the essential workers of today, in masks and scrubs, walking around the campus; the temporary morgue container, installed beside one of the buildings, that houses those lost to coronavirus.

What can we learn from past pandemics? So many of us are asking this question. The exercise can provide a measure of relief, helping us imagine a future when a vaccine is found or, failing that, one in which we learn to live with our stranger. Perhaps this is why I took the trip, and why the words you're reading I spoke out loud, into my phone, surrounded by the pavilions. This site can be folded. Creased just so, two pandemics touch. But if I had expected to find clarity, then I'm sorely mistaken. Here, there is nothing but overgrowth.

IMAGES

p. 264

Tyler Coburn, *Overgrowth*, 2020. Photo: the artist.

2020

Prepared Remarks

seventeen time capsules were sealed in 2020
today, they are due to be opened
and we will learn what their makers felt
should stay cloistered for the past twenty-five years

2045, on its face, is not an obvious choice
one can't cleanly divide a century into forty-five parts
a cake with forty-five candles triggers a midlife crisis
the only reason the year stands out is that
Ray Kurzweil, the former futurist
predicted an event called
"The Singularity"
when machines would make emphatic the fact that
we are nincompoops

"The Singularity" has not arrived
or if it did, we barely noticed
each year brings less novelty
and more obligations
to open the capsules that travel
very slowly
from the past
to treat the curios contained therein
as something more than junk
waiting, in sealed garbage cans
for future sanitation workers

when people make a capsule
they put their best foot forward
were we to judge the past only by this means
its humans would be elegance and erudition
millinery and religion, cosmetics and sober reflection
realism is the exception, reality a light suggestion
the capsule buried at Expo '70 in Osaka

was said to include a string of imitation pearls
reflecting the fact that the average Japanese woman of the time
couldn't afford the real thing
surely this distinction won't be lost
upon the beings tasked with opening it
in 6970

if we want to know how humans actually lived
we'd do better to visit a landfill
for the stories told through discarded effects
are far more revealing
the number of drinks you claim to have in a week
the actual pile of bottles
every blender and flexer and fad gadget
a testament to the churn of the capitalist machine
trash, our most durable medium
so stubbornly everywhere capsules are not
to dig for one is to find the other

the capsule is a modern phenomenon
dating back to 1876 when
a large iron safe
began a hundred-year journey
from Philadelphia to Philadelphia
before then, votive offerings were embedded in cornerstones
and hoards amassed to prepare for the afterlife
only through the ingenuity of Americans
were things hidden with the purpose of being retrieved

Plug-and-Play Ancestors

Kameelah Janan Rasheed

Time capsules occupy a specific place in collective and personal memory. In the 1990s, my siblings and I watched sitcoms in which high school students stow away objects for future societies to explore. Today, as we face uncertainty on all fronts, the emergence of certain technologies has expanded the concept of the time capsule: Where it was once a box from the 1990s that someone in 2025 opens, new developments, particularly in AI and biohacking, have enlarged the scope of what can be conserved, preserved, and reanimated for future use.

In the early 2000s, I developed a deep interest in the transhumanist movement and the kindred efforts to extend ecosystems, human life, and objects beyond the point of a "natural" end. These initiatives yielded proposals as varied as an Earth that can be rebooted after a civilization-ending event through an all-encompassing data file (see: Arch Mission); a body that can reverse age and persist well beyond life expectancy in excellent health (see: Bryan Johnson); a deceased family member you can communicate with through a deathbot programmed in their likeness (see: HereAfter); and an artwork so well conserved that future generations can view it in its "original form" as a stable object (see: museum conservation practices). Particularly weird are the post-Earth depositories that Arch Mission is sending to the moon, which encapsulate civilization in a series of discs for reboot.

Corporations have convinced us of many things, but my favorite fabulations are: a) that the nuances of humanity can be compressed into twenty-five nickel silver discs; b) that this can be done without the influence of contemporary bias; and c) that our version of humanity is worth the rerun or reboot. Humanity is not plug-and-play. I convinced myself that my not-so-casual obsession with efforts to stop, stabilize, and seduce time had to do with a fear of death and endings, and how such fear can be marketed back to us. While this is part of it, I find that I am most concerned with transgression and porosity—what it means to push beyond established limits and spill where you are not "supposed to." I think this is a question about how data lubricates transgression, or how our nearly religious faith in data, as embodied and comprehensive, normalizes the reanimation of people, places, and things that have met their "natural" end without ever consenting to such use.

While reading Mark Fisher's 2016 book *The Weird and the Eerie*, I stumbled across a reference to H.G. Wells's short story "The Door in the Wall," in which the narrator, Redmond, recounts incidents in the life of his friend Lionel Wallace.[1] At age five, Wallace, who lived under the watch of the nursery governess and a negligent father, goes through a green door set in a white wall and encounters an expansive garden, kind beasts, and joyful playmates, only to be thrust back out into a "grey" world. This leaves Wallace "haunted by something . . . that fills [him] with longings." As he resigns himself to the fact that he no longer has access to what Redmond calls "immortal realities," he experiences a sense of "ungovernable grief." This "ungovernable grief," one might imagine, leads to his death in adulthood: He enters an unfastened doorway for workmen; his body is later found in a deep excavation. As I read on, like a planchette roaming the Ouija board that is Fisher's book, my eyes yielded to a repeated word: *presence*. This felt not accidental but familiar, the repetition an invitation evoking Gertrude Stein's realization of "the inevitable repetition in human expression that [is] not repetition but insistence."[2] Ceding to this insistence, I wondered about what an ungovernable presence could be in the world of grief and death industries powered by machine learning—what scholars like James Hutson and Jay Ratican are calling "digital necromancy":

> the practice of using advanced technologies, such as artificial intelligence (AI) and robotics, to recreate or simulate the presence of deceased individuals or to interact with digital representations of their personalities. It involves harnessing data from various sources, including online profiles, voice recordings, images, and other digital artifacts, to construct virtual versions of individuals, enabling their continued existence in digital form.[3]

About five years ago, I wrote a funding proposal that drew connections between deathbots and zombies in Haitian folklore, who are reanimated to continue laboring, unpaid. As Sarah Juliet Lauro writes, the zombie emerges from African soul capture myths, and "in its earliest iteration, the *zombi* was read as symbolic of the Caribbean country's past as a plantation economy built on slave labor: drained of its own resources and existing only for the benefit of others."[4] At the time, I argued that reanimating the dead as chatbots or holograms to satisfy our desire for just one more chance with the deceased was akin to making a zombie.

Deathbots, or grief bots, are AI-powered chatbots designed to mimic the language, personality, and essence of deceased loved ones. To build these chatbots, all available and "processable" pre- and post-mortem material authored by the deceased is collected as a "corpus" and given over to a company that will clean and curate this data for use in training an LLM, or large language model. Following Colin Koopman, the deathbot can be understood as predicated on the rise of so-called informational persons. Citing Ian Hacking's research on confessional technologies in the scholarship of Michel Foucault—not unrelated to Maria Inigo Clavo's notion of "confessional ontology"[5]—Koopman notes that these have "brought a new kind of man into being, the man whose essence was plotted by a thousand numbers."[6]

Before deathbots, there was (and continues to be) ancestral communication—an embodied technology that does not seek to reanimate the dead so much as nurture an evolving relationship. Where a deathbot user may power up a chat client programmed with available data, a communication ritual might include reanimating corporeal data (as gesture, as repeated movement, as material juxtaposition) to engage with the dead. This is not an on-demand service. It is a labor-intensive relational practice that grants agency to both parties: The living can make the "call," and the ancestral spirit might respond—not instantly but in due time; not through predictable, concatenated text strings but in other ways. A Zulu practitioner and friend reminds me that when he burns *impepho*, the response is not immediate. Instead, the living must stay attuned to noise and signal, stretching our traditional perception practices. The response may eventually come as an event or in a dream.

What happens in ancestral communication cannot be replicated or captured, and this is where I think (some) power lies. In an essay I often cite,

"A Sea of Data: Apophenia and Pattern (Mis-)Recognition," Hito Steyerl discusses *dirty data*—that which is frequently "dismissed" due to redundancy, unintelligibility, or incompleteness.[7] She reminds us of a mythical story retold by Jacques Rancière about how the separation of signal and noise might have been engineered in Ancient Greece: "Sounds produced by affluent male locals were defined as speech, whereas women, children, slaves, and foreigners were assumed to produce garbled noise."[8] This distinction, she continues, serves as a "political spam filter": We hear, see, and acknowledge the signal and discard all else as "irrelevant, irrational, and potentially dangerous nuisances."[9] The data harvesting, curation, and training necessary for deathbots is its own form of "political spam filter." A system built on pattern recognition cannot make sense of divergence, while unintelligible bits, insider references, coded vernacular, non-Latin letters, and any extralinguistic reality are filtered out. But isn't the "content" of a life found precisely in the messy noise, rather than in immaculate and legible signals?

Artist Nolan Oswald Dennis describes the process of sifting through this noise as a kind of "precovery,"

> digging through residual data, the backgrounds of images and other superfluous material produced in the process of doing other, unrelated, astronomical work. Looking for as-yet-unperceived objects in existing observations. Reprocessing noise to locate signals which were always already there, in what [Fred] Moten calls, our "supersensible and nonsensical surround." Surrounded. In a perception space overdetermined by the fact of observation—the regulation of apparition—precovery suggests the necessity of an alter-perceptive programme.[10]

This practice, albeit a delayed reverence for noise, reminds me that some of the best things in life are hidden from us and from datafication. The "alter-perceptive programme" Dennis calls for requires a demythologizing of certainty and capture. It also requires a different relationship to time, according to which returning to the past to (re)look is an expansion of the future.

Deathbots, I fear, freeze us in time. They can trap the dead in narrative loops and lock the living into terraformed realities. Deathbots are optimized to filter out the noise and create a cradle of comfort and predictability. This keeps customers returning but alienates us from the process of grief, which is inconvenient, messy, and unpredictable. Grief is a learning process. What are the pedagogical values that animate the deathbot? What sort of relational politics is this deathbot designed to exhibit? What habits and beliefs are formed with the use of deathbots? These are questions we must ask of any knowledge and memory management tool that promises to collect and categorize everything we encounter, automate efficient retrieval, and predict future collection choices. In an increasingly on-demand culture, a deathbot may become yet another optimization service—we count the books we read, the miles we've run, the meals we've cooked, and now we can clock "productive" hours with our deathbot, making grieving efficient so we can get back to work more quickly, and expediting healing so we can microdose death counseling in fifteen-minute high-intensity sessions between meetings.

1. Mark Fisher, *The Weird and the Eerie* (London: Repeater Books, 2016). See also H.G. Wells, "The Door in the Wall," *Daily Chronicle*, July 14, 1906.

2. Gertrude Stein, "Portraits and Repetition," *Lectures in America* (Boston: Beacon Press, 1957 [1935]), 168.

3. James Hutson and Jay Ratican, "Life, Death, and AI: Exploring Digital Necromancy in Popular Culture—Ethical Considerations, Technological Limitations, and the Pet Cemetery Conundrum," *Faculty Scholarship* (2023): 1–2. https://digitalcommons.lindenwood.edu/faculty-research-papers/478.

4. Sarah Juliet Lauro, introduction to *Zombie Theory: A Reader*, ed. Sarah Juliet Lauro (Minneapolis: University of Minnesota Press, 2017), x.

5. See Maria Inigo Clavo, "Traces, Signs, and Symptoms of the Untranslatable," *e-flux journal*, no. 118 (April 2020), https://www.e-flux.com/journal/108/325859/traces-signs-and-symptoms-of-the-untranslatable/.

6. Ian Hacking, *The Taming of Chance* (Cambridge: Cambridge University Press, 2006 [1990]), 34, cited in Colin Koopman, *How We Became Our Data: A Genealogy of the Informational Person* (Chicago: University of Chicago Press, 2019), 15.

7. Hito Steyerl, "A Sea of Data: Apophenia and Pattern (Mis-)Recognition," *e-flux journal*, no. 72 (April 2016), https://www.e-flux.com/journal/72/60480/a-sea-of-data-apophenia-and-pattern-mis-recognition.

8. Jacques Rancière, "Ten Theses on Politics," trans. Rachel Bowlby and Davide Panagia, *Theory & Event* 5, no. 3 (2001), https://dx.doi.org/10.1353/tae.2001.0028.

9. Steyerl, "A Sea of Data."

10. Nolan Oswald Dennis, "Throwers (space-rock notes pt. 1)," *Serpentine Reader*, no. 1, February 26, 2025, https://www.serpentinegalleries.org/reader/issues/issue-1/.

2016–

Ergonomic Futures

In the beginning, there's a model—specifically, there's the tree. Sometimes it grows upward from root to tip; sometimes the branches get longer with each generation, like the neck of a giraffe; sometimes they sprout leaves of as many kinds as there are beaks of a finch; sometimes the tree is cut, and on its stump are the intricate veins I'm told are us; and sometimes it's allowed to grow in the most novel ways, the branches feeding back into other parts of tree, building you, me, and every eukaryote we know.

Sometimes the tree isn't a tree but a chain, which once hung all the way from heaven to hell—which was intimately known by our ancestors, for it held them in perfect harmony. Everything was linked in the chain, even the ugly stone, the treacherous snake, and the louse. Nothing was an error of creation, because everything had a place.

The trouble came with the human, who occupied a sensitive link between heaven and earth. Here was a creature whose wit and will distinguished him from his fellow animals, yet a creature substantially less perfect than even the stupidest angel. Surely God hadn't erred in designing the chain. Surely everything had a place. Surely, the scholars of the Enlightenment reasoned, it was the Elizabethans who had drawn the chain wrong—who left out links between humans and angels, to be filled not by the creatures of the known world, but by those from other planets: suprahuman, sub-angelic beings.

Unlike the extraterrestrials of the present age, those of the Enlightenment weren't foreign to humankind. They fit hand in glove with its logics.

A few years ago, a group of alien "believers" approached Shara Bailey, an anthropologist at NYU working on the dental morphology of early humans. They claimed to have found an ancient jaw, and they were pretty certain that it belonged to an extraterrestrial . . .

Shara agreed to talk with the television reporter covering the story. She said something to the effect of: "In my professional opinion, this jaw is a fake. There's nothing on earth that looks like this." Well, Shara's first sentence was cut from the segment, so she'll forever be remembered by the "believer" community as the scientist who said, on broadcast television: "There's nothing on earth that looks like this."

Shara told me this story a while back, when I visited her office. I had originally reached out because I wanted her to imagine a scenario, at some point between now and the bitter end of the universe, when our bodies experience such a degree of evolutionary change that the biological, ontological, and legal criteria of the human come undone—when we undergo speciation.

In Shara's opinion, outside of genetic engineering, the only way we'll see drastic change is if humankind fragments into groups, isolated by geography, culture, or ideology. Owing to their limited scale, each group would experience low genetic variation, meaning that over generations, recessive traits would have the possibility of becoming prominent.

This phenomenon is often known as the "founder effect," suggesting that the founders of a given community can have a huge influence on its gene pool.

There are a few famous cases of the "founder effect":

There are the Amish, who suffer from Ellis-van Creveld Syndrome. This syndrome wreaks havoc on the skeletal system, causing dwarfism and cleft palates, and growing extra fingers and toes.

There is a famous community in the Dominican Republic in which most of the children are born female. Around the age of twelve, some develop penises and become—biologically and culturally—boys.

There are the "Blue Fugates," a family that has lived in Kentucky since the 1820s, near the towns of Hazard and Troublesome Creek Times. The founders of the Fugates were Martin and Elizabeth, who shared a rare genetic disorder. Their blood produced a surplus of hemoglobin that couldn't release oxygen into the body, thus turning their skin blue. As Martin and Elizabeth lived in geographical isolation, their condition spread over generations . . . The human equivalent of the Smurf clan was born.

One of the Blue Fugates showed his family tree to a reporter. "You'll notice," he remarked, that "I'm kin to myself."

Baby

Sometimes a tree isn't a tree but a chain. And sometimes a chain is a chart, its links compressed into tiny statistical points where the beggar, the ignorant, and the deaf—where every human has a place.

The stone, the louse, and the snake can live on the charts of a different field. For social statisticians of the nineteenth century like Adolphe Quetelet, the chain is a human chain, the coil a human coil, its length stretched not from heaven to earth but curved around an invisible bell and centered on "the average man."

Who is "the average man"? His figure, his face? How is life lived on the fiftieth percentile? It's strange to speak of an empirical fiction, but this human surely was one. Every time Quetelet added data to the chart, his "average man" grew less lifelike and less precise.

There were some other problems with Quetelet's model, particularly for members of the nascent eugenics movement. For one, the bell curve made "the average man" the norm. The scope of deviation thus included both the shorter and the taller, the dumber and the smarter, the browner and the whiter. To remedy this spread, the eugenicist Francis Galton reimagined the norm to be less a statistical "reality" than an aspiration: a want for social betterment, for selective breeding, for a kingdom of the taller, the smarter, and the whiter . . .

"The average man" was one of the nineteenth century's many hallucinations; Galton's composite portraits were among the most notorious. In these images, a different empirical fiction is on display: Three, five, sometimes nine portraits of criminals have been merged to reveal their common facial traits—to expose the fundamental likeness of "the criminal type."

Digital technology could intensify this technique—pixel by pixel, layer upon infinite layer—but alas, composite photography is a thing of the past: another tombstone in the graveyard of pseudoscience. The norm no longer lives on the surface of images but deep in the grain of the self.

The Human Genome Project, according to David Serlin, is also a composite: an empirical fiction that invents norms from a genome in constant change. Donna J. Haraway has called it a "standard reference work" that purports to tame the unruly diversity of our species by the sheer power of exhaustive code.

By sequencing our genes, we follow in the footsteps of Adolphe Quetelet. We add data to "the average man." We observe the scope of deviation. But to engineer the perfect human, we have to move in Francis Galton's direction. Galton had to rework Quetelet's bell curve in justifying eugenic practices. Genetics, in turn, must strive to do more than plot and measure our genome. To engineer the perfect human—to incubate a designer baby—it must rid our genome of its every last fault.

From 2015 to 2016, I approached a number of people, like I approached Shara, and I posed the same question: Is it possible, somewhere between now and the suspension of everything, for our bodies to experience such a degree of evolutionary change that the biological, ontological, and legal criteria of the human come undone—when the human, as we know it, fragments or even ceases to exist?

I wanted to know how a designer would answer this question, so I called Jonathan Olivares, who wrote the 2011 book *A Taxonomy of Office Chairs*. Jonathan remarked that evolutionary change can't be envisaged in a vacuum. We need to consider the geographical, cultural, and ideological qualities of a community, as Shara had said. We need to study the broader environment. We also need to look to design—and particularly, to ergonomics. These are fields that can respond to the practical needs of the human. Moreover, they can prescribe and evolve those needs.

Ergonomics is a young discipline—a child of the Taylorist years, when its main task was to increase the efficiency of the working body: to minimize wasteful movements; to keep the eye trained on its machine; to quicken the pace of materials as they raced toward the market. We know ergonomics better in its modern sense, popularized in Henry Dreyfuss's 1955 book *Designing for People*. Dreyfuss's ergonomics focuses on enhancing the comfort of the human body in the workplace and beyond. The more comfortable a worker feels—at his seat, within his machine—the more productive he will be.

Dreyfuss was an interesting figure. In his early career, he designed theater sets in New York, which led to a commission for the 1939 World's Fair to create Democracity, a diorama in the round that scaled democracy to the size of a future city. This was a Greenfield City par excellence, where each and every resident could enjoy a garden apartment, a bucolic view, the landscaped highway to his job downtown, the landscaped highway for a swift retreat. Democracity claimed to depict the world in a hundred years' time, though suburbia arrived much sooner.

In the sixteen years between Democracity and *Designing for People*, Dreyfuss zoomed in from his Greenfield City to the intimate lives of its users—from utopian theater to the intricacies of ergonomics.

The protagonists of *Designing for People* are "Joe and Josephine": paragons of mid-century American gender. Joe can be found working on a linotype or in a tank, and Josephine over an ironing table, or at the switchboard.

Ergonomics didn't limit itself to templates like Joe and Josephine. Books from that era include design for the elderly and disabled, for children and the obese, for the standard US male body of Black, white, and Japanese descent—for the standard US female body of the same provenance. Their diagrams appear to be more complicated than the charts of Adolphe Quetelet, but don't mistake what they share. The norm has gone granular, yet "the average man" persists. The visuals change. The tendency to typologize remains the same.

Church

I approached Shara and Jonathan. And still, the question remained: Is it possible, sometime between now and oblivion, that our bodies experience such a degree of evolutionary change that the biological, ontological, and legal criteria of the human come undone—that the kernel of anthropocentric egotism is ground down beyond repair?

I took my question to Seth Shipman, a fellow in geneticist George Church's lab. Seth and I discussed the 2014 symposium "Genetics and Society," where Church claimed to have found the genes that should be modified to make the human body survive better in "extraterrestrial environments": modifications to give us extra-strong bones, lean muscles, and lower cancer risk.

Taking Church's human to its historical precedent, we arrive at a 1960 NASA research proposal that imagines a human perfectly adapted to space—who can live in "space qua natura." This human, according to the authors, could breathe without lungs and spacewalk without suits.

What this required were exogenous devices: fuel cells to replace the lungs, intravenous feeding tubes to save the labor of mastication. Pressure pumps would be injected beneath the skin, triggering drug infusions to stave off the ravaging effects of radiation. When these mechanisms functioned effectively, they'd be so integrated into their user as to operate "unconsciously."

When they didn't function effectively, the human was presumed to be the problem. In such cases, drug infusions could be triggered from Houston or by a fellow crew member. For nearly every conceivable problem, drugs were the obvious solution.

NASA's model astronaut was a human freed from the limits of biology yet bound by imperfect devices and doped to ease the pain of those imperfections—doped to palliate the anxieties of being haplessly invaded by the future. To describe this new human, the authors invented a term: "cyborg."

Chimera

Sometimes a tree isn't a tree but a chain. And sometimes a chain is a chart, left outside for so long that when found again, it's yellowed and tattered: pieces missing, pieces torn. The perfect model is beyond our reach, and what's left are oddities, embarrassments, and chimeric monstrosities.

The chimeras of lore had lions for heads, goats for bodies, and snakes for tails. Sometimes, they had the claws of dragons; sometimes, glorious manes; always, mouths filled with fire that imperiled any who stood too close.

Chimeras are still among us, though we can scarcely distinguish them from the rest. Chimeras can even live in human guise, unaware of their fearsome gifts.

Consider Lydia Fairchild. By chance, two of her mother's eggs fused before insemination, causing Fairchild to be born with forty-six chromosomes, or two DNA signatures. Unbeknownst to her, Fairchild was multiple people.

This fact finally came to light in the early 2000s. Fairchild applied for public assistance, which required her and her children to take DNA tests. The results revealed that Fairchild was not the mother of her children, leading the state to suspect that she was attempting welfare fraud.

Eventually, an additional DNA test was given to a baby that Fairchild *had just birthed*—again, with the same results. And so, the odd but correct conclusion was finally reached: that Fairchild was both the mother and the aunt of her children.

Fairchild's case illuminates a larger trend, as personal testimony is losing credibility against genetic evidence. The latter, according to Aaron T. Norton and Ozzie Zehner, amounts to a "technological confession" for someone like Fairchild "through a privileged objectification of her biological attributes."

Though genetics is usually credited as being objective, there are some telling exceptions. Recent years have seen cases of transgender parents who have a genetic relationship to their children yet find their parental rights nullified for not matching their original sex.

What this example reveals is that, far from being an objective force in contemporary jurisprudence, genetics is selectively deemed to be objective when it aids and abets social norms, affirming traditionalist thinking about identity and parenthood.

Sometimes you judge a book by its content, though usually you just glance at the cover.

Great Chain

The Great Chain wasn't the invention of the Elizabethans but the Greeks: less a chain at first than the product of paranoia, not a model of anything but the madness of Zeus. It dates back to the Trojan War, when the gods were vying to stack the decks—to be far more than bystanders to glorious war. Zeus responded with a warning: Any gods who played a role in the war would suffer no less a fate than exile. And any attempt to overthrow his authority would be tantamount to folly. He was too powerful to budge.

Say the gods latched a chain to the heavens in an effort to yank him down. Well, Zeus would simply pick it up, give it a tug, and the rebel gods, their earthly minions, *the entire carnal world*, would be flung through the cosmos to an untimely end. With a mere twist of his finger, Zeus could take control of the chain: as a weapon, a keepsake, a necklace for the peak of Olympus.

Zeus never acted on this threat, but his gauntlet kept hanging. With each passing era, it grew ever more like a chain. The natural world took a liking to this object. Creatures began to clamber up and take shelter in its links. By all accounts, they loved the altitude and the elliptical life.

Gods come and go, and still the chain keeps hanging. Trees have sprung up around it, but if we look closely, we can see it: a weathered thing, more rust than metal; a testament to all we've forgotten to remember—to the worlds of old epistemologies, to the aliens of the Enlightenment.

At some point, the future may reclaim this chain:

For the ugly stone, the cyborg, the deaf, and the telepath to join together in lasting congress.

For designer babies to have a trinket that reminds them of the world before human perfection.

For mechanical overlords to ensnare the last vestiges of earthly life, pulling chain links around necks as a hangman would.

For the founders of space colonies to climb their way to the stars—to spread their genetic stock throughout this galaxy and the next.

For citizens to have a cautionary tale of what comes from living within empirical fictions written by models, charts, and norms.

Whatever purpose the chain will hold for those to come, it will keep hanging.

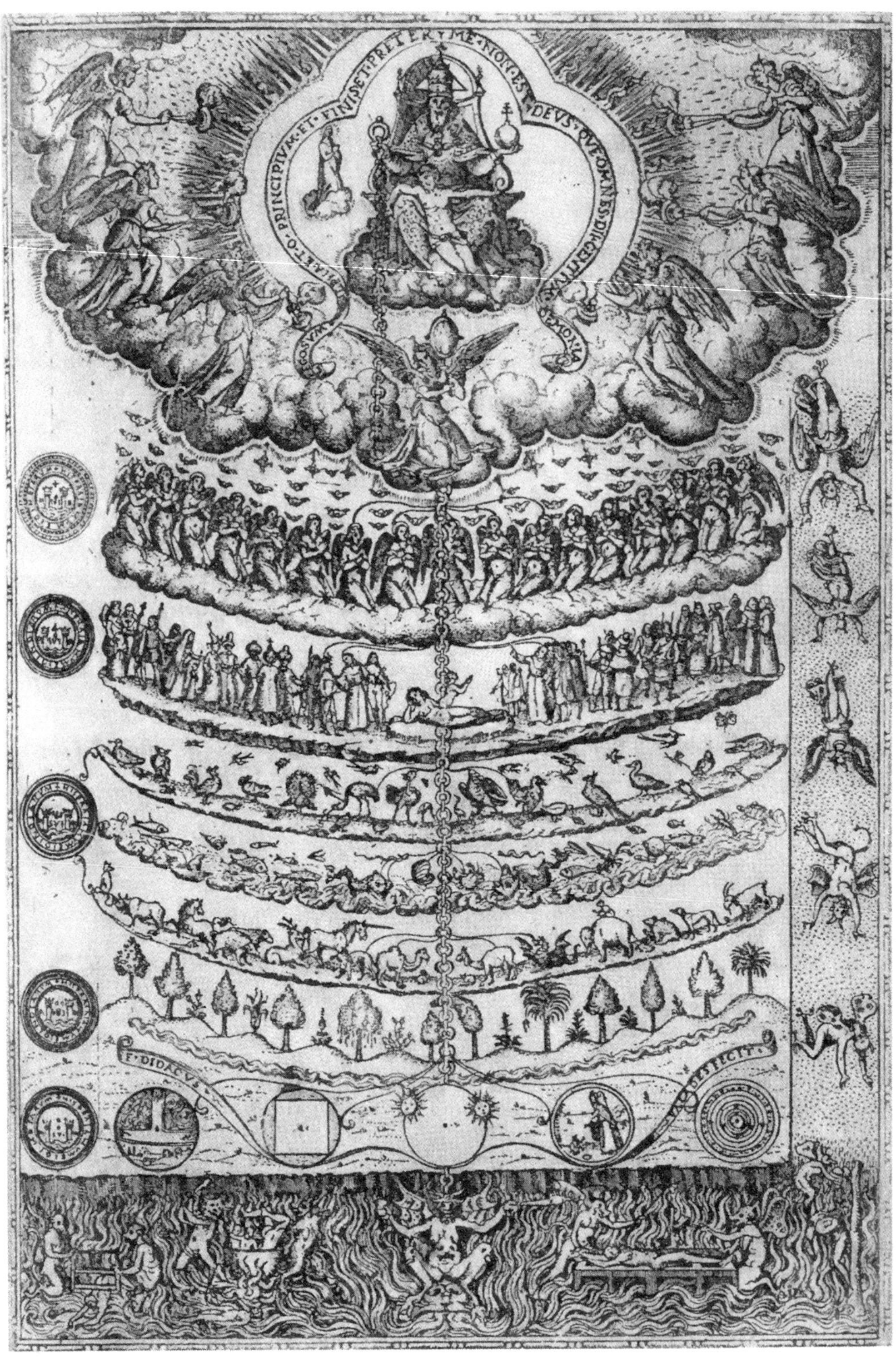

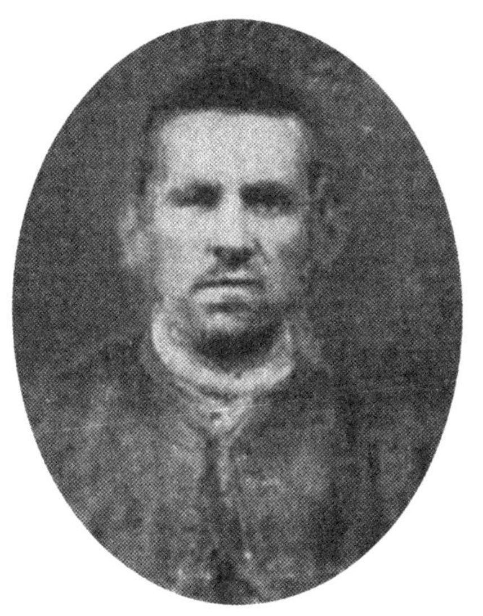

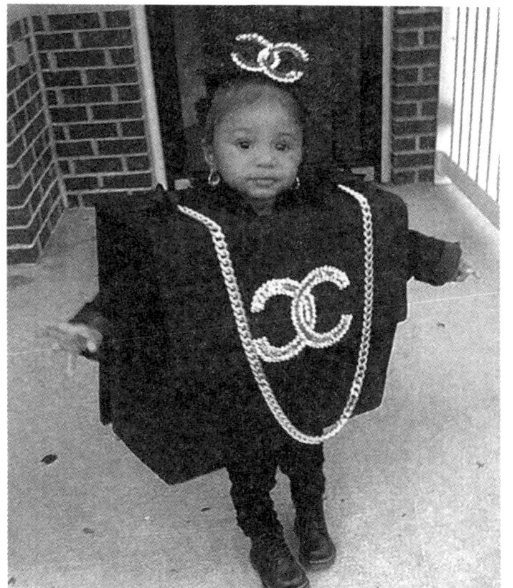

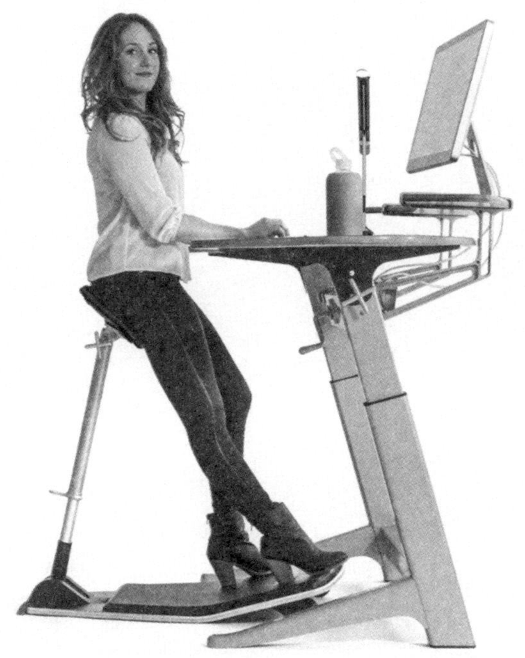

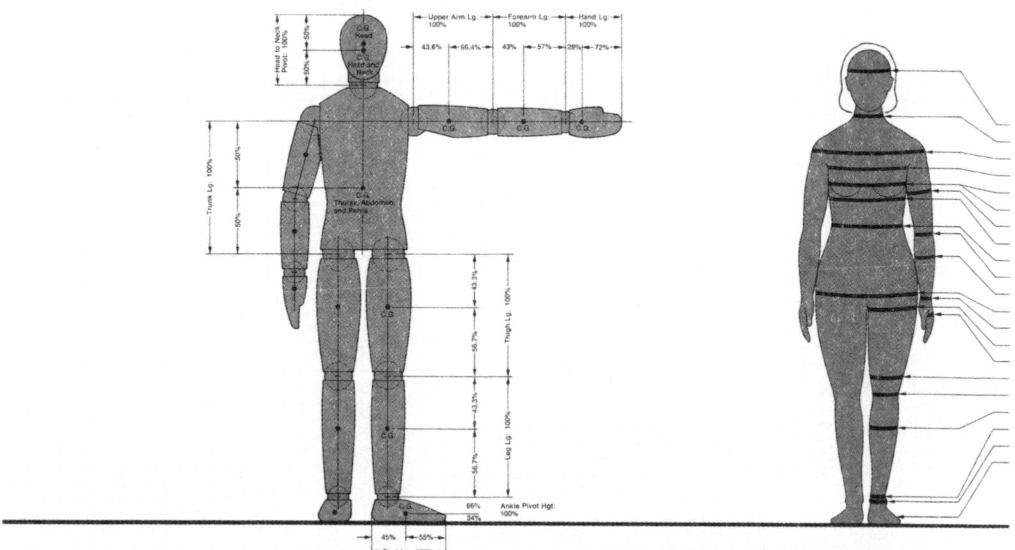

Head to Neck Pivot: 100%
50%
50%
C.G. Head
C.G. Head and Neck
Upper Arm Lg.: 100%
Forearm Lg.: 100%
Hand Lg.: 100%
43.6%
56.4%
43%
57%
28%
72%
C.G.
C.G.
C.G.
Trunk Lg.: 100%
50%
50%
C.G. Thorax, Abdomen, and Pelvis
43.3%
56.7%
Thigh Lg.: 100%
C.G.
43.3%
56.7%
Leg Lg.: 100%
C.G.
C.G.
66%
34%
Ankle Pivot Hgt: 100%
45%
55%
Foot Lg.: 100%

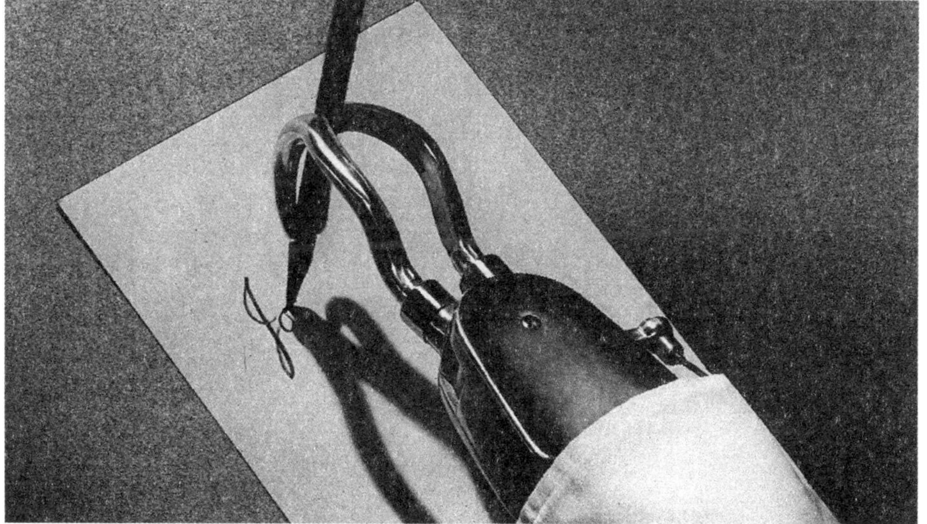

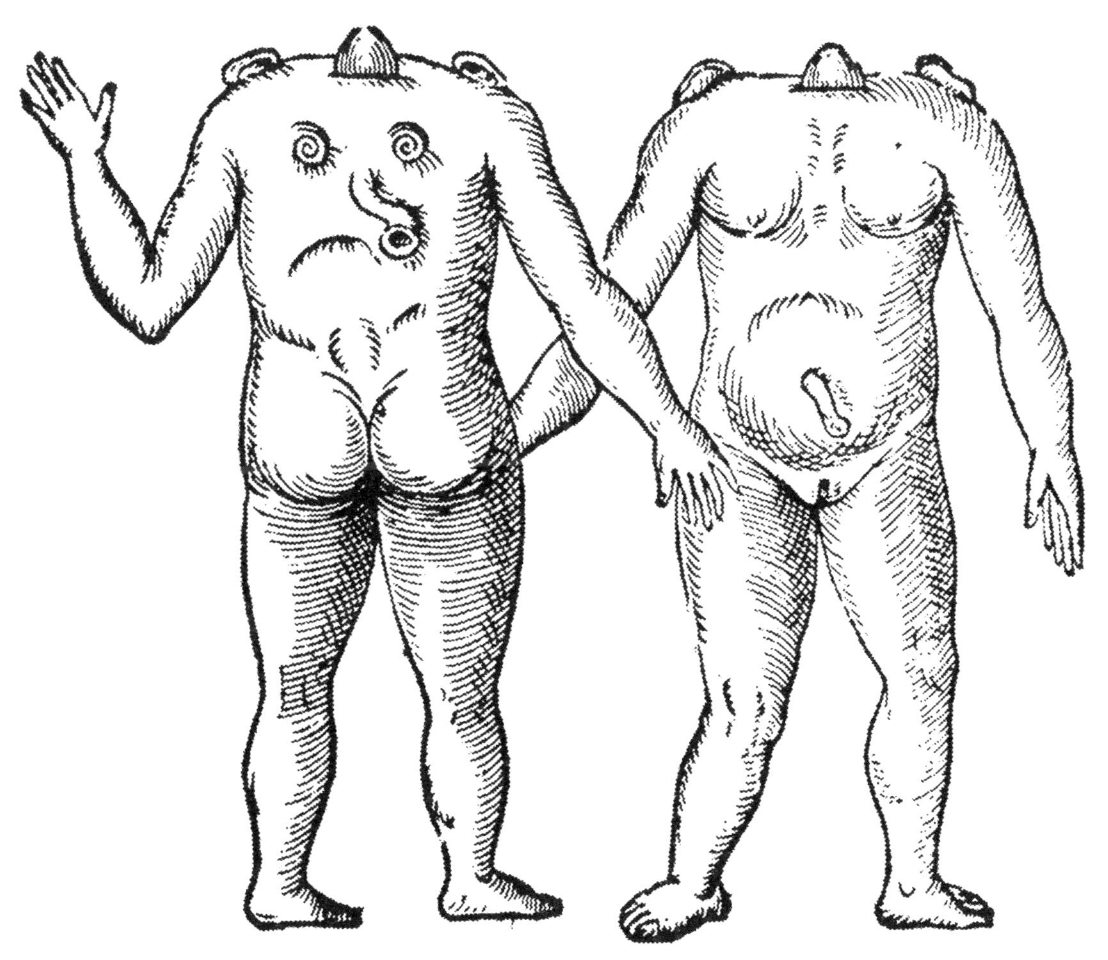

i am sleepy

Théo Robine-Langlois

My four limbs are going in every direction

i don't see any clear differences
between my hands and my feet
my shoulders and my knees
here & there
it's a bit hard for me to move around
i just do it like a snake
or a snail
i'm sweating
wetting the floor
i feel the ground
sometimes accidents in the construction elevate me
i am always sleepy
here & there
but when one of my siblings
puts my hands or my feet on someone's wound
it heals them
i depend on my siblings to feed me
with a lot of melon & tomato juice
i am connected
not as you think
but with those you know
everybody you know
an infinite repertoire
i hear their voices
not in my head
but in my body
constant vibrations
that's why i am always sleepy
melon & tomato juice
i am exhausted
i can't stand
i am always on the floor
i have no awareness of time
it's a bit embarrassing
for my relations
for my relatives
to meet them
in proper conditions
it's hard for me to remember
dead & alive
precisely when an event took place
a constant present
a constant vibration
a bug
here & there
a buzz
i feel sometimes
that my body is big
not too big
but some parts of it
are not very well articulated to the others
because of their size
so i have to be careful

t is two seat a seat is a seat is two seat a seat is a seat is two seat a seat is a seat is two seat a seat is a seat is two seat a seat is a seat is two seat a seat is a seat is two seat a seat is

as i move
not to disarticulate myself
not to lose myself
i have some difficulty using my body
here & there
that's why i am always lying
in order to exist
i need to be two
not only to have a discussion
but to stay alive
someone needs to help me move
with délicatesse
to keep breathing
as i am constantly asleep
i am calm
my body is weak
and i feel it
as i discover the world, slowly
here & there
i find a special object
i wrap myself
around this form
someone can sit with me
we can have a conversation
not with words
but between two bodies connected to each other
smoothies & bubble teas
even during our dreams
around our new nest
some artefacts
activating our thoughts
even if we can't see them
because we are looking at the ceiling
feeling the same things
or feeling the void behind
the difference between us and the next solid object
we feel it the same way
so we are here
vibing around
a fusional relationship
not only between us
but between two bodies and the world
here & there
spreading our toxicity
inhalation & exhalation
absorbing polluted air
air conditioning
filtered particles
floating
unfortunately none of us are able to feed ourselves
a bad alliance
a lack of strategy
dead & alive
two dysfunctional bodies
so what we do now
what we do
in order to survive
is to drink smoothies & bubble teas

o seat a seat is a seat is two seat a seat is a seat is two seat a seat is a seat is a seat is two seat a seat is a seat is a seat is two seat a seat is a seat is two seat a seat is a seat is two seat a seat is a seat

i try to call my siblings
in my head
cheap telepathy
but they're all gone
they have others things to do
maybe we can separate our bodies
let some limbs wander by themselves
and get some food
or at least something to drink
we don't need that much
as we are always sleepy zzzzzzzzzzzzzzzzzzzzzzzz here & there
low energy consumption
we can also attract other providers
with our fancy outfits
ugly colors and baroque garments
new haircuts
discreet seduction
then go back to our dreams
full, satisfied, content
we smell the past around us
and even if a leg or an arm is missing
we don't need to be complete
to think
and move without moving
we need only to stay in the same place
so sleepy zzzzzzzzzzzzzzzzzzzzzzzz here & there
eyes wide
hooked by the fictions we hear
sometimes we loan each other our limbs
if needed
we stay in this little island we inhabit
we talk about a hypothetical separation
we study every angle of our relationship
sometimes we even separate for real
but we are always coming back
slowly zzzzzzzzzzzzzzzzzzzzzzzz dead & alive
to our sleepy situation
my body is your body is a body zzzzzzzzzzzzzzzzzzzzzzzz here & there
blah blah blah blah blah blah blah
the old people of our village
sit on benches
constantly commenting on the world
they know exactly what everyone is doing
just by looking at the passing cars
it's a lot
but something is missing
we never learn how to deal with the end
the information we get keeps us unlimited
so we look for sensible frontlines
in our interwined nightmares
feelings of ubiquity
time synchronicity
physical fragmentation
dead & alive

eat a seat is a seat is two seat a seat is a seat is two seat a seat is a seat is two seat a seat is a seat is two seat a seat is a my body is your body is a body my body is your body i

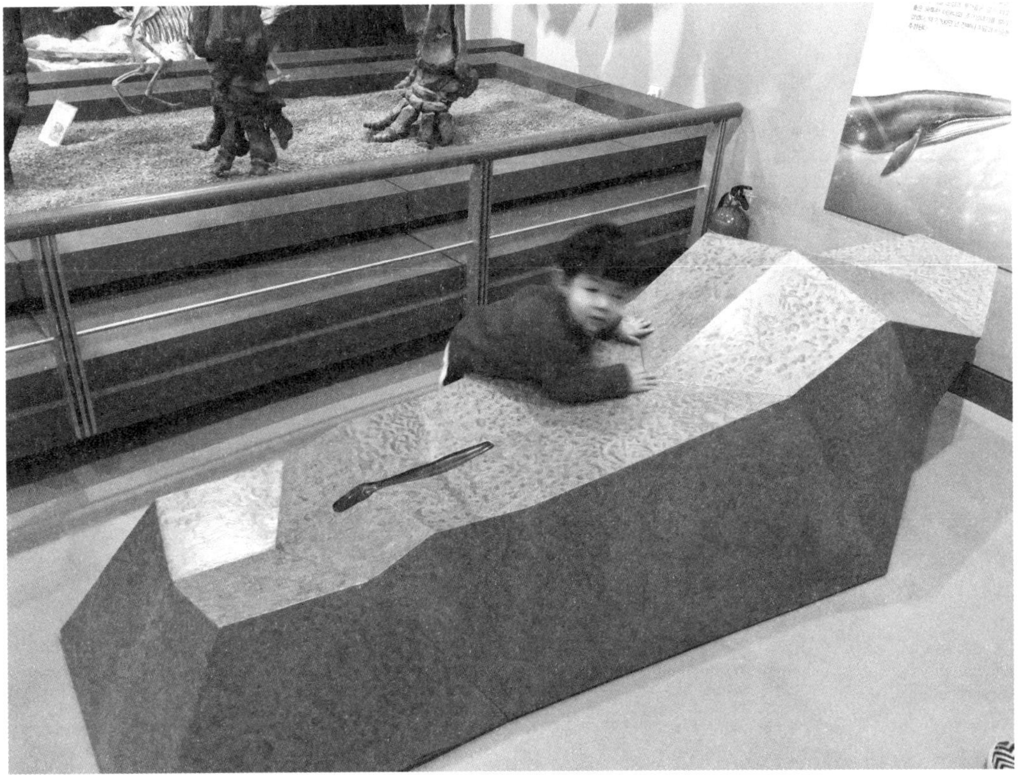

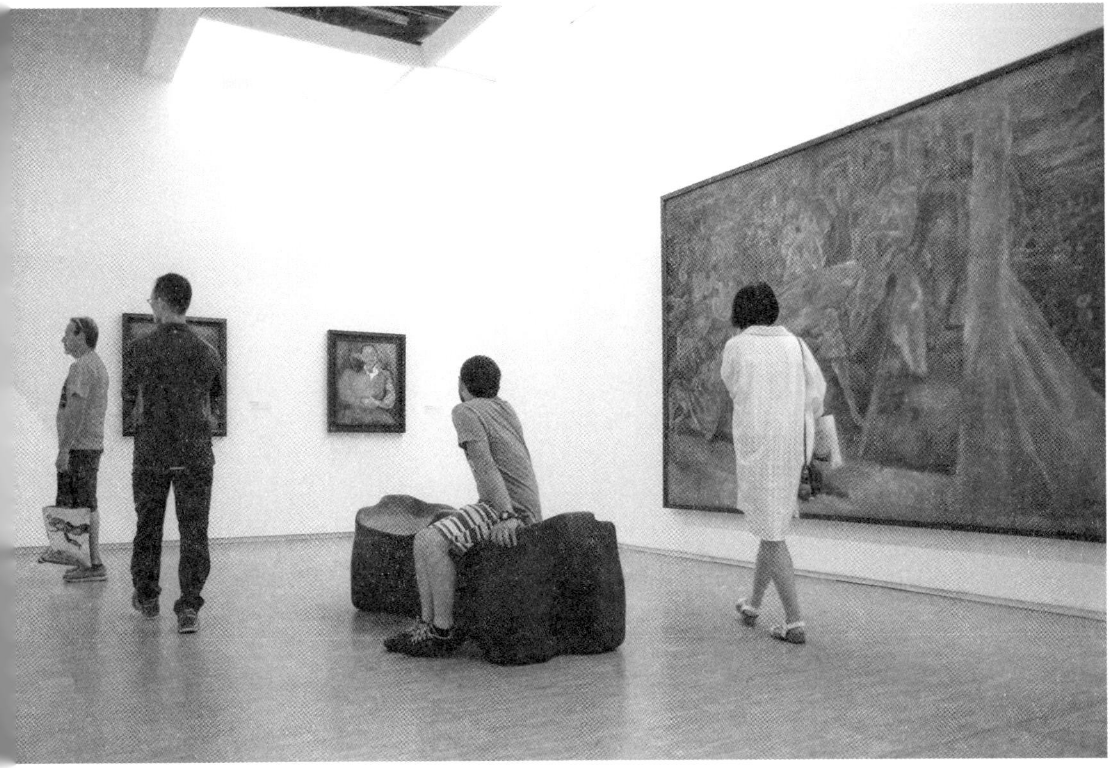

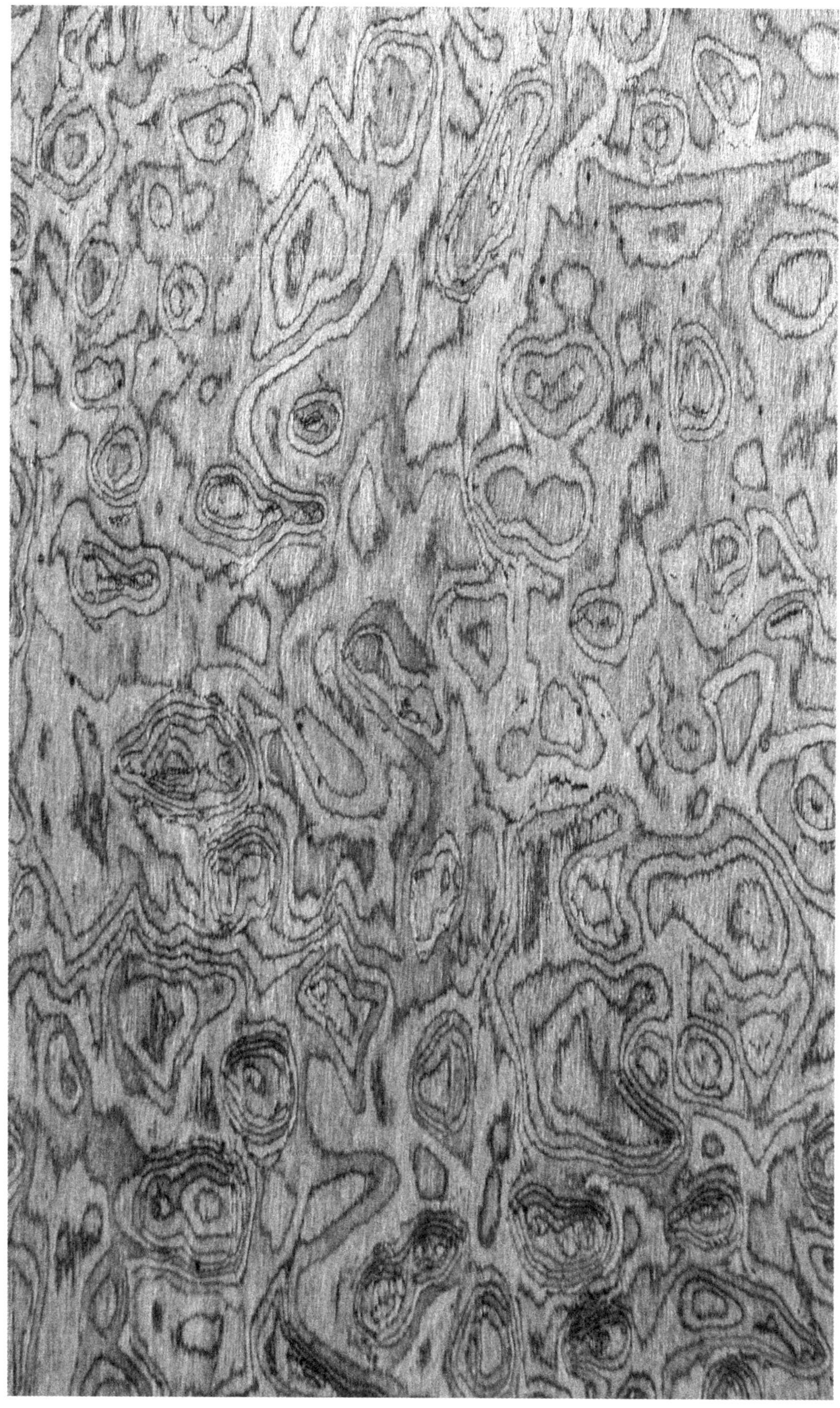

Chang, Kenneth. "Beings Not Made for Space." *New York Times*, January 27, 2014.

Clynes, Manfred E., and Nathan S. Kline. "Cyborgs and Space." *Astronautics* 5, no. 9 (September 1960): 26–27, 74–76.

Davis, Lennard J., ed. *The Disability Studies Reader*, 2nd ed. New York: Routledge, 2006.

———. "The End of Identity Politics and the Beginning of Dismodernism: On Disability as an Unstable Category." In Davis, *The Disability Studies Reader*, 231–42.

Dreyfuss, Henry. *Designing for People*. New York: Simon and Schuster, 1955.

Egan, Gabriel. "Gaia and the Great Chain of Being." *Ecocritical Shakespeare*, edited by Lynne Bruckner and Daniel Brayton. Farnham, UK: Ashgate, 2011.

Friedman, Lauren F. "The Stranger-Than-Fiction Story of a Woman Who Was Her Own Twin." *Business Insider*, February 2, 2014. http://www.businessinsider.com/lydia-fairchild-is-her-own-twin-2014-2.

Fudge, Erica. "How a Man Differs from a Dog." *History Today* 53, no. 6 (June 2003): 38–44.

Galton, Francis. "Generic Images." In *Notices of the Proceedings at the Meetings of the Members of the Royal Institution of Great Britain*, vol. 9, *1879–1881* (London: William Clowes and Sons, 1882).

Gelertner, David. *1939: The Lost World of the Fair*. New York: Free Press, 1995.

Church, George. "The Future of Human Genomics and Synthetic Biology." Lecture, September 19, 2014. Posted October 29, 2014, by Genetic Engineering and Society Center. YouTube, 28:24, https://www.youtube.com/watch?v=0E0a5ZaE6Gk.

Haraway, Donna J. *Simians, Cyborgs, and Women: The Reinvention of Nature*. New York: Routledge, 1991.

Knapton, Sarah. "The Astonishing Village Where Little Girls Turn into Boys Aged 12." *Telegraph*, September 20, 2015. http://www.telegraph.co.uk/science/2016/03/12/the-astonishing-village-where-little-girls- turn-into-boys-aged-1/.

National Space Biomedical Research Institute, "The Body in Space." http://nsbri.org/the-body-in-space.

Norton Aaron T., and Ozzie Zehner. "Which Half Is Mommy? Tetragametic Chimerism and Trans- Subjectivity." *Women's Studies Quarterly* 36, no. 3–4 (Fall–Winter 2008): 106–125.

Provine, W.B. "Ernst Mayr: Genetics and Speciation." *Genetics* 167, no. 3 (July 2004): 1041–46.

Sekula, Allan. "The Body and the Archive." *October* 39 (Winter 1986): 3–64

Serlin, David. "The Other Arms Race." In Davis, *The Disability Studies Reader*, 67–75.

Stephenson, Neal. *Seveneves*. New York: William Morrow, 2015.

Templeton, A.R. "The Theory of Speciation Via the Founder Principle." *Genetics* 94, no. 4 (April 1980): 1011–38.

Tillyard, E. M. W. *The Elizabethan World Picture*. New York: Vintage Books, 1959.

Trost, Cathy. "The Blue People of Troublesome Creek." *Science* 82 (November 1982).

IMAGES

p. 300

Illustration of "The Great Chain of Being" from Didacus Valadés Fecit, *Rhetorica Christiana* (1579).

p. 301

Francis Galton's composite portraits of criminals. Plate XXVII from Karl Pearson, *The Life, Letters and Labours of Francis Galton*, vol. 2 (London: Cambridge University Press, 1924).

Photograph from Pinterest, accessed October 1, 2016, https://www.pinterest.com/pin/422281208998702/.

Photograph of "Focal Upright Sphere Bundle Pro," from the website Standing Desk Nation, accessed September 14, 2016, https://www.standingdesknation.com/products/focal-upright-sphere-bundle-pro

p. 303

Illustration from Niels Diffrient, et. al., *Humanscale 7/8/9: A Portfolio of Information* (Cambridge, MA: MIT Press, 1981).

Photograph from Henry Dreyfuss, *Designing for People* (New York: Simon and Schuster, 1955).

p. 305

Illustration from Ambroise Paré, *On Monsters and Marvels*, trans. Janis L. Pallister (Chicago: Chicago University Press, 1983). Originally published in 1573.

p. 311

Tyler Coburn, *Ergonomic Futures*, 2016–. Installation view, Seodaemun Museum of Natural History, Seoul. Photo: Doosung Baek.

Tyler Coburn, *Ergonomic Futures*, 2016–. Installation view, Centre Pompidou, Paris. Photo: the artist.

p. 313

Tyler Coburn, *Ergonomic Futures*, 2016–. Installation detail, 11th Gwangju Biennale, Gwangju, 2016. Photo: the artist.

About *Some Monologues*

I'M THAT ANGEL, 2011–

Book written to be read aloud in data centers, tour, lecture, essay
pp. 13–60

I'm that angel is the story of a "content farmer": an online journalist contracted to generate articles based on words peaking in Google Trends. The project takes four forms.

First, it mashes quotes, trending language, anecdotes, notes, and rants into a book. Paraliterary, confessional, and epistolary modes rub up against online vernaculars. The writing style might be best described as *inattentional*.

Second, in an effort to disenchant the seeming groundlessness of "the cloud," readings of the book often occur in data centers, followed by facility tours led by employees. What results is an uncanny experience in which audience members encounter the material doubles of their online selves in the form of data servers.

Finally, as a "postscript" to this ongoing project, a lecture and essay describe the themes of the book, the state of content farming and cloud computing, and various things that happened during readings and tours at data centers.

Credits

I'm that angel, book published by the artist, 2011
Designed by Eric Nylund and edited by Jeffrey K. Miller

First readings by Justin Sayre at California Point of Presence, Los Angeles, April 9–12, 2012, as Coburn's MFA thesis at the USC Roski School of Fine Arts, Los Angeles; by Coburn at Bahnhof, Stockholm, May 27, 2013, in collaboration with the Visions of the Now festival

"Postscript on *I'm that angel*," lecture first delivered at Koenig & Clinton, New York, October 2, 2013

"My Life in the Cloud," essay published on *Motherboard*, September 22, 2015, https://www.vice.com/en/article/my-life-in-the-cloud

A. E. Benenson, Excerpt from "Order_30763_6," July 2013. Courtesy of the author

NATURALLYSPEAKING, 2013–2015

Text, screensaver, monitors, furniture, floor paint, performance by Susan Bennett (the original voice of Siri)
pp. 61–93

NaturallySpeaking uses the training copy of Macintosh speech recognition software to retell famous stories of the voice, from Edison's attempt to make his phonograph replay every sound in the history of the world to the robotic dogs and chatbots of early AI, and the scene in Rabelais's *Gargantua and Pantagruel* when the warming air thaws the frozen sounds of a past battle.

Since its inception, this project has taken multiple forms, including a published text and an installation with an MDF daybed and two monitors—one displaying the text, the other a screensaver of a melting ice sculpture of Pantagruel's ship. In 2015, Susan Bennett read the essay live at Judson Memorial Church, New York, where the Judson Dance Theater once developed a vocabulary of pedestrian- and task-based movement. Apple's taskmaster guided listeners through prescribed and errant registers of speech.

Credits

"NaturallySpeaking," text originally published in *You Are Here: Art After the Internet*, edited by Omar Kholeif, published by Cornerhouse Books/SPACE, 2014

Installation produced for *La Voix Humaine*, Kunstverein Munich, January 25–March 30, 2014

Performance by Susan Bennett for the program *USER AGENT*, curated by Rachel Valinsky, presented by New York Performance Artists Collective (NYPAC) at Judson Memorial Church, New York, March 29, 2015

TRATTEGGIO, 2018

Performance by Norio, the accessibility robot of Château d'Oiron, France
pp. 95–111

Tratteggio was produced for the group exhibition *Déclassement*, which looked at contemporary protocols for the conservation, restoration, and support of cultural heritage. The venue, Château d'Oiron, is notable for operating as both a historical monument and contemporary art collection including works by On Kawara, James Lee Byars, and Marina Abramović.

Drawing from his ongoing research about automation, robotics, and telepresence, Coburn proposed a collaboration with Norio, an accessibility robot that Château d'Oiron commissioned and employs. Visitors unable to climb to the second floor can telenavigate the robot from a console on the first, which allows them to see the artwork through its eyes. At the time, Norio was the only robot of its kind in a museum in France.

For *Tratteggio*, Coburn cast Norio in an additional role. Over the course of the exhibition, when not providing accessibility services, the robot faced the windows at the end of the Gallery of Paintings and looped a text-based monologue on its screen. Norio described past and potential restorations of the room, wondering if it would also be preserved for the benefit of posterity.

The term *tratteggio* refers to the practice, mentioned in the monologue, of a conservator making marks that reveal their interventions in an artwork.

Credits

Produced by Château d'Oiron, Centre des monuments nationaux, in the context of the exhibition *Déclassement*, curated by Barbara Sirieix, Château d'Oiron, France, June 23–September 30, 2018

CANDLESTICK MAN, 2023

Performance, *gofun*, candlesticks, hand-dipped candles made of beeswax and oil infused with lichens collected on Tanegashima, Japan
pp. 113–144

Candlestick Man looks at Japanese portrayals of the first Europeans to arrive in the country, with a particular focus on historical and speculative relationships between human migration and the spread of disease. As part of his research, Coburn visited Tanegashima, the island where the Portuguese landed in 1543. The monument to their arrival is covered with lichens, which gives it the misleading appearance of being sick.

The installation of this work centered on two replicas of *Oribe Nanbanjin* candlesticks depicting Europeans, which Coburn and actor Wataru Naganuma engaged—for small audiences—in English- and Japanese-language performances. On the gallery walls was a sculpture in *gofun*, a white pigment made of oyster shells that dots the lichens in traditional Japanese painting. Misusing *gofun* as putty, Coburn copied the lichen dots from two early-seventeenth-century folding screens by Kanō Sanraku showing the Portuguese in transit to Nagasaki. Lastly, he fashioned candles from beeswax and oil infused with lichens collected on Tanegashima. When lit during the performances, these candles opened sensory channels to the past.

Credits

Produced during the Tokyo Arts and Space International Creator Residency Program, 2023

First performed by Coburn and Naganuma at OPEN STUDIO, Tokyo Arts and Space, Tokyo, March 17 and 19, 2023

First exhibited in *As Above, So Below*, TOKAS Hongo, Tokyo, July 1–August 6, 2023

Script translated into Japanese by Penguin Translation

Candlesticks made by Jiro Sasaki and an unknown creator

SEVEN PORTRAITS ON A CORREALIST ROCKER, 2009

Performance on a replica of Frederick Kiesler's *Correalist Rocker*
pp. 145–174

When designing Peggy Guggenheim's Art of This Century gallery in New York, Frederick Kiesler created the *Correalist Rocker*, an object with seven intended positions as a chair, stand, and plinth. *Seven Portraits on a Correalist Rocker* turns this object into a storyteller's seat. Coburn rotates an MDF replica seven times and adapts his body accordingly. In each configuration, he describes a portrait of Peggy Guggenheim. Some are actual renderings by her contemporaries like Max Ernst, Man Ray, and Virgil Thomson. Others are loosely based on her work with Maya Deren, Marcel Duchamp, and Kiesler. One is a portrait given by the *Correalist Rocker* itself.

At the time Coburn made this performance, he was working for a commercial gallery and thinking about how "representation" is the common way to describe a dealer's relationship to their artists. *Seven Portraits on a Correalist Rocker* inverts this dynamic, representing Guggenheim from the perspectives of the people she championed and claimed.

Credits

First performed at Renwick Gallery, New York, April 4, 2009

Replica designed and produced in collaboration with Jonathan Butt

RICHARD ROE, 2017–

Orchid hybrid "Aranda Richard Roe,"
custom glass potting, memoir, reading
pp. 175–196

Richard Roe is at once an orchid hybrid that Coburn named after the legal person "Richard Roe," a fictional memoir by Roe, and a performance of this text. The project builds on a convention particular to Singapore in which orchid hybrids are named after politicians and celebrities—effectively, as a means of cultural diplomacy.

In 2017, Coburn developed a relationship with Hongyi Zhou of Toh Garden, which cultivates many of Singapore's famous hybrids. Coburn obtained Zhuo's permission to legally name one of them, and called it "Richard Roe," a fictional name used in American and British law when the real name of a person is unknown or withheld. Now that this name has entered the registry of the Royal Horticultural Society in the United Kingdom, it is bound to every one of these hybrids in the world.

Since the naming, "Aranda Richard Roe" has occasionally appeared on the front desks of art institutions, where it passes as a decorative object. Placed alongside it, a published version of Roe's memoir—written by Coburn—describes the legal fictions that creep around the margins of selfhood and increasingly play a role in the political and economic spheres.

Taken as a whole, *Richard Roe* is a natural thing made to perform as a legal fiction, at once circulating through flower markets, art institutions, and the fictive spaces of the law.

Credits

Commissioned by Thyssen-Bornemisza Art Contemporary, Vienna, and curated by Cory Scozzari
Additional support by NTU Centre for Contemporary Art Singapore and Beeler Gallery at Columbus College of Art & Design

"Aranda Richard Roe" hybridized by Toh Garden, Singapore
Potting designed by Coburn and manufactured by Verreum, Prague

Richard Roe, memoir published by Sternberg Press and Thyssen-Bornemisza Art Contemporary, 2019
Designed by Luke Gould, edited by Annie Godfrey Larmon, and copyedited by Orit Gat
Illustrations by Krisia Ayala, Mummalaneni Bharath, Sampathkumar J, Skye Luchiano, Robert McKinnon, Valeria Denisse Millan, Ana Rivera, Angela Skinner, and Rachelle Sawatsky

First performed by Birgit Huppuch at The Poetry Project, New York, April 27, 2018; by Coburn at NTU Centre for Contemporary Art Singapore, October 16, 2018

"Peeling off the Voice," essay by Coburn about *Richard Roe*, in *Master of Voice*, edited by Lisette Smits, published by Sternberg Press, 2020

RESONATOR, 2016–

Performance for one person, .zip file, printed takeaway, ingots
pp. 197–226

Supposedly, most things in the world have one or more resonant frequencies, and if exposed to them, will vibrate in sympathy—at greater and greater amplitude—to potentially therapeutic or destructive effect. In a famous demonstration, Nikola Tesla once affixed a pocket oscillator to a building under construction in Wall Street, threatening to bring it crashing down. His experiment was cut short, but when viewed allegorically (and somewhat whimsically), it attests to the capacity of resonance to destroy capitalism—or at least, to beleaguer its infrastructure.

Resonator departs from this anecdote, imagining that resonance can serve as a vibrational and conceptual tool to help shift our relationship to finance, logistics, and love. The project centers on a script Coburn wrote while on a container ship from Elizabeth, New Jersey to Ashdod, Israel. In the resulting work, first performed in Hong Kong near a container terminal, he shares a bench with a single attendee each hour, discusses the sympathies and vulnerabilities that can come from mutual resonance, and employs techniques of mimicry and mirroring to try to come into resonance with them.

Coburn's trip was organized by the Container Artist Residency and supported by the Israeli shipping company ZIM. His contract stipulated that he gift an artwork which ZIM could sell, with proceeds donated to a charity or good cause. Coburn decided to use bullets made by Israeli Military Industries, which are shipped by ZIM to the United States and sold domestically by Federal Independence Ammo. The lead extracted from these bullets became two ingots, respectively cast from molds of tuning forks vibrating at 256 Hz and 274 Hz. If struck at the same time, they generate an interval of 18 Hz—the resonant frequency of the eye. Studies have shown that eyes exposed to this frequency can experience a smearing of vision to the point where apparition-like figures appear. By gifting one ingot to ZIM and keeping the other, Coburn intended to bring such apparitions to the fore.

Running alongside these elements was a collaboration with artist Byron Peters that drew influence from Alexander Geirot's "Labor Organ," an instrument designed in 1921 to communicate the conditions of work, powered by the excess energy of factories. In a .zip file of assorted materials, Coburn and Peters repurposed a 2013 patent for the "High Speed Processing of Financial Information," imagining a "Financial Organ" of comparable function for the present age.

Credits

Produced for Container Artist Residency 01, 2016

First performed at Lai King Estate, Hong Kong, December 3–4 and 9–11, 2016, as part of *Creative Operational Solutions*, Para Site, Hong Kong, December 10, 2016–March 5, 2017

Tuning fork molds created by Jessi Li, bullet lead extracted and cast by Gary Griffiths, and ingots refined by Rebecca Timman
Exhibited in *Creative Operational Solutions*

.zip file produced in collaboration with Byron Peters at the invitation of Am Nuden Da
First distributed in an email titled "with assumed responsibility of tyler coburn & byron peters," July 19, 2016, http://www.tylercoburn.com/da.zip

Printed takeaway produced in collaboration with Byron Peters and designed by Frédérique Gagnon, with drawings by Mummalaneni Bharath, for the exhibition *The House of Dust d'Alison Knowles*, curated by Art by Translation, Fonderie Darling, Montreal, June 15–August 20, 2017

Michelle Wun Tin Wong's "Junk Ride at Night" and Camille Richert's "Without Apparent Seams" were partly written on the benches where *Resonator* was originally performed. Richert's text is translated from the French by Rachel Valinsky

MEDIUM NO. 1 (MANHATTAN), 2008–2009

Transcripts of eighty-two walks across Manhattan, thermal roll fax machine, laminate wood flooring, plywood, mirror, drywall, fluorescents
pp. 227–261

From January 1 to March 22, 2009, Coburn sent transcripts of monologues and conversations, recorded on walks across Manhattan, to a thermal roll fax machine in the basement of SculptureCenter, New York. These daily transmissions formed a continuous scroll that unfurled on a twenty-five-foot-long triangular plinth.

The Manhattan grid served as the framework for the walks. Drafted for the 1811 Commissioner's Proposal, it must have seemed, as Rem Koolhaas writes in *Delirious New York* (1978), to be "the most courageous act of prediction in Western Civilization." When Coburn first read the proposal, he was surprised by the transparency of its economic intent: That the standardization of horizontal property would help maximize value, opening the vertical axis to the eventuality of the skyscraper.

Medium No. 1 (Manhattan) comprises a mode of walking—from 1st Street to 82nd Street, one end to the other—that completely adheres to the urban plan and seems eccentric by the standards of common pedestrian travel. Over the course of these excursions, Coburn and his fellow walkers explored noneconomic, even creative ways of inhabiting the grid.

Credits

Produced for *In Practice '09*, SculptureCenter, New York, 2009

Plinth manufactured by Nick Friend, with assistance from Morgan Edelbrock

Walking companions included Graham Anderson, Eric Anglés, Uri Aran, Alisa Baremboym, Ronnie Bass, Sarina Basta, Thomas Beard, David Bench, Tova Carlin, Ted Coburn, Trisha Coburn, Michael Connor, Noralen Curl, David Kennedy Cutler, Victoria Donner, Benjamin Farnsworth, Jeanne Gerrity, A.J. Glusman, Summer Guthery, Andrea Hill, Ellen Kenney, Josh Kline, Derek G. Larson, Lindsay Larson, Beverly Liang, Matthew Lutz-Kinoy, Joshua Mack, Liz Magic Laser, Candice Madey, Saskia Miller, Mariah Robertson, Bartholomew Ryan, Hana Scott-Suhrstedt, Luke Stettner, Eva Struble, Ryan Sullivan, Yulia Tikhonova, Josh Tonsfeldt, Lance Wakeling, Madeline Warren, Julia Weist, Logan Werschky, Sam Wilson, and Olivia Wyatt

OVERGROWTH, 2020

Text, photographs
pp. 263–271

In June 2020, after recovering from coronavirus, Coburn went to Sea View Hospital on Staten Island, New York. Carrying an audio recorder, a camera, and his research notes, he improvised a monologue beside the ruins of pavilions that once served patients with tuberculosis. The photographs he took of the site, and an edited transcript of the monologue, were later published as *Overgrowth*.

Credits

Commissioned for *HOMEWORK*, an online platform by Art Sonje Center, Seoul, that ran from May to November 2020

PREPARED REMARKS, 2020

Audio
pp. 273–285

In 1974, Stephen Antonakos sealed works by Richard Artschwager, Daniel Buren, Sol LeWitt, and Robert Ryman in steel boxes until the year 2000 (*Time Boxes 2000*, 1974). Decades later, Art by Translation invited seventeen artists to create time capsules, and additional artists—Coburn included—to imagine the sonic landscape of 2045: the year they are due to be opened.

Prepared Remarks is a speech delivered at the projected opening of the capsules. 2045 is notable, the speaker observes, for being the year Ray Kurzweil predicted the Singularity would come to pass, and humans would merge with artificial intelligence. The speaker claims this event "has not arrived." His voice, sounding more synthetic with each word, suggests otherwise.

Credits

Commissioned by Art by Translation and Lab'Bel for the exhibition *Time Capsule 2045*, Beaux-art de Paris, May 7-23, 2021, and Musée d'art et d'histoire de Genève, July 6-August 23, 2022

ERGONOMIC FUTURES, 2016–

Furniture, website
(www.ergonomicfutures.com)
pp. 287–316

Ergonomic Futures explores the subject of contemporary "fitness" through the lens of speculative evolution, informed by Coburn's research and interviews with paleoanthropologists, ergonomists, evolutionary biologists, and genetic engineers. To each he asked: Is it possible to imagine a future scenario when our bodies experience such a degree of evolutionary change that the biological, ontological, and legal criteria of the human come undone? And could this thought experiment put pressure on humanism, the humanities, and the frameworks and norms that maintain them?

The project takes a few forms. Working from his research and interviews, Coburn collaborated with architects Bureau V to design functional ergonomic seating for different future bodies. By exploiting a problematic tendency in the field of ergonomics—the production of body typologies—and imagining that those typologies don't yet exist, he stages a scenario in which no living user has the "normal" body for the seats. As it might take a while for those typologies to come into being, the seats can currently be used in art, anthropology, and natural history museums—parasitizing these institutional time capsules for the sake of their survival. The bodies that the seats are designed for are never disclosed, so museum-goers, using their knowledge of ergonomics, can engage in a tactile form of speculation.

Accompanying the seats is a website of Coburn's short stories, which were later adapted for performance and publication.

Credits

Commissioned by the 11th Gwangju Biennale, Gwangju, 2016, and Lafayette Anticipations, Paris, 2016

Furniture designed in collaboration with Bureau V, New York
Gwangju Biennale seat fabricated by Yong Chul Kim
Lafayette Anticipations seat produced with Dirk Meylaerts and Aude Mohammedi Merquiol, and fabricated by Creaform, Fontaine
Editions held by Centre Pompidou, Paris; Musée de l'Homme, Paris; Art Sonje Center, Seoul; and Seodaemun Museum of Natural History, Seoul

Website designed in collaboration with Luke Gould and Afonso Martins, and edited by Joanna Fiduccia

First performed at e-flux, New York, October 18, 2016

"Ergonomic Futures," script published in *e-flux journal*, no. 98 (March 2019)

Interviews for *Ergonomic Futures* conducted with Shara Bailey, Pierre Cassou-Nogues, Manny Halpern, Evelyne Heyer, Guillaume Lecointre, Philippe Morel, Samuel Myers, Jonathan Olivares, Ryan Raaum, Joel Sanders, and Seth Shipman

Théo Robine-Langlois's "i am sleepy" was partly written on Coburn's furniture in Centre Pompidou and Musée de l'Homme, Paris. His contribution is typeset in Linux Libertine, the same font used on www.ergonomicfutures.com

Yu Araki is an artist and filmmaker based in Kyoto, Japan. He is deeply engaged with the transmission of culture and intercultural encounters, particularly in the potential of mistranslations and misunderstandings that arise in these processes. In his recent video installations, Araki explores the differences that emerge between historical events and fiction through methodologies such as reenactment, reinterpretation, and reanimation. He received a BA in Fine Arts (Sculpture) in 2007 from the Sam Fox School of Design & Visual Arts at Washington University in St. Louis, and an MA in Film and New Media Studies in 2010 from Tokyo University of the Arts. In 2024, he was one of the recipients of the Pola Art Foundation's Grant for Overseas Study by Young Artists, which supported his fieldwork in Lisbon, Portugal.

A.E. Benenson is New York-based writer and editor. He is the creator of Ligature Press, an artists' book press, and with his wife, co-owns Harvesters, 1565, a bookstore in the Hudson Valley. He is interested in the histories of writing, reproduction, vernacular design, anachronism, and misuses of technology.

Tyler Coburn is an artist, writer, and professor based in New York. He received a 2024 Andy Warhol Foundation Arts Writers Grant, and his writing has appeared in *ArtReview*, *BOMB*, *C Magazine*, *Dis*, *e-flux journal*, *frieze*, *LEAP*, *Metropolis M*, *Mousse*, and *Rhizome*. Coburn is the author of four books: *I'm that angel* (self-published, 2012), *Robots Building Robots* (CCA Glasgow, 2013), *Richard Roe* (Sternberg Press and Thyssen-Bornemisza Art Contemporary, 2019), and *Solitary* (Sternberg and Art Sonje Center, 2022). He has presented artwork at such venues as Centre Pompidou, Paris; Bergen Kunsthall; Hayward Gallery, London; Para Site, Hong Kong; and Kunstverein Munich.

Mashinka Firunts Hakopian is an Associate Professor at ArtCenter College of Design, a 2025–27 Vera List Center Fellow, and a 2024–25 Cambridge Visual Culture Visiting Research Fellow. Her book *The Institute for Other Intelligences*, an artist book and work of speculative feminist media theory that presents lectures on data justice delivered by "artificial killjoys," was published by X Artists' Books in 2022. She holds a PhD in History of Art from the University of Pennsylvania. Her recent multidisciplinary collaboration, Բաժակ Նայող (*One Who Looks at the Cup*), uses community dataset creation to train a model to perform coffee reading, and has been presented at REDCAT and The Music Center in Los Angeles, and the 2024 Asian Art Biennial at the National Taiwan Museum of Fine Arts.

Sven Lütticken is an art historian and theorist. He started writing for art magazines in the mid-1990s and completed his PhD at the Vrije Universiteit Amsterdam in 2002. Lütticken teaches at the Vrije Universiteit, where he coordinates the research master's track in Critical Studies in Art and Culture, and since 2022, is also a senior lecturer at Leiden University's Academy of Creative and Performing Arts. He is the editor of the critical reader *Art and Autonomy* (Afterall, 2022), and the author, most recently, of *States of Divergence* (Minor Compositions, 2025), *Objections* (Sternberg Press, 2022)—the first in a two-part study on forms of abstraction—and *Cultural Revolution: Aesthetic Practice after Autonomy* (Sternberg Press, 2017), among others.

Spyros Papapetros teaches art and architectural history and theory in the School of Architecture and the program in Media and Modernity and is the Director of the Program in European Cultural Studies at Princeton University. He is the author of *On the Animation of the Inorganic: Art, Architecture, and the Extension of Life* (University of Chicago Press, 2012) and the coeditor of *Retracing the Expanded Field: Encounters between Art and Architecture* (MIT Press, 2014). He coedited the first edition of Frederick Kiesler's book project *Magic Architecture: The Story of Human Housing* (MIT Press, 2025) and co-curated the exhibition *pre-architectures* (CIVA, Brussels, 2024–25).

Camille Richert is an art historian, teacher, independent curator, and art critic who lives and works between Paris and Lyon. She studied at ENS Lyon before earning a PhD in art history from Sciences Po, Paris. Her research focuses on representations of labor in the West since 1968; the relationship between feminism, contemporary art, and labor; and democratic exhibition practices. Her monograph on the Hackney Flashers collective, *Parents must unite + fight* (Tombolo Presses, 2024), won the Most Beautiful Swiss Books award and led to the exhibition *Hope for change* at the CEAAC in Strasbourg (2025). She was the co-curator of *Chaleur humaine*, the second Art & Industry Triennial in Dunkirk (2023), and regularly collaborates with AWARE (Archives of Women Artists, Research & Exhibitions) and La Salle de bains in Lyon, where she co-curated *Ça commence souvent par des problèmes* on Carole Roussopoulos (2025).

Kameelah Janan Rasheed is a learner. Through her large-scale installations, multichannel video works, publications, software, performance, public archives, and learning platforms, Rasheed explores the relationship between language, mysticism, and disobedience.

Théo Robine-Langlois (1990) grew up in Juvisy, a small town near the Orly airport in France. His writings address the weight of ordinary fictions, untying them through a dysfunctional language in which words and images collide. They craft and call for other worlds, in and outside of the book—and do so with the help of plants, spell-casting grand-mothers, clouds, insurrections, or Xerox machines. A member of After 8 Books and Publication Studio Paris, he is also a correspondent for the online radio station *Duuu and produces videos with the collective la ville fumée. He organizes writing workshops in artistic and educational spaces. Robine-Langlois has published several books and vinyls including *Corbeau* (Riga Project, 2025), *Secrèt* (Dépense Défensive, 2024), *Le Gabion* (After 8 Books, 2021), and *[...]* (Nous, 2016).

Ian Wallace is a writer, curator, and art historian based in New York. He is currently Associate Curator at Amant.

Elvia Wilk is a writer and editor living in Brooklyn. She is the author of two novels, *Oval* (Soft Skull Press, 2019) and *A Diagnosis* (Graywolf/Peninsula Press, 2026), and the book of essays *Death by Landscape* (Soft Skull Press, 2022). She writes for many publications about art, books, ecology, architecture, and having a body.

Michelle Wun Ting Wong is a Hong Kong-based researcher who also curates and writes. She received her PhD in art history from the University of Hong Kong in 2025, where she studied the cultural modernity and artistic modernism emerging from post-WWII Hong Kong. Her current research focuses on how the travels of artists of Chinese descent in mid-twentieth century East and Southeast Asia mediated their projections of a cultural China. Her writing has been published in *Ambitious Alignments: New Histories of Southeast Asian Art, 1945–1990* (2018) and the journal *Southeast of Now* (2019). Wong was the lead researcher in a team of archivists at Asia Art Archive that organized and digitized the late Ha Bik Chuen's collection. Recent curatorial projects include *Reframing Strangeness: Ha Bik Chuen's Motherboards and Collagraphs* at Para Site, Hong Kong (2025).

Cover illustration by Mummalaneni Bharath, 2025
Drawing concept by Tyler Coburn

Document Series #13
First Edition, 2025
Edition of 1,000 copies
ISBN: 979-8-9909878-7-6
LCCN: 2025943107

Edited by Rachel Valinsky
Proofread by Tyler Coburn and Rachel Valinsky
Designed by Bryce Wilner
Typeset in Grotesque No. 3
Grayscale image retouching by Bryce Wilner
Color image retouching by Michel Sixou
Printed at Printon, Estonia

Distributed in the USA by Asterism Books
asterismbooks.com

Distributed in Europe/the UK by Antenne Books
antennebooks.com

The authorized representative in the EU for product safety and compliance is eucomply OÜ, Pärnu mnt 139b-14, 11317 Tallinn, Estonia, hello@eucompliancepartner.com, +33757690241. Our official distribution partner is Antenne books ltd.

Published by Wendy's Subway
379 Bushwick Avenue
Brooklyn, NY 11206
wendyssubway.com

Wendy's Subway is a non-profit reading room, writing space, and independent publisher located in Brooklyn.

The Document Series is an interdisciplinary publishing initiative that highlights work by time-based artists in printed form.

The Document Series is supported, in part, by the New York State Council on the Arts with support of the Office of the Governor and the New York State Legislature, and the Andy Warhol Foundation for the Visual Arts.

Some Monologues is supported, in part, by a School of the Art Institute of Chicago 2022–23 Faculty Enrichment Grant.

The artist would like to thank the Coburn family, Siqi Zhu, Sharon Lockhart, Michael Ned Holte, A.L. Steiner, Benjamin Weissman, Jeffrey K. Miller, Joanna Fiduccia, Samantha Culp, Anna Lundh, Pieter Verbeke, Stefan Wagner, Chiara Figone, Nicola Guy, Krist Gruijthuijsen, Anna Daneri, Anna Gritz, Auridas Gajauskas, Chris Fitzpatrick, Mary Leclere, Summer Guthery, Kari Cwynar, Kara Hamilton, Caitlin Jones, Allison Collins, Roy Huschenbeth, Lea Vene, Ana Kovačić, Sanja Sekelj, Margit Säde, Laurel Ptak, Florian Weigl, Vivian Sky Rehberg, Michael Conner, Rachel Valinsky, Bart van der Heide, Saim Demircan, Omar Kholeif, Karen Archey, Taraneh Fazeli, Samuel Quenault, Carine Guimbard, Kaori Otake, Ayumi Uno, Mio Hanaoka, Ayako Oshima, Ken Kondo, Hikaru Fujii, Mark Rappolt, Tom Eccles, Hana Saleh Al Saadi, Leslie Fritz, Christine Messineo, Margaret Liu Clinton, Caterina Riva, Ute Meta Bauer, Magdalena Magiera, Anna Lovecchio, Tatjana Günthner, Jo-ey Tang, Alana Odenweller, Nadine Droste, Jana Wieking, Susanne Leeb, Clemens Krümmel, Manuel Clancett, Maayan Strauss, Prem Krishnamurthy, Cosmin Costinas, Asher Mones, Olivia Chow, Dorothee Richter, Ronald Kolb, Pablo José Ramirez, Sam Simon, Adam Gibbons, Jesper List Thomsen, Lewis Ronald, Mary Ceruti, Sarina Basta, Heehyun Cho, Sébastien Pluot, Maud Jacquin, Jeff Guess, Maria Lind, Margarida Mendes, Anna Colin, François Quintin, Marie-Ange Brayer, Magdalena Ruiz Marmolejo, Sunjung Kim, Clara Suwon Chun, Doosung Baek, Jimin Lee, Marie de Brugerolle, Eva Wilson, Amal Issa, and Kaye Cain-Nielsen.